WHERE TO LIVE IN AUCKLAND

Published in New Zealand by Barbican Publishing Limited
PO Box 91572, Auckland

Phone:	64 9 376 4849
Fax:	64 9 376 4879
Email:	info@wheretoliveinauckland.co.nz
Website:	www.wheretoliveinauckland.co.nz

ISBN 0-476-01558-8

SOURCES:

Recorded property sales
(years ending December 2003, 2004) – Quotable Value New Zealand

Population statistics
(2001 Census data) – Statistics New Zealand

Mosaic neigbourhood classification system 2002
supplied by Pinpoint Target Marketing

Publisher	Stephen Hart
Assistant publisher	James Hodgson
Editor	Sharon Newey
Contributing writers	Robyn Welsh
	Alice Shopland
	Billy Leonard
	Charlotte Cossar
	Vicki Holder
Photographers	Simon Young
	Marcel Tromp
Sub-editing	Alice Bulmer
	Jane Binsley
Design	Liesl Strauss
	Brett Hutchinson
Imaging	Image Centre
Printing	PMP Print

Acknowledgments: Our sincere thanks and gratitude to the many industry sources, local authorities and individuals interviewed for this book. Special thanks to Quotable Value New Zealand, PMP Distribution Limited and Statistics New Zealand for their invaluable contributions. Thanks also to The National Bank of New Zealand for their support.

Cover image: House photographed (and sold by!) Andy Dye, Bayleys & Thompson, Mission Bay

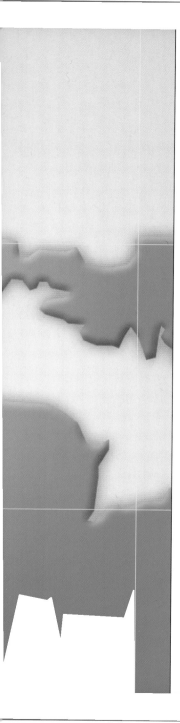

With over 50 branches and 27 Mobile Mortgage Managers in the Greater Auckland area alone, we've got Auckland covered. No matter where you are, or when you need us, we have branches open for extended hours and weekends, Mobile Mortgage Managers available anytime, and Call Centre staff who are also home loan specialists. For extensive local knowledge in the Auckland market call us on **0800 47 87 25**.

The National Bank
The thoroughbred among banks

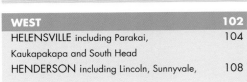

House hunting?

Your weapon of choice:

HomeFinders

taking the legwork and guess work out of homebuying...

*O*ur inside knowledge of the Auckland real estate market and expert negotiation skills can save you many hours and thousands of dollars!

We can help you with everything from finding the right home, to researching, negotiating and bidding at auction.

So whether it's your first time looking for Auckland property, whether you live in New Zealand or abroad, or you simply want to buy without the hassle, we can help.

Our objective is to ensure that the buyer secures the perfect property for the lowest price, in the shortest amount of time, with the minimum amount of fuss.

Our services include:

· Property search and evaluation
· Familiarisation tours
· Investment properties
· Negotiation advice
· Rental search and evaluation
· Project management
· Auction and tender advice

HomeFinders is run by Auckland property expert Stephen Hart, publisher of the best-selling book, **Where to Live in Auckland**, and co-presenter of TV2's top-rating, House Call programme.

Where to Live in Auckland is split into five geographical areas – Central, West, the North Shore, East and South. Each area is, in turn, divided into neighbourhoods – a collection of suburbs and areas close to each other and similar in nature. To find the neighbourhood you are interested in, either refer to the contents page or use the index at the back of the book.

Within each neighbourhood, we look at the character of the area, the people who live there, types of houses typical to the area, real estate trends and typical prices, as well as the amenities you can find there – the schools, shops, leisure facilities, open spaces, eateries and transport.

At the back of the book, you'll find even more interesting facts – a full and comprehensive list of Auckland schools, zoning maps for secondary schools with enrolment schemes, information about private schools and statistics giving a profile of Auckland's population.

Our star ratings: We've given the amenities in each neighbourhood a rating from one to five and we've also rated each neighbourhood from one to five, based on its desirability, house price level and general access to amenities.

Maps: Each neighbourhood has a map, coloured according to the types of people that live in the area.

It's an intriguing insight into the habits, likes and dislikes of your potential neighbours – do they like drinking wine or beer, like sport, use the internet?

Each colour relates to a particular population sector based on demographics, lifestyle and preferences. For an explanation of those see page 226.

Prices: Property values and prices quoted in our House Prices boxes are based on interviews with real estate agents, are anecdotal only and take into account some of the market forces brought to bare in certain areas such as school zones or sea views.

Working out where to live in Auckland?

Let us help

There are fundamental differences that make Barfoot & Thompson different from the rest:

Magnitude As the largest wholly New Zealand owned real estate company, we offer our customers a significant edge. Our sheer size and focus on Auckland and Northland maximises your chances of a sale. We have more listings, more contacts and more potential buyers.

Focus Barfoot & Thompson has never been interested in nationwide expansion. We choose to be experts in the Auckland and Northland property markets and, with 60 offices, you don't just get one real estate salesperson working for you, you get a team of over 950.

Trust & Integrity In the competitive real estate market, our approach to business stands out. We are a family owned business and place a strong emphasis on honesty, integrity and transparency. No matter which of our business divisions you deal with, we pride ourselves on having people who are easy to deal with, value their clients, give sound advice and provide good information about the properties they represent.

www.barfoot.co.nz Check out properties which suit your search criteria any time of the day or night on our dedicated website. We make it as easy as possible.

New Zealanders and their houses are a special partnership. In other countries, renting is the norm, or your house is merely a place to lay your head. The Kiwi attachment to his or her quarter-acre paradise is well documented. It's where we spend a lot of our time and it's where we raise our children. Pride in our homes is a particularly Kiwi characteristic – but then we are often blessed with large houses, set within generous gardens and close to all sorts of outdoor spaces and amenities.

The do-it-yourself phenomenon is also rooted deep in our psyche. Part of it stems from the Number 8 wire, make-do mentality and part of it from the simple fact that we can – our timber houses are easy to chop

and change. In generations gone by, if you were a male confessing to not being able to hammer in a nail, you would be hounded from the neighbourhood.

These days, Kiwis are still keen on renovating, but for different reasons. And it's all about location, location, location. Concentrating much more on the location and what the area has to offer, we are not as concerned about the particulars of the actual house – because you can change it, but you can't change where it is.

Buyers are not fazed about throwing renovation funds at a house to make it suit their needs, as long as the location is right and the section has the potential – like the right aspect for sun and enough space to fit a garage or extension. They know that, no matter whether the real estate market is booming or not, the Auckland sector is strong enough that if they stay put for a few years, they will recoup their investment.

Investing so much money and emotion in our houses is perhaps a particularly Auckland thing, too. The story goes that if you live in Christchurch, the question is which school you went to. If you live in Wellington, it's what movies you have seen lately. But if you live in Auckland, it's where do you live?

Auckland city is easily New Zealand's biggest city, sprawling over 63,000 hectares. Its population of just over 1.31 million in the greater Auckland area is about one-third of the whole country. And it's growing all the time – forecasts put the number of people living here at 1.65 million by the year 2021.

Despite being the nation's economic powerhouse, Auckland and its inhabitants seem to inspire extremes of emotion in other New Zealanders, being either admired or reviled. Aucklanders can also be heard complaining about the city's failings – it's a rat-race, it rains too much and the traffic is appalling.

We're also woefully ignorant of our own city. Ask a North Shore-ite where Glendene is and they'll confuse it with Glen Innes on the opposite side of town. Get a Mt Eden dweller to locate Clover Park and they might suggest Australia. But in such a sprawling city in which each area is so well serviced with amenities, venturing out of your own neighbourhood just isn't necessary.

So how is it that Auckland continues to grow? The truth is that Auckland's sub-tropical climate, its attractive clean harbours, the beaches and bush areas, its ethnic diversity, nightlife, cafes, universities, sporting facilities and large job market all make it a great place to live. Love it or not, the city is big, brassy and the closest New Zealand gets to an international cosmopolitan centre.

Auckland is located on the narrow isthmus of the Tamaki Peninsula, between the Waitemata and Manukau Harbours. In this city you're never far from the water – there's a mere 9km of land separating the Pacific Ocean from the Tasman Sea. Huge surf may be pounding the sparkly black sand of Auckland's west coast while on the same morning gentle waves are lapping the golden sand of the east coast beaches.

Another name for Auckland is City of Sails. It is said that Aucklanders own more boats per head of population than in any other city in the world.

The dramatic remodelling of the Viaduct Harbour, and the subsequent creation of a harbourside community of apartments and cafes has made the area a popular drawcard for tourists and locals alike.

Buying and selling property is another popular Auckland activity; on average Aucklanders sell their home once every seven years. The importance of Auckland's coastline is also reflected in real estate. In some North Shore suburbs, for instance, proximity to the beach decides the value.

The importance of water, boating and property converges in particular on the

Hauraki Gulf islands. Property prices on islands where you can buy permanent or weekend homes, in particular Waiheke Island, have skyrocketed along with their popularity.

It's thought that Maori first settled in the richly fertile Auckland region about 650 years ago. Today, one in seven Aucklanders identify themselves as Maori. Auckland is also a Polynesian centre; one-third of all Polynesian people over the entire Pacific region choose to live in Auckland.

Ngati Whatua are considered to be Auckland's first tribe. During the 1820s Maori were involved in fierce inter-tribal conflict, and by 1840 the colonising British had either beaten or bought them out. Captain William Hobson, New Zealand's first governor, chose Auckland as a name to honour his patron and former commander, Lord Auckland (at that time, the Viceroy of India). Many Auckland place names carry the influence of Hobson's patron.

On May 30, 1959, the four-lane Harbour Bridge was opened, connecting Auckland's downtown business centre with the city's northern shore – and true North Shore suburbia was born. Ten years later the bridge was expanded to eight lanes, using Japanese engineering commonly referred to as the "Nippon clip-on". The motorway system has been growing ever since. Auckland's sprawl and relatively limited public transport system means that it's hard to get by without a car.

In 1997 the Sky Tower, New Zealand's tallest building, was completed. Its top viewing platform is 300m above sea level, making it the highest outdoor public viewing platform in the southern hemisphere. In 2001 the city's skyline was dramatically altered again when the lone pine tree on the summit of One Tree Hill was removed following a chainsaw attack by a Maori activist. Auckland has abundant parks. The domain is home to the Auckland War Memorial Museum, opened in 1929 to commemorate World War I casualties from Auckland.

A potted history of housing

Auckland is ever-changing and varied, architecturally speaking. In its 160-year history, it has collected a range of house styles from early worker's cottages, villas, bungalows, state houses, brick-and-tile homes and units to today's terrace and freestanding townhouses, apartments, and plaster and masonry homes.

By 1881, the highest population densities in the whole of New Zealand were on the upper slopes of Freemans Bay and Grafton Gully and the neighbouring areas of Ponsonby and Newton. By 1896, Auckland's population of 50,000 mostly lived in an area 6.5km long and 2.5km wide, made up of the boroughs of Auckland, Parnell, Newmarket, Newton and Grafton. There were also settlements at Avondale, Mt Eden, Epsom and Ellerslie and the maritime suburbs of Northcote, Birkenhead and Devonport.

Access to plentiful timber made it easy to build worker's cottages, which changed rapidly to accommodate family needs. Cottages, however, with their bad sanitation and crowding into urban pockets, affronted Victorian sensibilities enough to spur the creation of the villa. Today, villas may be sought-after and trendy, but back then they

were never viewed very favourably. Villas were seen as architecturally inept and built like packing cases. The classic villa hallway was condemned as a conduit of cold air in the winter and dust in the summer. Burnley Tce in Mt Eden is a landmark example of mass-produced villas in New Zealand.

The housing styles of Auckland continued to evolve from international influences, including the Californian bungalow and various Spanish Mission-style stucco and Art Deco houses. Today, Auckland suburbs are an eclectic mix of styles, from traditional to ultra-modern. Whatever your preference, there's likely to be something to suit.

Real estate trends

The Auckland real estate market has been on a high for about three years, experiencing huge leaps in value. Tales abound of houses selling for $100,000 more than they fetched the year before, without being renovated.

Industry watchdogs put the rise in house values down to a number of influences. One is the return of ex-pat New Zealanders seeking a piece of clean, green land as an investment to which they can one day return. This trend has been around for a number of years, fuelled by the favourable exchange rate. However, as our dollar strengthened and the American dollar weakened in late 2004, there was a drop in the number of Americans coming here. Wealthy Brits and Australians weren't so deterred.

Interestingly, as we witness a worldwide backlash against US foreign policy, some wealthy American businesspeople are now seeking alternatives to the more traditional real estate investments at home. New

Zealand, so far away from the rest of the world, is seen as just the place to diversify and Auckland's large commercial heart is central to that focus.

The stability of the economy in the past few years has helped boost interest in housing as an investment. The steadiness and the relatively low level of mortgage interest rates encouraged people to upgrade their house or area. Inner-city suburbs are where most of the frenzy has been concentrated, but this has expanded to surrounding suburbs as supply has decreased.

Mortgage interest rates started to increase again in late 2004 and it was thought the housing market would start to suffer. But just as predictions for a market slide began to emerge, an interest rate war between the banks seemed to unleash another wave of enthusiasm for property. As most people fixed their mortgages for longer terms, they felt safe to continue buying and selling.

Confidence in the general economy

remains high and there are still some heady sales being made, especially for well-presented properties in the sought-after inner-city suburbs.

Despite the positive environment, there are signs that the housing market is past its peak. Properties are taking longer to sell, which is always an indicator of an easing market. On the back of higher floating interest rates and falling immigration, housing construction is at last pulling back from a 30-year high.

Rents are starting to fall by 5 to 10% in many areas, which is encouraging potential first home buyers and investors to stay out of the housing market for the time being.

While there is no evidence of a market-wide crash, and overall demand for apartments remains strong, lower quality city apartments are suffering a "market correction". Most affected are the small apartments let to students. They were often bought by heavily leveraged investors but with a fall in the number of immigrants and foreign students, who traditionally underpin the apartment rental market, prices for these units have fallen.

The big question is – where to now? The Auckland market is anything but predictable. It has always been characterised by peaks and troughs.

As this book went to press, some economists were predicting a 10% drop during the next three years and a 5% drop in 2005 alone. Tumbling net migration was cited as one of the main contributing factors for the predicted falls. Numbers have gone from a record 12-month gain of 43,000 people in May 2003 to 12,800 in January 2005.

Zone 8 regulations

In 2003 Auckland City Council created a new zone, Residential 8, which allows for "urban intensification" in certain areas. The zone is one way Auckland City plans to cater for the estimated 140,000 people Auckland stands to gain by 2021.

Although it allows for more compact living, Residential 8 is not a blueprint for overcrowding or high rises. It aims to put an end to "battery hen" apartments by requiring a minimum floor area of 40m2 and has guidelines to ensure good urban design, including criteria for visual and acoustic privacy, landscaping, private open space, energy efficiency and neighbourhood character.

The zone will not be applied in character or heritage areas and, to comply, public transport options must already be in place. The new rules will typically apply around town centres, or within 2km of the CBD, on land areas greater than one hectare in size.

Areas that will not see Residential 8 are those already zoned Residential 1, 2 or 3. Otherwise, anyone, anywhere in the city can apply for a site to be re-zoned for terrace housing and apartments. After fulfilling certain requirements, developers will be able to erect apartment blocks up to five stories high within 2km of the town centre. Within a five to 10-minute walk of suburban centres, these blocks could be up to three or four storeys high.

Re-zoning will require community consultation and developers must also go through an intensive application process. Areas that could be re-zoned Residential 8 are Avondale, Stoddard Rd, Mt Albert,

Sandringham, Balmoral/Dominion Rd, Surrey Crescent in Grey Lynn, Newmarket, Pt Chevalier, Mt Roskill, the former Mt Wellington Quarry, Onehunga, Royal Oak, Remuera, Ellerslie, Mt Wellington/Sylvia Park and Otahuhu. As we went to print, Glen Innes and Panmure are going through the consultation process to have Residential 8 applied. These are suburbs the council believes can accept more people.

Transportation

Some facts and figures about transport in the Auckland region (source: Census 2001):

- Approximately 630,000 cars and 95,000 heavy motor vehicles are registered in the Auckland region – one for every two people.
- On an average weekday, nearly 50% of morning peak journeys are work related and another 40% are to schools or other educational institutions.
- Each car carries only 1.3 occupants on average in peak periods.
- Approximately 8% of people in the

Auckland region use public transport to get to and from work.

Auckland's transport problems continue to be at the forefront of its residents' minds. A survey published in 2004 suggests that 52% of the Auckland region's population find traffic congestion the thing they most dislike about living in Auckland. Finding the perfect route to a destination, avoiding peak-hour traffic – which seems constant at all hours of the day – and escaping the constant threat of road rage (yours and other drivers') all adds to the pressure of living in this dynamic city.

Road and transportation issues are the subject of hot debates and strong emotions, and any number of political footballs.

Auckland City Mayor Dick Hubbard assures us that Auckland is on the verge of some of the biggest changes in its history with dozens of transport projects – road, bus and rail – on the boil. Auckland's political leaders have given a big tick to maximum public-transport spending. The influential Auckland Regional Lane Transport Committee voted for a 10-year strategic

package which gives public transport as much money as new roading projects.

Hubbard's predecessor, John Banks, promoted big roading projects to solve the city's problems, including the controversial eastern corridor which sent some landowners into a panic, particularly those whose lovely Orakei Basin view would have been destroyed. The motorway was to link Auckland's CBD to Botany Downs and while the land is still designated, construction plans have been shelved.

The current council is not so keen on a new motorway going ahead north of Glen Innes. It recognises that Auckland's transport must improve and says it is keen to develop roading links through the Tamaki area. Whatever is decided, any council only has security of tenure for three years, so anything may happen in the future.

A dedicated busway is being built on State Highway 1 to provide more efficient access between the CBD to the North Shore. Many of the city's existing bus lanes have been extended and some are enforced at all times rather than just during peak periods.

A central transit corridor designed for high frequency bus services is proposed between Britomart Rail Station and Newmarket, stopping at Auckland Hospital.

Auckland's rail system is being improved as well. Auckland only has three lines – one heads west to Waitakere; another loops east then joins with the southern lines at Mt Wellington then continues on to Papakura. The North Shore has no rail system. The Auckland Regional Transport Authority aims to have 10 minute peak frequencies on all lines. This will, however, require double tracking in the west, to be completed within two years.

Trains are being modernised and stations upgraded, and a decision will be made on whether the rail system should be electrified.

There are also improvements underway to relieve motorway congestion. The Western Ring Road is proposed as an alternative four lane motorway around the Auckland isthmus from Manukau to Albany. It will divert traffic away from the southern and northern motorway, and in particular the heavily congested Spaghetti Junction by the CBD. When completed, north-bound motorists will exit near Rainbow's End amusement park in Manukau City, curve to the west through Mangere Bridge, Mt Roskill, Avondale, link on to the north-western motorway, through Hobsonville, past Greenhithe and join the northern motorway at Albany.

While most of the road is either being built and or due to start, the specific route of the Avondale link hasn't been determined nor resource consent sought.

Moving out to the city rim

A recent phenomenon in Auckland sees many families and retired couples moving away from Auckland's central suburbs and out to the city's rim. Property in suburbs on the

outskirts of Auckland generally offers better value for money with bigger sections and houses and with no neighbours butted up to your back fence. A rural or bush outlook often replaces views of clotheslines and rooftops, and the streets are a lot quieter. One downside is the time spent commuting to work in peak-hour traffic.

Another reason why so people move further out of town is simple – they've been priced out of the central Auckland market and don't have a choice.

With the increased regularity of ferry trips from the CBD, Waiheke Island has also experienced huge growth. Living here, people can enjoy a sense of escapism within a short stroll of the beach, charming cafes, top class restaurants and myriad wineries, without forgoing city amenities.

Many luxurious new homes with expansive views have recently been built here, which to some extent, has changed the laid-back, slightly off-beat flavour of the island to one that is more sophisticated – and helped real estate values soar faster than any other area of Auckland. Between 2002 and 2004, the median price increased from $170,000 to $400,000, an increase of 74% over 2002.

The apartment and terrace house market

More and more people are opting for the security and ease of apartment living. According to a recent Bayleys Real Estate survey, there are now more than 10,500 apartments in 135 complexes in the CBD; 24 complexes were completed in 2004, adding close to 2900 apartments. Another 38 complexes are under construction and will add 3920 apartments during 2005 and another 1585 in 2006. Growth is expected to tail off in 2007 due to rising costs, rising land values and the sheer volume of existing city apartments.

At the upper end of the apartment market, stylish character conversions are at the top of the wish list along with the higher quality viaduct apartments.

The apartment market will play a significant role in shaping Auckland during the next couple of years. Predictably, as immigration slows, there has been a fall-off in cheap, small units of dubious quality which had been pitched at the foreign student market. A recent report in the New Zealand Herald (March 2005) stated that rents for low-quality one-bedroom inner-city apartments let to students had fallen from an average of $330 a week in October 2004 to $290 a week.

Concern over tiny apartments prompted Auckland City Council to establish a minimum size of 30m2 in early in 2004. This hasn't been related to bedroom numbers, however, so an apartment can measure 60m2 but contain three tiny bedrooms.

Outside the CBD, a number of new boutique terrace house developments have been built, especially in Parnell, Remuera and Ponsonby.

Leaky building syndrome

The leaky and rotten building scandal of 2002 took a backseat to other issues for a while, yet it has by no means disappeared. Tens of thousands of owners of townhouses and terrace houses have been caught up in frustrating and costly court battles with developers, architects, builders and

contractors which, for the most part, have not delivered satisfying results.

Auckland City has paid at least $5 million to settle claims and faces possibly another 1000 or more claims in forthcoming court or resolution services. Many developers have hidden behind the Limited Liabilities Act and because they've not been at the building coalface, the courts have found that they didn't contravene the Building Code.

Set up in 2002, the Weathertight Homes Resolution Service was intended as a cheaper and quicker alternative to the courts. In its first 18 months, it resolved only about 150 of more than 2000 claims received. This weathertightness issue did become the catalyst for the new Building Act which came into being in April 2005. Its focus is for better building controls, better administration with more reliable inspections and code of compliance requirements, more competent building practitioners and better informed and protected consumers.

The Auckland Regional Council and city councils have lobbied hard to get a review of the Unit Titles Act, which governs the management of multi-unit developments. In early 2004, the Government agreed to review the legislation, and released a discussion document in early 2005.

The ARC also wants changes to the Building Act to prevent any further leaky building problems. It is soon to become a signatory of the New Zealand Urban Design Protocol, which aims to encourage a higher standard of design.

Urban growth and development are priority issues for Auckland but it's not just about fitting everyone in. In April 2005, Mayor Hubbard announced a mayoral taskforce to overhaul the city's development controls. Armed with a landmark High Court decision stating that the council could set rules on design, Hubbard said the council would insist on an aesthetically pleasing city environment that residents would be proud of. A taskforce of leading architects, developers, property and landscape people has been set up to fast-track the planning approval process to improve urban design.

Building a rental empire
By Gez Johns, editor of **Kiwi Property Investor Magazine**

Although trends are slowly changing, in the UK, and probably the majority of Western Europe, if you own and rent out a second property, then you're a landlord; a home-provider – more often than not viewed by those you house as a direct descendent of the feudal aristocracy, and begrudgingly respected as such. Here on the other side of the globe, however, it would appear that we care little for such medieval fantasy. Own a second property in New Zealand or Australia, and first and foremost you're an investor. Good landlording is however just as important as making good investment decisions ... but more on this later.

The reason why we take property so much more seriously in this country is that, without the safety mat of a state pension, it represents the most understandable and accessible means of providing for our future.

Although many invest in rental properties as part of a well-researched financial strategy, others have done so, particularly of late, out of fear – a knee-jerk reaction to the apocalyptical warnings of self-proclaimed property experts; that those who don't invest in property will be left with nothing.

This has certainly been a key driver behind the sustained property boom of the past couple of years. Indeed, for Aucklanders, owning a second property has become as de rigueur as walking a small dog down Ponsonby Rd or tailgating on the north-western motorway.

Such increased competition for housing stock has, however, led new investors to parts of the country they may never have previously considered, with one-mill North Island towns such as Tokoroa competing with the Costa Del Invercargill as unlikely hotspots. But for all this geographical diversity, opportunities still remain closer to home: they're just not quite as evident as they used to be.

With a worst-case scenario of property values dipping by 5-10% during the coming year, bargain hunting is just not that easy. Worse still for new investors is that weekly rental rates, as reported by the Ministry of Housing, have been pretty static for the last year, meaning the returns on investment are falling. Nevertheless, with Australian buyers still snapping up apartments off-the-plans, from a global perspective the city remains prominently on the radar, not least because of this country's investor-friendly tax laws.

Yields and taxes
Investments of all types are generally rated on the yield that they offer: essentially the return on investment before tax. To calculate the yield of any prospective property purchase, simply divide the yearly total value

of the rental income by the purchase price. A good tip here is not to simply multiply the weekly rent by 52, since inevitable periods of vacancy between tenancies should be factored in to the equation.

For example, the average price for a two-bedroom house in Mt Roskill today is around $300,000, with a median weekly rental of $300. Catering for three weeks of vacancy, the yield right now for this sort of property would then be less than 5% (300 x 49 / 300,000). Given that long-in-the-tooth investors will happily regale you with stories of yields of over treble this, "back in the day", this perhaps doesn't sound too promising – particularly with interest rates sitting comfortably above this.

However, as a new investor what you should really be interested in is the net return, which takes into account all incomings, outgoings and numerous tax advantages, and will allow you to work out whether or not the property will be "cashflow positive" after tax – in other words, return more income than you pay out on it.

At the heart of these tax savings is how you structure the ownership of your property. These days the most heavily favoured option is to detach yourself from personal ownership and place investment properties in an LAQC, or Loss Attributing Qualifying Company. In brief, an LAQC will allow losses from the rental property or properties to be allocated to its individual shareholders (ie, you) to offset against personal income, thus minimising the amount of tax you would have to pay. There are obviously many specific rules and regulations involved in setting up a structure such as this, therefore it is vital to consult an expert accountant.

Just as much a friend to investors is depreciation. As Australian financial expert and regular KPI Magazine contributor Margaret Lomas explains: "In New Zealand you may make a range of depreciation claims on your tax return which serve to create a loss which is on-paper only. These on-paper claims give you back some of the tax you have paid on your income, often more than you need to close the gap between income and expenses on your property." To maximize the depreciation you can claim, it is vital to carry out a full chattels apportionment, which breaks down the individual worth of each component of a property, from the letterbox to the kitchen carpet, which, according to IRD guidelines depreciate from a tax perspective at different rates.

While gaining intimate knowledge of this country's depreciation schedule before even thinking about buying an investment property might seem to be like trying to run before you can walk, it does underline that to go about investing profitably, you need to have carried out plenty of research. After all, these are not insignificant amounts of money we're talking about.

Where, oh where?

So having armed yourself with enough background knowledge of the "hows" and "whys", what about the "wheres"?

One of the most common misconceptions is that you can buy property either for cashflow or capital gain; that the two are mutually exclusive. Of course, real estate in prime locations, such as Herne Bay or Parnell, is more likely to appreciate in perceived value than housing stock in the lower socio-economic areas during boom periods. However to borrow a nautical analogy befitting of the City of Sails, a rising tide lifts all boats. According to statistics released by the National Property Data Centre, Otara, Mangere and Otahuhu, between 1994-2004, witnessed respective 10-year growth rates of 116%, 101% and 86%. And probably provided their fair share of positive cashflow properties for investors, too.

On the basis that you're approaching the concept of property investing as a means of achieving financial security, rather than a quasi-altruistic hobby afforded by already-established wealth, then perhaps the most important factor to remember is that you are not buying a house that you would be happy to live in, rather one suitable for your target tenant's needs.

As this sort of first-time investor, the chances are you will want to be investing in a property that is cashflow positive, which, unless you look for properties with a twist, such as home and incomes, or purpose-built student accommodation, today would invariably lead you south, where house prices are more affordable and therefore returns higher. Which brings us back full circle to the importance of good landlording.

Being a landlord

If owning and renting out a property in certain parts of South Auckland, whilst theoretically profitable, is pushing you a little too far out of your comfort zone, then it could be time to call in the professionals. For a fee of 7–10% of the weekly rent, you can sign over your feudal role to a modern-day squire: the property manager, who will take responsibility for the day-to-day running of the property, its profitability and its maintenance.

But if the ideal of being a hands-on landlord is what has attracted you to investing in property rather than in something less tangible, then you are going to need to familiarise yourself very quickly with the RTA: the Residential Tenancies Act. The RTA, which

is available from Tenancy Services at www.dbh.govt.nz outlines the responsibilities of both landlord and tenant … of which there are many. Failure to comply with these can lead rapidly to the landlord's worst nightmare: The Tenancy Tribunal. "If you've seen the TV show, Judge Judy, it runs a bit like that," explains leading Auckland property manager Pat Allen. "Adjudicators are less aggressive than Judge Judy … but not as humorous."

Although this may all sound a little scary, it doesn't have to be. Making friends with your tenants is ill-advised, as is letting to existing friends or family, since emotional detachment will allow you to concentrate more on the fact that your reason for investing was to make money. Nevertheless, ensuring your tenants are confident in your, or your property manager's, skills as a landlord, through responding promptly to requests for maintenance or accommodating a few individual quirks, or simply adding a carport or alarm, will help you retain your tenants long term and at market rate rent. This will then keep supplying your investments with the lifeblood they need to provide for your future.

Your move.

When you're planning to move into your first home, we have a comprehensive Home Buyer's Pack to guide you on your way. It's full of useful information – from doing your sums to things to look for when buying your home. To find out how you can get your Home Buyer's Pack, call us on **0800 47 87 25** or visit any branch.

The National Bank
The thoroughbred among banks

NBH 6955

Buying and moving house is one of the most stressful times in your life, and buying property is one of the biggest investments you will make. To start you on your way, here is our guide to financing a home, looking for one and how you go about making it your own.

The content in this section is not provided by The National Bank. It was independently researched and written by Where to Live in Auckland. We believe that everyone will find something of value in this guide, but inevitably it does not take into account your own individual personal circumstances. We recommend that you take professional advice before acting on the information.

Finance first

Buying a house is all about how much you can afford, or are willing to spend on a property. Most of us calmly and rationally set ourselves a budget – then end up spending more than we thought we would. Knowing how much you can or want to spend underpins all of the decisions you make about buying. It will determine how big the house can be, where it will be and in what condition. However in inner-city suburbs, unrenovated houses can sell for as much as their spruced-up neighbours, bought by people happy to have a blank canvas on which to create their own masterpiece of renovation.

Your pot of money will normally consist of a deposit – money you have saved up – and a mortgage. Under certain conditions, most banks will lend up to 90% of a house's registered value. If you are borrowing a high proportion of the purchase price, the bank may insist on mortgage protection insurance in the event of you losing your income for some reason – injury, death or redundancy.

Your bank will ask you to complete a budget summary showing income and expenses, to determine how much money they think you can comfortably afford to repay.

Banks can also provide you with a pre-purchase finance approval that will enable you to make offers on houses that are free of any finance condition clause, or let you bid comfortably at auction knowing how much you have to play with.

Your ability to meet repayments is only one factor. The bank needs to be happy that the property being offered for security is satisfactory, so depending on the proportion of your loan, they may need a pre-purchase valuation. Pre-approval will speed up the processing of the actual mortgage once you have bought.

So, once you know how much you can spend, you can go house-hunting. Check our neighbourhood information for house prices, to find out what areas or types of houses are best suited to your budget.

Visiting the bank

In years gone by, there wasn't much choice about which lending institution to ask for a mortgage – it was the one where you did your day-to-day banking. That's no longer the case. You can shop around, and banks are always advertising special rates or conditions in the hope of netting new mortgage customers. Chances are, if you have your mortgage with one bank, you will take your day-to-day banking with you. Some banks insist on it anyway.

So as well as checking out the home loans your own bank has to offer, research the rest too. Compare not only interest rates and types of loans available but also charges for processing a home loan and other conditions. For example, can you make lump sum payments on a fixed interest loan without incurring penalties? To top it off, consider which bank you feel best about – which one has given you good service and good advice.

Types of loans

Consider which type of loan suits your ability to pay and your lifestyle.

Table: this is the more common type of loan which spreads regular payments over the term of the loan, which only change when the prevailing interest rate changes. Initially, a bigger portion is made

One-off costs
When doing your budget, don't forget the one-off costs of buying a house. These might include:
- legal fees
- a valuation
- a builder's, engineer's or architect's report
- moving costs (not just the truck, but also reconnections for phone, Sky TV etc)
- insurance (house and possibly mortgage protection)
- bank administration fees
- urgent maintenance

Does the house need any urgent renovations or repairs before you move in? Talk to the bank about extra finance for these.

Need a Home Loan Specialist?

NBH 6955

up of interest and a smaller portion of the principal, but that reverses over time. The benefit of this type of loan is that it lets you budget well with a set amount each fortnight or month.

Reducing: this type of loan starts off high but reduces with each payment. Each repayment includes the same amount of principal. If you can cope with the higher initial payments, it's rewarding to see your principal steadily reducing. Also, over the term of the loan, you will have paid less in interest than with a table mortgage.

Interest only: some lending institutions will allow you to pay just the interest and none of the principal, but usually only for a short time and under certain circumstances.

Mixed: many banks offer essentially tailor-made loans that suit your particular circumstances, made up of a mix of different types of loan and interest. Check with your bank about this option.

The types of interest rates

Floating interest: this is the more commonly used, and allows you to benefit from any reductions in the floating interest rate. Conversely, your payments will increase if the rate goes up. Floating interest rates have been relatively low and steady recently.

Fixed: this is when the interest rate is fixed for a certain term (anything from six months to several years) and is not affected by fluctuations in the floating rate. Depending on the economy, these may be offered at slightly below or slightly above the floating rate. You gain the benefit if the floating rate stays above the fixed rate or, better still, rises. In more volatile times, however, you risk the floating rate dropping below your once-attractive fixed rate. Lump sum payments usually can't be made on fixed interest loans without incurring penalties.

Mixed: a combination may be best so that you can benefit from the advantages of both floating and fixed. Any lump sum payments can be made on your floating mortgage. Once the term of the fixed-interest loan is up, you can either negotiate another fixed term or put it in with the floating interest loan.

The term of the loan will affect the payments. The longer the term, the lower the payments will be but at the end of the term you would have ended up paying more interest. You can also choose the frequency of payments, the options usually being fortnightly or monthly, whichever suits your income and payment structure.

Going shopping – the area

Once you have done your mortgage homework, you can start looking for your perfect house. Read about the areas you have identified as having potential in the following chapters. Are they likely to include the type of house you prefer? Will you have like-minded people as your neighbours? Does the area have the amenities you need - shops, schools, parks? Does it match your budget? Check the commuting distance to work or public transport routes. What sort of setting would you like - quiet cul-de-sac, busy urban, established, new?

Drive around the areas, maybe refining your choices into certain streets.

The house

What type of house do you want or need? The style (villa, bungalow, 1970s family home, ex-state, contemporary etc) will determine not only the general characteristics but also maintenance levels and costs. Are you prepared to renovate, or do you just want to arrive and unpack?

If you're buying the house with someone else, discuss everything in detail. Is storage for the windsurfer more important than a dishwasher? Work it out. Buying a house is stressful enough, without having it threaten your relationship.

You may like to make up a score card and

use one for each house, so you don't have to rely on memory when you have been to numerous open homes. Split your list of requirements into two – the must-haves and the would-likes.

- How many bedrooms? Do you also need a study or home office, or will a desk in the corner of the family room do?
- Do you need a guest room?
- How many bathrooms? Would an extra toilet be handy?
- A separate laundry? Or will a cupboard or back of the garage do?
- How many living areas?
- Formal dining?
- Do you prefer open-plan living?
- Off-street parking? A garage? Double? Internal access?
- Aspect: do you want living areas to be north-facing for the sun?
- Is outdoor living important? Should it flow well from internal living areas?
- How big a garden do you need, if any? Big enough for a kids' cricket game, or is a small courtyard fine? Does it need to be fully fenced for the dog or toddlers?
- What sort of mod-cons do you want? Dishwasher? Filtered water tap? Underfloor bathroom heating?
- What level of security? Alarm? Video intercom?
- How much storage do you need, or are you going to be brave and have a big clean-out between moves?

The hidden things

Many faults can't be seen with a cruise through the open home. If you are not going to use a builder to inspect the property, watch for:

 How much can you afford?

NBH 6955

- level floors and sound piling
- rot in the weatherboards and joinery
- insulation
- water pressure – turn on the taps and flush the toilet
- noisy neighbours
- dampness (smell and/or mildew)
- leaks

In light of the leaking building syndrome, a building inspection on any plaster-clad house would be extremely sensible.

Armed with your wish list, start looking at the houses advertised - check the *New Zealand Herald's* Weekend Real Estate section, *Property Extra* and *Property Press*. Peruse local real estate agency windows. Check out websites – most real estate agencies put all listings on the internet.

Ring agents and visit open homes to see what type of houses are available. Start to consolidate your ideas. Be prepared for any eventuality – you may fall in love with the first house you see, or it may take months to find the perfect home. Make sure you visit the property at least twice before you buy it, preferably at different times of the day.

Buying methods

Selling by negotiation used to be the favoured way of marketing a house, with only very special properties or rural land being put up for auction. Now, auctions and tenders are much more common. In a volatile market, it may be difficult to assess a house's worth so an auction or tender allows the upper limit to be left wide open.

Some houses are marketed by negotiation but without an asking price. After one or two open homes, the agent may give an indication of value – this may be a price range or it may just be the bottom limit.

For a buyer, these methods of selling make it harder to know if you can afford a particular house. You have to do more homework, look at comparative recent sales in the area (ask the agent for a list of these) and visit lots of open homes. A house's CV (capital valuation) may be of some help. Even if it is out of date, you may be able to compare the CVs of recent sales with the actual sale price or ask real estate agents how much houses in the area are selling for in comparison to CV. Then you can apply that formula to the CVs of houses you are interested in.

If you are interested in a house being sold privately, make sure your lawyer thoroughly checks any contracts before you sign. If you don't feel comfortable negotiating directly with the homeowner, ask a friend to help.

Sale by negotiation

Agents have standard contracts for making offers on a house. You may want your lawyer to check it over and help you with the wording of any conditional clauses you might add. Remember that the real estate agent is working for the vendor, so it is best to get independent advice.

A conditional contract is one which gives you a set time, say one or two weeks, to sort out various things. Common conditions may be:
- finance (so you can organise a mortgage) – make sure you stipulate that the finance is satisfactory to you, not just the bank
- a valuation (which will probably be part of the mortgage requirement anyway)
- a title search, checking for easements, covenants or restrictions
- a Land Information Memorandum (LIM) from council. The LIM is used to highlight

anything that exists on the property that may not be permitted. If there's a garage or a deck that's higher than one metre from the ground on the property but no permits showing for these on the LIM, alarm bells should ring. Once you have bought the property, the onus shifts on to you to remedy these problems

- a satisfactory builder's or engineer's report
- sale of the buyer's own house

The vendor may add a "cash-out" clause to any conditional offer, which means that if they receive an attractive back-up offer, they give the first buyer a set time (usually about three days) to satisfy the conditions.

If not all of the conditions are satisfied, it doesn't mean you should walk away from the deal. If you are still keen on the house you may renegotiate a drop in the sale price in compensation or add a clause that the vendor has to remedy the situation before settlement.

The offer will specify the chattels to be left in the house (curtains, dishwasher, etc) and a settlement or completion date, which is when you pay over all the money in exchange for the key. A common time frame is six weeks, although it can be shorter or much, much longer (called a delayed settlement). If you are needing to sell your existing house, a delayed settlement may be more attractive to the vendor than an offer conditional on you selling, but will still give you the time to take action.

Once your offer is drawn up, it is presented to the seller (or vendor in real estate speak) and they will usually counter-offer. More counter-offers may follow and the negotiations will either be successful or fail.

Auctions

Many houses are taken to auction these days to take advantage of the competitive Auckland market. Some agents and homeowners also find it difficult to judge the value of a particular property, so will let the market decide, as such.

Auctions normally follow a fairly high-profile advertising campaign that lasts three or four weeks. You may not have all of this time, however, to make up your mind, as some houses sell before auction. A buyer wants to guarantee they are going to get the house of their dreams, so will offer an amount that's too good to refuse.

On the other hand, beware of the agent who tells you something is going to sell before auction in order to prise an offer out of you – this may mean that they have identified you as the only real bidder in the running, but still want you to believe you are in a competitive situation. Or agents may use pre-auction offers to assess the sort of money people are prepared to pay to help guide the vendors on a reserve price, but then still take the property to auction.

If you are serious about a house that is being sold by auction (or tender), make sure you let the agent know. Don't be coy, or you may find out the property has already been sold and you've missed out on the chance. To buy at auction you need to be sure of your finance. An auction sale is cash and unconditional and you must front up a cheque for 10% of the sale price straight after the bidding. This means doing any homework on the property beforehand, which can involve some costs – for example, if you want a LIM or a valuer's report. Real

 Investing in residential property?

estate agents selling auction properties will often prepare a pack of information for you, including such things as a copy of the title and maybe even a LIM. They'll provide a copy of the sale contract with the usual details such as the settlement date, etc, for you and/or your lawyer to peruse.

The actual auction is an emotion-charged and fast-paced affair. You might want to go to another auction beforehand, just to watch what happens. Try to be calm. Go along with your top bid in mind and be prepared to stick to it. Be confident and firm – it will help psyche out the other bidders. If you don't feel confident at all, an agent can bid on your behalf.

The vendors would have set a reserve, which is the minimum price they want for the property. A property cannot be sold "under the hammer" until the bidding has reached that reserve. Once the bidding has reached the reserve, the auctioneer will say something like "this property is now on the market", which lets you know that from now on, the top bid wins and that the buyer is committed.

If the bidding doesn't reach the reserve, the property is "passed in" and normally negotiations will ensue between the vendor and the top bidder.

Tenders

A tender is like an auction but without the public bidding. Essentially, you fill out an offer document that states a price. On the day the tender closes, all of the tender offers are opened and the most acceptable (if any) chosen.

For a vendor, a tender gives the benefit of privacy – the sale price isn't shouted out in an auction room. They also don't have to accept any of the tenders. If they are not happy with the price or conditions, they will ask the agent to negotiate with one or more of the potential buyers to see if an agreement can be reached. They normally have five days to do this.

One buyer may be so keen, they will offer a good deal more than the others, so the vendor gets a premium price. This is a common characteristic of tenders.

It's trickier for a buyer, because you have no idea what level your competitors are at. The idea is to do your homework, study the market, get advice from a valuer and give it your best shot if you are serious about buying. Unlike other methods of selling, you probably won't get a chance to make another offer and you need to ask yourself how you would feel if you missed out by a thousand dollars.

One advantage is that you are able to ask that certain conditions be added to the tender offer, much like a negotiated sale – but remember that a cleaner offer is always more attractive to the vendor. Most tenders are "closed" or "blind", where buyers cannot be told what the other bids are.

Buying land

Usable land is scarce in the more established parts of Auckland. A good percentage of subdividable sections have already been cut up and infill housing is now a feature of many suburbs. In desparation to fulfil the building dream, some people buy a section with an exisitng house and remove it.

When buying land, there are certain things to check. Make sure there is a clear title to the property. If it has only just been subdivided, the paperwork may still be going through council, so any offer should be conditional to clear title.

Check that there are no covenants or caveats on the land, or if there are, that you are happy with them. If it's someone's back yard you are buying, they may have lodged a caveat on the title stipulating that you can't build within so many metres of their boundary, or that your new house must be designed in such a way as to not encroach on their privacy.

In a new subdivision, there may be covenants restricting the types of building materials or the style of house you may use, in order to keep the neighbourhood up to a certain standard.

Many developers will offer land and design packages, where you have a choice of sections and a choice of house designs. They then build for you and will often offer their own finance packages. Although these sorts of deals are standard, always have your own lawyer check the contract. You might want to add a penalty clause for completion, for example, if the developer doesn't build the house in the time they say they will, they incur financial penalties.

Your lawyer

Whenever property is bought or sold, the ownership has to be legally transferred – known as conveyancing. This is normally carried out by a solicitor, either your regular one or there are specialists set up, often offering set fees.

Conveyancing includes things like searching and approving the title, checking the sale agreement, making sure the mortgage documents are in order and properly signed, explaining the documents to you and registering them.

The cost of conveyancing will vary depending on the complexity of each deal, and may range from $600 to $1200.

Settlement day

Before settlement day, you are entitled to a pre-settlement inspection of the property. This is to check that the property is in the condition agreed upon and that nothing has happened to it between signing the contract and moving in - like any sort of damage, or removal of stated chattels.

It's best to do this as close to settlement as possible, preferable once the previous owners have moved out, although this may be tricky. This allows you to see the condition of the property much more clearly.

If you do notice a problem, inform your lawyer, who will inform the vendor's lawyer. Your lawyer may decide to withhold some of the money until the problem is remedied.

Once the funds have gone through to the vendor (often electronically these days rather than by bank cheque), you get the key and move in. Break open the champagne and congratulate yourself on your new home.

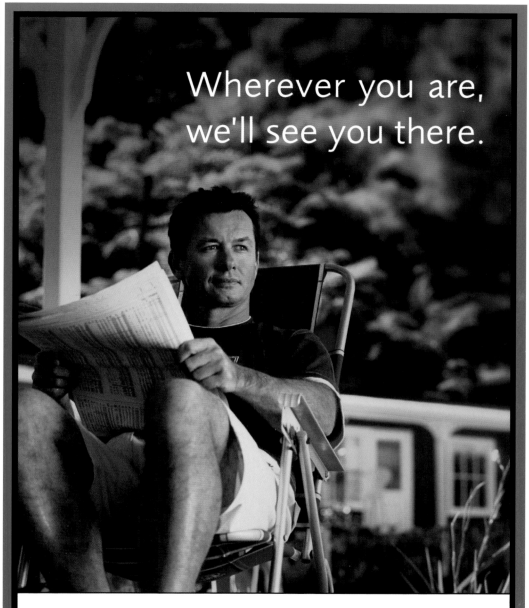

Wherever you are, we'll see you there.

Wherever you want to live in Auckland, our Mobile Mortgage Managers can help you get there. Local and knowledgeable, they are specialists in the Auckland market. Call anytime on **0800 47 87 25**.

The National Bank
The thoroughbred among banks

NBH 6955

Central

The central suburbs of Auckland are where it all began. It's from here that Auckland has sprawled, around its two harbours and edging ever further north and south, to become the largest city in New Zealand. The central suburbs is where most of Auckland's history lies and where most of its prestige real estate can be found. The apartment boom of recent years means that Auckland's central business district now has an energy it once lacked. The other growth area is Waiheke Island, which buyers are making their permanent home rather than just a holiday destination.

Auckland central encompasses a large area, from the southern edge of the Waitemata Harbour, west to Avondale, east to Panmure and south to Onehunga.

The central suburbs are where any new real estate trends are first felt, and in boom times,

this is where price increases are at their highest. As areas like Ponsonby, Parnell, Remuera and Mt Eden become more expensive, attention turns to the next suburban ring. Suburbs that used to be called "outer" are now "fringe", and the list of suburbs referred to as "inner" gets longer.

The rest of Auckland's homeowners wonder why inner-city residents continue to pay huge sums for houses with no garaging that sit so close together you can hear your neighbour sneeze. Conversely, people who have prised themselves away from the inner areas marvel at the space they can buy for half the price out west or on the shore. And you can still get a decent cup of coffee!

the sparkling Waitemata
coffee and cafés
high energy nights
high-ticket houses

Central Auckland is where you find the most of the truly luxurious real estate. Blue chip suburbs like Remuera, Herne Bay, Parnell and Epsom boast some gracious properties with large houses and plenty of room for swimming pools and even tennis courts.

With Auckland's ongoing road congestion woes, the central city is an attraction for CBD workers keen on spending as little time commuting as they can. The abundance of new apartments and townhouses mean that living near the city is still affordable, whether you are buying or renting – rental prices have not kept increasing at the same rate as housing prices in recent years.

The amenities for central dwellers are plenty and long-established. Great shopping, plenty of big parks, the sparkling Waitemata Harbour, top restaurants and cafes, plenty of sporting facilities and clubs.

The housing architecture is hugely varied. Much of it is older – villas, bungalows, state cottages – while many new and snazzy homes now share the land with their older neighbours. Whatever type or age of house you are seeking, you can find it somewhere in central Auckland.

AUCKLAND

CENTRAL

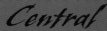

Reduce your risk

Thinking about buying or renovating a house?

If you do your homework well, you can considerably reduce the risks associated with buying or renovating.

Purchasing a Land information Memorandum (LIM) from Auckland City Council is one of the key tools in helping to reduce the risk when you are either buying or renovating a property. LIMs can now be ordered via our website and shortly will be available to you in electronic format.

You can also find more details about a property at our property information centre, where our staff will help you with:

- LIMs
- council valuations and aerial photographs
- property maps showing zoning and limitations special land features, contours and drainage
- consent plans such as floor, site boundaries elevations and structural details
- building and resource consents including code compliance certificates, specifications calculations, inspections, soil and other reports.

A small investment at the beginning can save you thousands later on.

Find out more

■ Call Auckland City on 379 2020 or
  visit the property information centre at 35 Graham Street, Auckland Central

■ Visit www.aucklandcity.govt.nz and click on 'apply for a LIM online'

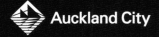

Vibrant and cosmopolitan, full of apartments, students and restaurants and with the Viaduct Harbour on its doorstep ... this is just one of the more obvious ways to describe the atmosphere and make-up of Auckland's inner city. It took us a while to cotton on but now, like other major world cities, we see our CBD as a place to live not just work and play. Auckland's central city residents are not all young and trendy. Many aged 50 and more are making the city their home, attracted by the security and ease of apartments, and closeness to entertainment. The city is obviously suited to those not yearning for the quarter acre or lifestyle block – and judging by latest trends, this is an increasing number of Aucklanders. The popularity of city living is soaring.

Who lives there?

As well as the ageing baby boomers (particularly the never-married and now divorced ones) who feel more at home in the heart of cosmopolitanism than the suburbs, central Auckland is home to many young people. Despite recent bad press among the Asian communities, there are still numerous tertiary and language school students living in inner city apartments. As language schools have diversified their markets, students of other nationalities have moved in with "newer" nationalities including Russians and other eastern Europeans, and lately Brazilians and Argentineans.

Many residents choose to live in the city because they can walk to work, universities, schools and entertainment. Other than students, working inner city residents tend to

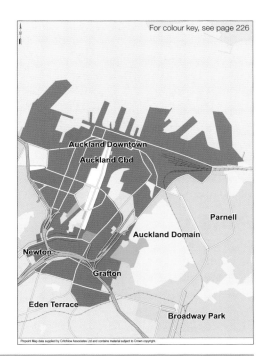

For colour key, see page 226

Auckland Downtown
Auckland Cbd
Parnell
Auckland Domain
Newton
Grafton
Eden Terrace
Broadway Park

Pinpoint Map data supplied by Critchlow Associates Ltd and contains material subject to Crown copyright.

Population profile	Population in 2001 11,193	% Aged Under 15 years 4.02	% Aged over 65 Years 4.1
% European 51.38	% Maori 5.49	% Pacific Peoples 3.46	% Asian 31.2

be professionals, in fields such as law, management consultancy, finance and property. Despite recent immigration downturns, the city is still a magnet for new arrivals and many ex-pats are choosing to live here as well.

Typical dwellings

As you'd expect, the city scene is apartments, apartments and more apartments, ranging in size and style. New apartment buildings just keep emerging, despite dire warnings from industry commentators and economists alike who say we're headed for an oversupply. Interestingly, most apartments are sold before completion, albeit that some purchasers are ever-optimistic investors.

There are older houses in nearby Grafton and Newton, but many of the grand villas have been removed to make way for terrace housing developments.

Many city apartments are of variable quality in terms of both design and construction. There is the top end, some medium end – and some that may well become slums of the future. It is a case of buyer beware, and it should also be noted that not all apartments are freehold. Leasehold apartments are found particularly around the viaduct, Princes Wharf and the railway station developments.

Amenities
Schools ★★

Demand for schooling in the central city is not great. The eastern part is in zone for Auckland Grammar School. Others include Freemans Bay Primary, private Jewish school Kadimah College, which is open to all children, Senior College and Auckland Girls Grammar School. For a full list, see page 272.

Shops ★★★★

After spending some time in the doldrums when people flocked to suburban malls instead, Queen St shopping is once again attracting serious shoppers. Fashionable new chain stores sit alongside established outlets such as Smith & Caughey.

Newmarket and St Lukes mall are relatively close and two large supermarkets, the new Foodtown near Britomart and New World in Freemans Bay, give inner city dwellers plenty of choice for food shopping.

Leisure ★★★★

It's relaxing to walk around the central city waterfront. There's plenty of boat watching, with superyachts still moored in Viaduct Harbour. The viaduct cafes, bars and restaurants are still the place to be seen, for trendy Aucklanders and out-of-towner tourists alike. Auckland City Council has developed a draft plan to upgrade the waterfront, extending walkways and turning the former America's Cup base into a marine events centre. Beyond the harbour, the central city has plenty of tempting cafes for people watching from all angles. There are quite a few green spaces in the inner city area, including Albert Park, Myers Park and Victoria Park – and the Auckland Domain isn't far for joggers.

Real Estate
Trends

The only certain trend in the Auckland property market at the moment is the increased sales of small inner city apartments.

With houses taking longer to sell and the prices in many suburbs falling or levelling off, commentators attribute the recent Auckland median house price drop to the number of lower-end inner city apartments that have recently changed hands.

With apartment building after apartment building interrupting the skyline, most people thought that these too-small-to-swing-a-cat-style apartments would sit on the market and not sell. It seems they were wrong.

Foreign investors looking to include New Zealand real estate in their portfolios are snapping up these cribs by the dozen. One inner city high density residential apartment block is reported to have sold groups of one and two bedroom apartments to Australian investors, with many others selling to Russian women and Asian students.

Leaky building syndrome continues to affect buyer demand for afflicted properties, but changes to the building code mean that many newer developments aren't tarred by the same brush.

Savvy buyers are also well aware of council air rights and look for apartments where they can not be built out. Buildings that are identified in the District Plan as not having such rights often take longer to sell.

Many inner city dwellings – more than a third – don't include car parks. Parking facilities can cost anywhere from $35,000 extra and are often on a separate title.

Local Hero: Britomart Transport Centre

Aucklanders waited with baited breath for the opening of the $204 million new central transport hub in July 2003. Centred around the historic Chief Post Office building at the bottom of town, it was one of the largest projects ever undertaken by a local authority and now links ferry services from across Quay St, buses from the reconfigured Queen Elizabeth Square in front and rail services in a new terminal behind. Despite early complaints about lack of train reliability, it has settled in to become a well-used facility.

The stunning post office building, built in 1912 and now beautifully restored, and its adjoining terminal also house numerous shops and eateries. The original part of the building features an historic banking chamber, stained glass domes and elaborate stone carvings. It's linked to the railway station, which has three platforms and five rail lines, by a glasshouse made from louvred panels.

Rental and investment

This area will always attract a steady stream of renters and investors, with plenty of choice for both parties. According to the Auckland City Council, about half of the CBD apartments are owner occupied and half rented.

Best buildings

Many of the apartment buildings in the viaduct are considered good, including The Point, Lighter Quay and The Parc complex of apartments. Top freehold buildings in the city include the Metropolis, Highgate, Quay West and the Connaught – although this can change almost annually, with new and improved buildings always on the rise.

Converted loft-style apartments in heritage buildings are also considered prime real estate.

Look Out ⓘ

Do your homework if you're investing in an apartment. Watch out for immigration and student trends that may affect your returns. Small apartments can provide good returns, but many are only 20m2 in size, have poor ventilation, no sound-proofing or windows and little natural light. If the rental market slows, these are the apartments that will stand empty.

Smart Buy ⊘

A soundly constructed, well-located, central city apartment close to the university and Queen St would be a sound investment. It is predicted that by 2020, 80% of all home occupiers will be singles with high disposable incomes, with many finding the central city very attractive. Also, with commuting times increasing and people moving out of the city, the need for central crash pads is increasing. Newton, in particular, is seen as a good place for first-home buyers and singles to get a toe in the market.

House prices

Studio apartment
Price	$100,000 plus

Entry-level apartment
Bedroom	🛏
Price	$120,000 plus

More spacious apartment
Bedroom	🛏
Price	$250,000 plus

Apartment with views
Bedrooms	🛏 🛏
Price	$280,000 plus

Older loft-style apartment
Bedrooms	🛏 🛏 🛏
Price	$400,000 plus

Viaduct apartment
Bedroom	🛏
Price	$400,000 plus

Larger viaduct apartment
Bedrooms	🛏 🛏
Price	$500,000 plus

Rental prices

Apartment
Bedroom	🛏
Price	$250 – $350/wk
Bedrooms	🛏 🛏
Price	$350 – $475/wk
Bedrooms	🛏 🛏 🛏
Price	$500 – $600/wk

Travel times

The transport facilities are great – everything starts and ends in downtown Auckland. The Intercity bus terminal is under Sky City Casino. The ferry terminal services the gulf islands, the North Shore, Gulf Harbour and Half Moon Bay. And Britomart has brought trains into the central city, as well as providing a central connection point for bus, ferry and rail.

How did such an innocent suburb get to be associated with horror? The middle-aged among us know Avondale for its historic Hollywood Cinema, and its amazing 10-year run of the classic cult movie The Rocky Horror Picture Show. For others, the most enduring image is of the large hairy spiders that take their name from the suburb. But really, Avondale is a very unscary, established suburb close to the city and very popular with its discerning residents. It's one of Auckland's oldest suburbs, with the first European settlement as early as 1843. Originally part of the Whau District (an area reaching from near Mt Roskill to Henderson), the suburb was called Avondale in 1882 and became exemplified by its brick yards and market gardens.

Who lives there?

With trouble-free access to the city and a good array of amenities in west Auckland, the Avondale area is now popular with numerous professionals seeking character family houses on large sections.

Avondale also attracts first-home buyers and immigrants, who like it for its good schools, job opportunities and lively community spirit. There's also a large Polynesian influence.

It's always been multi-cultural and in some parts staunchly blue collar. The influx of yuppies and dinkies who have been scared off by the prices of some other inner-city suburbs is changing the profile of the area's people.

Many of these new residents are also impressed by the magnificent potential of the area.

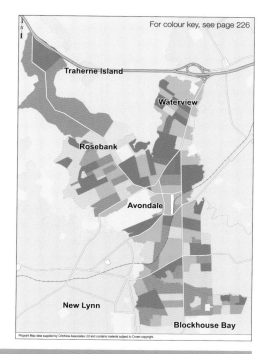

For colour key, see page 226

Traherne Island

Waterview

Rosebank

Avondale

New Lynn

Blockhouse Bay

Pinpoint Map data supplied by Critchlow Associates Ltd and contains material subject to Crown copyright.

Population profile	Population in 2001 25,206	% Aged Under 15 years 22.8	% Aged over 65 Years 10.08
% European 45.11	% Maori 10.93	% Pacific Peoples 24.57	% Asian 20.02

Typical dwellings

There is probably no typical dwelling in Avondale. There are, in fact, numerous renovated villas and bungalows plus an abundant supply of 1930s through to 1960s brick and tile or weatherboard family homes. The past two decades have seen a number of modern infill plaster or brick and tile townhouses. Although created in 1861, Waterview was slow to develop – the area is now sought after however for its waterside location.

Amenities
Schools ★★★

Generally, schooling in the area is above average. Avondale College is very highly regarded and people will move into the suburb for this reason alone.

For a full list of schools, see pg 272.

Shops ★★★

Lynn Mall and St Lukes are close by and that has had an obvious impact on suburban strip shopping in Avondale itself. Avondale centre recently had a revamp with a newly paved town square, a stage, modern toilets and a 3m high spider sculpture, and that's attracted new shops and cafés.

Every Sunday, the local market – popular

with many from outside the area – at the racecourse sells local produce, arts, crafts, foods and second-hand goods.

Leisure ★★★

Avondale is famed for its race course and jockey club in Ash St. There are also other sporting clubs, including bowls.

West Coast beaches are easy to reach, and Pt Chevalier beach is just down the road. There are plenty of parks and reserves.

Waterview has nearby mangrove wetlands accessible via Waterview Park and Howlett St Reserve. Backing Waterview is the Motu Manawa/Pollen Island Marine Reserve.

Heron Park is in limbo pending further motorway development.

Local facilities include numerous gyms and sports clubs and a number of sports facilities at the college. Restaurants abound and cultural and educational facilities including libraries and community centres are available. Avondale College runs an extensive community education programme.

Real Estate
Trends

Values in Avondale have increased appreciably during the past decade, driven by the good public transport and demand for land by developers and homeowners. The nearby industrial and commercial areas have attracted businesses locating from other parts of the city, so there's work handy and increased economic activity generally. All of this, and the proposed motorway extensions, make this an area likely to continue growing in value. At the moment it's still a reasonably affordable area close to the city. Properties around Rosebank Rd are cheaper than the elevated properties above Great North Rd towards New Windsor.

Rental and investment

There is a shortage of rental accommodation in the area. Numerous ex-rentals have been renovated and on-sold to owner-occupiers. Much of the demand for rental is driven by education – tertiary in the form of Unitec and secondary in Avondale College. There's also a more recent demand from city workers.

Best streets

Blockhouse Bay Rd and Holly St. Also Avondale Heights, including Cradock St, Himikera Ave and Powell St. The streets near Unitec are highly regarded at present.

Look Out ⊘

The extension of State Highway 20 through Avondale – it may be a nightmare while under construction, but will be great when finished. It will link to the north-western motorway (SH16) and the upper harbour motorway (SH18). Traffic will be able to bypass existing clog-ups through the central city and the harbour bridge.

Smart Buy ⊘

Avondale is a colourful and relatively affordable city fringe option – for the time being. Edged with water and close to good shopping, it is well worth a look. Although, remember, it's not Ponsonby and never will be. Albeit that many agents will try and convince you that it is! Also appealing is Waterview, which is small and isolated, and many of its homes have sea views.

House prices

Unit or townhouse	
Bedrooms	🛏 🛏
Price	$250,000
Older house	
Bedrooms	🛏 🛏
Price	$180,000 – $250,000
Bedrooms	🛏 🛏 🛏
Price	$380,000 – $650,000
Bungalow and villa	
Price	$400,000 plus

Rental prices

Flat	
Bedroom	🛏
Price	$173 – $210/wk
Bedrooms	🛏 🛏
Price	$250 – $280/wk
Bedrooms	🛏 🛏 🛏
Price	$300 – $331/wk
House	
Bedroom	🛏
Price	$197 – $245/wk
Bedrooms	🛏 🛏
Price	$265 – $300/wk
Bedrooms	🛏 🛏 🛏
Price	$306 – $360/wk

Travel times

From Avondale shops

CBD	off-peak 10 min
	peak 30 min
North-western motorway	off-peak 5 min
	peak 15 min
Airport	30 min
Lynn Mall	3-4 min
St Lukes mall	8 min

The train currently travels up Rosebank Rd and along the top of Blockhouse Bay Rd. One idea is to have it come into the centre of town along Crayford St. The area is well served by buses.

This may be a fairly low-profile part of the city but Blockhouse Bay offers some hidden treasures in terms of lifestyle and environment. Sitting on the southern edge of the Manukau Harbour many houses have outstanding sea views. The harbour is a continual source of interest, with ships and seabirds coming and going. By night you can see the lights of Glenbrook Steel Mill on the southern horizon. On the city side of Blockhouse Bay, some streets look across surrounding suburbs while others get a view of the Sky Tower. Lynfield is on a point of land which means there is no through traffic. It's quiet and residents love it. The name Blockhouse Bay refers to fortifications built in the mid-19th century when European settlers feared Maori attack.

Who lives there?

This area has traditionally been a suburb for middle-class, Pakeha families. Recent decades have seen the area become a lot more cosmopolitan and it's now home to a mix of nationalities, including Fijian Indians and Asian immigrants. Popular with first-home buyers and investors, the area has many young families who move here for the numerous schools. Lately, the frantic pace of the Auckland property market has seen many first-home purchasers now being unable to afford houses here. Many owner-occupiers are in the 30-plus age group and consider Blockhouse Bay a good stepping stone to suburbs closer to the city.

Lynfield College's strong reputation attracts education-conscious migrants who also see the district as a good starting point in the

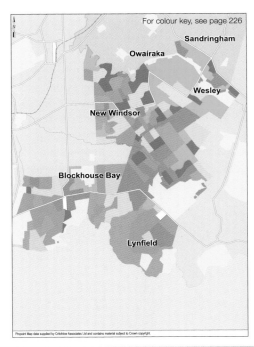

For colour key, see page 226

Sandringham
Owairaka
Wesley
New Windsor
Blockhouse Bay
Lynfield

Pinpoint Map data supplied by Critchlow Associates Ltd and contains material subject to Crown copyright.

Population profile	Population in 2001 26,283	% Aged Under 15 years 22.44	% Aged over 65 Years 12.24
% European 50.43	% Maori 5.95	% Pacific Peoples 14.67	% Asian 29.06

Auckland market. Blockhouse Bay, Wesley and New Windsor are a mix of rental and owner-occupied properties.

Typical dwellings

The most common houses in this area are weatherboard bungalows built between 25 and 35 years ago, usually with a brick or concrete base and iron roofs. There are also a number of solid brick and tile homes. There is some terrace housing at the bottom of Blockhouse Bay. Infill housing is common, typically with an older bungalow on the front section, and a 10 or 20-year-old house at the rear. There is a state housing area at the bottom of Blockhouse Bay.

Amenities
Schools ★★★

The area is well served with schools, including the well-regarded Lynfield College. For a full list, see page 272.

Shops ★★★

The Blockhouse Bay shopping centre has a village atmosphere, with about 20 shops including cafes, a butcher, florist, medical centres and a supermarket. Lynfield has a modern shopping complex including several new fast food outlets and a supermarket.

Leisure ★★★

Local sporting amenities include excellent recreational parks, a skateboard park, an ice skating rink, The Portage Trust Tennis Centre in Rathlin St (indoor and outdoor), the recently refurbished Blockhouse Bay Boat Club, bowling clubs and rugby clubs. On a cultural note, there is a good library and many artistic and creative events take place throughout the year. There are several places with street access to the harbour. It's possible to swim at Blockhouse Bay and Wattle Bay - the beaches are tidal, but there are beautiful parks with children's play areas nearby. The region is well supplied with parks, including Craigavon, Avondale South Domain, Manukau Domain and Wattle Bay Reserve. It is also handy to the Waitakere Ranges.

The local restaurant and café scene is gradually improving, with a few cafes and restaurants in Blockhouse Bay village. More refined dining can be found at nearby Titirangi.

Real Estate Trends

Seeing rapid rises since 2002 and only slowing in late 2004, the area has a reasonably high turnover of properties. Gone are the days of nine out of 10 properties selling above vendor's expectations, although prices are still buoyant. Because this is an average-priced Auckland suburb, buyers are always going to look here before viewing less desirable areas and, generally, there are still some good buys to be had. The area has many long-term Kiwi owners who tend to be very stable.

By contrast, immigrant families often buy

and sell within a couple of years to consolidate their equity. Other properties coming onto the market are through elderly couples selling to go to retirement villages.

Land size makes a difference. Anything larger than 750m2 is snapped up for its subdivision potential. Properties near the new motorway extension in New Windsor are taking longer to sell.

Rental and investment

This is a high rental area, but the range of prices is relatively small.

Best streets

Gilfillan St, Mitchell St, Endeavour St and the seaward end of Blockhouse Bay Rd.

Smart Buy ⊘

The area is still considered a good buy within reasonable travelling distance of central Auckland. Sea views, little crime and good facilities for the elderly attract a decent calibre of buyers, who help solidify the area. Quality schools continue to attract younger families. And the good news is that you could possibly get change from $350,000!

House prices

Unit	
Bedrooms	🛏 🛏
Price	$170,000 – $260,000
House	
Bedrooms	🛏 🛏 🛏
Price	$300,000 plus
Older renovated house	
Price	$400,000 – $600,000
Executive house with harbour views	
Bedrooms	🛏 🛏 🛏 🛏 🛏
Price	$1 million

Rental prices

Flat	
Bedroom	🛏
Price	$180 – $200/wk
Bedrooms	🛏 🛏
Price	$230 – $260/wk
House	
Bedrooms	🛏 🛏
Price	$240 – $290/wk
Bedrooms	🛏 🛏 🛏
Price	$310 – $350/wk
Bedrooms	🛏 🛏 🛏 🛏
Price	$360 – $480/wk

Travel times

From Blockhouse Bay shops	
CBD	off-peak 20 min
	peak 30 min
North-western motorway	10 min
Airport	20 min
St Lukes mall	10 min
Lynn Mall	5 min

Stagecoach Auckland provides a regular bus service from Blockhouse Bay and Lynfield. The coming SH20 motorway extension from Hillsborough through to the north-western will be all benefit (drivers will get places faster) without the disadvantages (it's not close enough to be noisy).

This group of suburbs reflects all that is aspirational about Auckland – history, a sense of grandeur, an interesting demographic range and a social and wealth structure which embraces both old and new money. Living in the eastern bays carries unquenchable, unshakeable status for Aucklanders, not to mention a very pleasant lifestyle. The harbour views, the white sand beaches, the parade of waterfront cafes, the leafy bays … St Heliers, Glendowie, Mission Bay, Kohimarama and Orakei roll into one fabulous stretch but each manages to retain its own separate character and charm. With the eastern corridor still having an uncertain future, the pleasant – if rather slow – drive to the CBD each morning provides a reality check for many residents.

Who lives there?

Many residents are second or third generation owners – and the wiser ones fully appreciate that they're sitting on a goldmine. Many newly wealthy Aucklanders and a number of migrants aspire to live in the area as well. Residents choose to live here because while it's close to the CBD, the life-style is quite distinct from inner-city living.

Foreign currency trends have made the eastern bays tempting to returning ex-pats, as well as new immigrants and other overseas buyers. Many residents move around the bays, or relocate from neighbouring suburbs. Older owners of large homes on big sections may trade them in for an apartment or relocate to retirement complexes such as the Grace Joel village in St Heliers.

Kohimarama attracts both families and

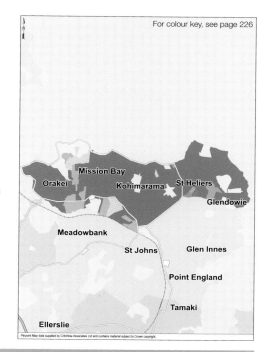

For colour key, see page 226

retired people with its facilities – locals enjoy being able to walk to the waterfront for casual strolls or more energetic runs, with superlative views of Rangitoto Island.

Mission Bay and St Heliers are locations to be seen in, and many choose to purchase in these suburbs for that reason alone. Bastion Pt is owned by the Ngati Whatua tribe, which hosts many cultural events including highly popular Kapa Haka concerts.

Typical dwellings

The eastern bays are not really the place to look for character villas or bungalows but they have every other type of dwelling – from the opulent mansions along Orakei's Paritai Dr to state housing in some pockets of the various suburbs. A number of ex-state homes have been privatised and revitalised so now command premium prices for their location.

Some of the state houses along Kitemoana St in Orakei have some of the best sea views in the entire city.

The continued development of the beaches at Mission Bay (including a beauitfully made boardwalk) means that the area is high on the priority list for buyers seeking a relaxed lifestyle.

Amenities
Schools ★★★★
Local schooling is of a high quality, with many sought-after primary and intermediate schools. Co-educational Selwyn College and Glendowie College and Catholic boys' school Sacred Heart are the local secondary schools.

For a full list, see page 272.

Shops ★★★
Shopping facilities are spread throughout the bays, with a village atmosphere at St Heliers and a preponderance of eateries at Mission Bay.

There's limited grocery shopping locally – although there is Eastridge shopping centre at the back of Kohimarama, and Meadowbank Foodtown is reasonably close. Many locals make weekend shopping trips to Newmarket and Botany Town Centre.

Leisure ★★★★★
There's plenty to do for both landlubbers and water sports enthusiasts. All the bays are tidal but suitable for swimming. The reserve bordering Mission Bay is well frequented by picnickers, walkers and sunbathers. The Glendowie sandspit and Tahuna Torea bird sanctuary have fabulous walks. And then there's Tamaki Dr for walking, running, cycling, stroller-pushing or rollerblading.

There are numerous green areas including Orakei Domain, the quaintly named Dingle

Dell, Glover Park, Madill's Farm, Kepa Bush Park, family friendly Churchill Park and many smaller reserves.

Local icons such as Tamaki Yacht Club – location of choice for many social functions – and Kohi Yacht Club are well patronised. Mission Bay has cinemas as well as numerous restaurants and cafes. St Heliers is also noted for its cuisine. Kelly Tarlton's Underwater World is enjoyed by tourists and locals alike.

Needless to say, this is cafe country. Latte lovers flock to the bays for daily or weekly fixes. With the cafe strip buzzing at night and all weekend, it's often said that locals leave the area for a bit of peace!

other parts of fringe inner-city Auckland, do-ups or subdividable properties are particularly sought after.

With such a large area and with diverse housing, prices range hugely, from early $200,000s to $8 million.

Rental and investment

The popularity of the area means the rental market is strong. People seeking the lifestyle often decide to rent long term rather than buy.

Best streets

Paritai Dr in Orakei, Cliff Rd and Spring-combe Rd in St Heliers and The Rise and Riddell Rd in Glendowie.

Real Estate
Trends

Properties in this area will always be in demand and command good prices. Heavily affected by the boom in recent years, the market is easing off a little. This isn't impacting so much in the mid range of homes but top-end palatial pads are taking longer to sell, and often have to have a price adjustment. Homes across the road from the water continue to sell well.

Entry-point properties, like classic brick and tile units, are being snapped up, bought by professional couples, who enjoy waterfront living but can't afford a standalone house.

Glendowie, a once less-desirable area, is now considered a good option. The views are not as good but the local schools are excellent and prices are relatively low, all of which makes it attractive to families. Also, many sections are larger here and there isn't as much infill housing as in the bays. As with

Local Hero: the new Kohimarama beach

Gleaming in all its new sandy glory, Kohimarama Beach has been completely transformed from a rather sad version of a beach into one even North Shore dwellers would admire.

Although it would be a stretch of the imagination to equate it to Australia's Gold Coast beach, the arrival of 50,000 cubic metres of imported sand has definitely improved the attractiveness of this popular weekend destination.

The beach, which now features an 800m strip of sand 5m to 15m in width at high tide, had gradually eroded during the past few decades. Summer now sees the beach full of bathers and bakers, all eager to soak up the atmosphere and enjoying not only the new sand but the enhanced boardwalk and reserve.

Smart Buy ⊘

You can't really lose in this part of Auckland. The eastern bays are unique for their leisure facilities and lifestyle opportunities, yet they're so close to the city.

House prices

Unit	
Bedrooms	🛏 🛏
Price	$250,000 plus
Small freestanding townhouse	
Price	$380,000 plus
Ex-state house on a half site	
Price	$400,000 plus
House do-up	
Bedrooms	🛏 🛏 🛏
Price	$400,000 plus
House on full site or new townhouse	
Price	$600,000 plus
Clifftop home	
Price	Multi-millions

Rental prices

Flat or apartment	
Bedroom	🛏
Price	$220 – $340/wk
House or apartment	
Bedrooms	🛏 🛏
Price	$350 – $440/wk
House	
Bedrooms	🛏 🛏 🛏
Price	$400 – $550/wk
Bedrooms	🛏 🛏 🛏 🛏
Price	$500 – $890/wk

Travel times

From Mission Bay (add 5 min for St Heliers)	
CBD off-peak	15-20 min
	peak 30 min
Britomart CBD by train	8 min
Greenlane interchange	15 min
Airport	25 min
Newmarket	15 min

Buses run regularly to St Heliers. A train runs between Glen Innes and Meadowbank and along the bottom of Orakei Rd.

You could call Epsom the dignified elder statesman of Auckland City – very dignified and proper. It has some famous residents and residences, and is full of leafy streets and truly magnificent old houses. Even the presence of some major arterial routes running through it towards the city doesn't dent the overriding feeling of peace and gentility. It has access to some of the city's top secondary schools, which has seen many parents move across town from places like Herne Bay – they used to think Epsom was too staid, now they're more interested in the good-quality free education it offers. While some residents bemoan the arrival of sterile infill housing during the past decade, the area remains popular with a wide variety of people.

Who lives there?

The faces of Epsom have changed noticeably in recent years with many "education aware" Asians making the area their home. Many of the suburb's decades-old family names, finding the upkeep of their grounds costly and time consuming, have moved on. Rightly or wrongly, many of their homesteads have been flattened and replaced with modern townhouses.

Many families choose to live in Epsom, especially those with secondary school-age children. The closeness to numerous quality private and public schools makes Epsom an idyllic choice for parents not wanting to travel too far for the school round. So close are the schools that some children will even walk to school – a phenomenon virtually unheard of in recent years. The suburb is

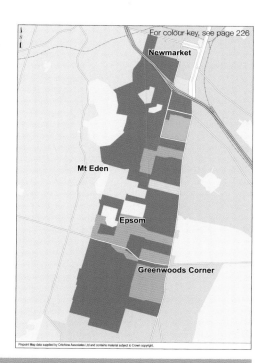

For colour key, see page 226

Newmarket

Mt Eden

Epsom

Greenwoods Corner

Pinpoint Map data supplied by Critchlow Associates Ltd and contains material subject to Crown copyright.

Population Profile	Population in 2001 9,849	% Aged Under 15 years 20.32	% Aged over 65 Years 9.53
% European 61.29	% Maori 2.56	% Pacific Peoples 1.83	% Asian 32.32

definitely upper middle class in its outlook – and the impact of school zoning on property prices places even greater pressures on those wishing to buy.

Although mostly full of moneyed families, Epsom is still a suburb for young professionals, as long as they are earning big dollars. Some are ex-pats, mostly from Britain. There is also a trend for young but well-off families from other inner-city suburbs to move here seeking good schooling for their growing children.

Typical dwellings

Epsom was settled mainly around the turn of the century, so there are many villas of 1900-1920s vintage as well as 1920s and 1930s bungalows. Most of these houses are on large sections. Infill housing constructed over the past decade means there are now also many large townhouses, mostly of brick-and-tile or plaster construction. Small units, sometimes in blocks, complete the spectrum of properties.

Amenities
Schools ★★★★★

The schooling is definitely top quality, including many of the sought-after public and private schools, both secondary and primary. Girls are especially well-catered for with the public Epsom Girls and two top-notch private schools. For a full list of schools, see page 272.

Shops ★★★

Apart from the collection of antique and other small shops at Greenwoods Corner, Epsom itself is not big on shops. But with Newmarket down the road, and the city and the improved St Lukes mall close by, residents want for nothing when it comes to retail therapy. The lovely villages of Mt Eden and Remuera are also nearby, as is Royal Oak.

Leisure ★★★★

Epsom has plenty of sports clubs for hockey, football, bowling, croquet, tennis and netball as well as the Auckland Trotting Club. There is the refurbished Lido Cinema, the Epsom library and Epsom Community Centre.

Eateries abound; there is some delightful ethnic cuisine in the form of Haveli India, One Italy, Phoenix Garden Chinese and the Sake Bar Nippon.

Real Estate
Trends

Notwithstanding the large number of desirable houses in Epsom, education is a major driver of demand – and high prices. The supply of families wishing to buy in the Auckland (for boys) and Epsom Girls gram-

mar school zones isn't easing. Currently, a house in the grammar zone will command a premium of more than $100,000 compared to an identical house outside the zone.

Epsom values definitely keep pace with Remuera, and suburbs on the boundaries of Epsom now refer to themselves as an east, north, south or west variant. Prices have trended upwards during the past three to four years and the worst case scenario could be a high levelling off.

Rental and investment

Schooling also drives a frantic demand for rentals. Investors don't necessarily take advantage though as buying a rental property doesn't come cheap.

Best streets

Mountain Rd, Shipherds Ave, Brightside Rd, Almorah Rd and Omana Ave.

Look Out ⚠

Mention of a new public co-ed secondary school in the area may cause flutters of anxiety among residents who have paid more handsomely for a house that's in the Auckland or Epsom Girls grammar zones. If a house suddenly changes zone, it's value could drop. The Ministry of Education had tagged land it owned near Alexander Park for a new 2000-pupil co-ed seconadary but ran into resource consent problems. Now, the University of Auckland is considering releasing its Epsom campus (the former Auckland College of Education) for a new college to ease the pressure on other inner-city schools. Watch this space!

House prices

Units	
Bedrooms	🛏 🛏
Price	$350,000 – $400,000
Bungalow or villa outside grammar zone	
Bedrooms	🛏 🛏 🛏
Price	$650,000 plus
Large house in zone	
Bedrooms	🛏 🛏 🛏 🛏
Price	$1.4 million plus
Renovated older house in zone	
Price	$1 million plus

Rental prices

Unit	
Bedroom	🛏
Price	$225 – $270/wk
Bedrooms	🛏 🛏
Price	$300 – $390/wk
House	
Bedrooms	🛏 🛏 🛏
Price	$432 – $585/wk
Bedrooms	🛏 🛏 🛏 🛏
Price	$550 – $750/wk

Travel times

CBD	off-peak 10 min
	peak 25 min
North-western motorway	10 min
Southern motorway	1 – 5 min
Airport	15 min
Royal Oak shop	5 min
Newmarket	5 min

Stagecoach Auckland has a regular bus service to Epsom, many travelling along the major roads of Gillies Ave and Manukau Rd. The major arterial of Gilles Ave is both a blessing and curse for local commuters; getting on at peak time is a tedious exercise but once on, you're well connected.

The mention of Glen Innes and Pt England may set the noses wrinkling of those from upmarket neighbouring areas who see them as a bit rough. But these often overlooked suburbs have a richness of another kind. Like cultural diversity and a strong community spirit. Popular with first-home buyers and investors, the area was mainly paddocks until World War II but now has many 1950s two-storey duplexes, some lovingly renovated ex-State gems and pockets of infill housing. Sitting between the Tamaki River and the railway, Glen Innes and Pt England cover a relatively small area. Pt England is a little more upmarket although Housing New Zealand is still a big property owner here. Glen Innes has large sections, few of which can be subdivided, so there are plenty of big family-friendly back lawns. And there are a lot of churches in the neighbourhood, which is always a good sign.

Who lives there?

The area has great ethnic diversity – lots of Maori, Pacific Islanders and Asians. There are many immigrants including Arabs and Albanians. Many Asian immigrants have moved to Glen Innes and Pt England, attracted by the lower rents and house prices. Being home to the Tamaki campus of the University of Auckland, it is popular with students, especially on the hill at the St Johns Rd end of the suburb. Which, in turn, makes it popular with investors as there is never a shortage of tenants.

With the prevalence of state housing, it's an area of blue collar workers. Residents have lots of pride in the area and there's a strong community spirit. They love their beer and their sports. Young couples and professionals have come into the area, buying up ex-state

For colour key, see page 226

Glendowie

Glen Innes

Point England

Tamaki

Pinpoint Map data supplied by Critchlow Associates Ltd and contains material subject to Crown copyright.

Population profile	Population in 2001 16,125	% Aged Under 15 years 26.98	% Aged over 65 Years 11.81
% European 46.79	% Maori 15.5	% Pacific Peoples 31.83	% Asian 8.89

houses and restoring these solid little homes. Many of these first-time home buyers will move closer to the sea in subsequent moves.

Typical dwellings

Archetypal houses are current and former state houses and bungalows of 1940s vintage onwards, including typical 1950s two-storey duplexes. Some ex-state houses have been nicely renovated. Wai o Taiki Bay is a pleasant mix of new houses constructed by developers, and state homes.

Recent state housing developments have progressed in Maybury St and Rowena Cres. Since the late 1980s, some parts of Glen Innes, such as Ropata Ave, have seen a fair amount of infill housing, typically of the single-level variety. There are still many two-bedroom houses on large plots.

The Talbot Park area is under redevelopment by Housing New Zealand. The plan is to provide better housing by refurbishing units and homes.

Amenities
Schools ★★★

Glen Innes is popular with families and there are at least three primary schools, one intermediate and a secondary school in the area. They are within walking distance of most parts of the suburb.

The secondary school, Tamaki College, has a reasonably small roll and is a popular choice for people in Glen Innes and the surrounding area.

For a full list, see page 272.

Shops ★★★

Known mostly for its food shopping, Glen Innes is packed with butchers, fruit and vegetable shops and a popular supermarket. Rumour has it that a new shopping complex is in the pipeline for the area. It is a popular destination with residents in surrounding areas as well as the locals as a great place to do your weekly shop.

Leisure ★★★

The area has a great sporting complex with a pool, and it is bordered by the Merton Rd sports grounds, which cater for rugby, cricket, soccer, tennis and soon new netball courts. The estuary has a walking track from Mt Wellington along the coastline to Glendowie which passes a native bird sanctuary.

Real Estate
Trends

It is generally hard to find houses for sale in Glen Innes because they are well priced and are snapped up by first-time home buyers and investors. Also, so much of the housing

stock remains in state ownership. The sought-after ex-state homes don't stay on the market for long.

The houses that are on the hill overlooking the estuary have spectacular views across to Bucklands Beach and Pakuranga. These houses, mainly in the area called Wai o Taiki Bay, are sought after and command some of the higher prices in the area.

On the flat in the heart of Glen Innes, the houses are a little cheaper. Glen Innes is very popular with families because schools are close by.

Rental and investment

The area's rental market is very strong, with generally more demand than supply. Housing New Zealand uses privately owned rentals to cater for their overflow which adds to the pressure.

Best streets

In Glen Innes, the top end off West Tamaki Rd, Weybridge Cres and Paddington St. In Pt England, Dunkirk Rd, and Riki Rd. In Wai o Taiki Bay, Silverton Ave and Inglewood St.

Smart Buy ⊘

Still relatively cheap in Auckland terms, the area is picking up. It is close to the waterfront, the city and all of the new amenities of the eastern suburbs such as Botany Downs. With Housing New Zealand likely to be a strong property owner for the near future, it may take a while to really come into its own, but it is still worth a look, especially around the edges.

House prices

For Wai o Taiki Bay, add $50,000

Unit	
Bedroom	🛏
Price	$150,000 plus
Bedrooms	🛏🛏
Price	$269,000 plus
Ex-state house	
Bedrooms	🛏🛏🛏
Price	$289,000 – $310,000
Modern townhouse	
Bedrooms	🛏🛏🛏
Price	$350,000 plus
House	
Bedrooms	🛏🛏🛏🛏
Price	$370,000 plus

Rental prices

Flat	
Bedroom	🛏
Price	$175 – $200/wk
Bedrooms	🛏🛏
Price	$230 – $260/wk
Bedrooms	🛏🛏🛏
Price	$250 – $315/wk
House	
Bedroom	🛏
Price	$200 – $260/wk
Bedrooms	🛏🛏
Price	$260 – $295/wk
Bedrooms	🛏🛏🛏
Price	$330 – $350/wk

Travel times

From Glen Innes shops

CBD	off-peak 20 min
	peak 40 min
Southern motorway	15 min
Airport	30 min

The area is well serviced by Stagecoach Auckland buses and the Tranz Metro train.

Cosmopolitan to its very core, Grey Lynn typifies everything that is socialist chic in Auckland city. While neighbouring Ponsonby claims much of the kudos for leading the central city's gentrification during the past 30 years or so, Grey Lynn attracts the same sort of sensitive but wealthy bohemian into its folds – just take a stroll through Grey Lynn Foodtown to do some celebrity spotting. Westmere and Pt Chevalier outwardly exhibit some of the same tendencies of Grey Lynn but beneath the liberal veneer, there are slightly more conservative concerns. Seen as slightly less desirable, Arch Hill attracts younger professional couples and singles buying the trendy – if sometimes small – villas which overlook the beginnings of the north-western motorway.

Who lives there?

Home to a melting pot of cultures, Grey Lynn has been the suburb of choice for many interesting and varied residents during its frequent face changes. Once an almost ghetto suburb, home to many students, it's now full of trendy go-getters wanting to live in the right part of Auckland. As with many of the inner-city suburbs, the trendy bohemi-anism and artistic flair of the past couple of decades has been replaced somewhat with more mundane concerns such as mortgage interest rates and school zones.

These suburbs attract young hipster renters who want to be close to the city centre, and the clubs and cafes along Ponsonby, Kings-land and Karangahape Rds. Significant num-bers of older people who have lived in the area for most of their lives choose to remain

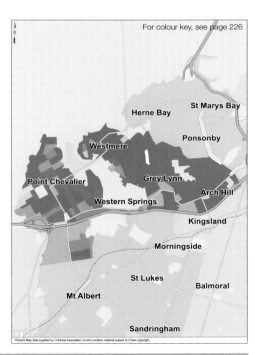

Population profile	Population in 2001 23,781	% Aged Under 15 years 18.09	% Aged over 65 Years 9.84
% European 73.05	% Maori 8.58	% Pacific Peoples 14.82	% Asian 8.14

and there is a sizeable number of Maori and Polynesian families living in long-held family homes.

The suburb is sought after by young couples and professionals, who want to live in the inner city but can't stretch to the higher price tags of neighbouring Ponsonby.

Westmere and Pt Chevalier are not as outwardly arty as Grey Lynn, however the suburbs are very multi-cultural – with a community of new immigrants and second and third-generation Indians and Pakistani.

Being a waterfront suburb, Westmere's attraction to professionals has increased markedly in the past decade. It is definitely a suburb to be proud of as one's address.

Pt Chevalier has always been popular with older people. Before Meola Rd linked it to Westmere in the late 1970s, the peninsula suburb was a backwater. Now, it is in demand from young professionals and families as a commuter suburb, appealing particularly to upwardly mobile single women.

Typical dwellings

Grey Lynn and Arch Hill remain known as older suburbs dominated by villas and bungalows, with occasional blocks of flats. The houses are mostly 100-year-old, three-bedroom villas and cottage villas made of kauri. Intermixed with these are small pockets of replica homes that have been built in the past 15 years to maintain the quaint, old world feel of the area. There are not so many new houses, but they do arise occasionally usually in one hit like the large Somerfield Villa terrace house development on the old Sleepyhead factory site a few years ago.

Arch Hill has narrower streets and smaller worker's cottages. There are still many do-

ups to be found, unlike its trendy neighbours.

Westmere and Pt Chevalier were originally developed as bungalow suburbs in the 1920s and grew directly along the tram routes. Westmere has a variety of wooden bungalows, but also brick and tile ex-state homes and the occasional stucco-clad art deco house. There has been a greater amount of new house construction in these suburbs and subdividing is a popular option with many of Pt Chevalier's larger sections.

Amenities
Schools ★★★
Standards of local schools have improved markedly in recent years and include private and public schools. For a full list, see page 272.

Shops ★★★
The Grey Lynn Foodtown is something of a local icon, however you still have to be careful what night you shop and what veggies you put in your trolley – it's common knowledge that some evenings are dominated by singles or gay singles, who express interest or availability by the way they place their bananas! Woolworths also has a super-

market on Richmond Rd. There are numerous trendy shops in the area, including Petropolis, a lifestyle store for pets and Zeitgeist for genuine retro furniture. The corner of Williamson Ave and Great North Rd is popular for cafes and at West Lynn on Richmond Rd the shops include cafes, a boutique wine shop Weta, clothing store Moa and well-known Harvest Wholefoods.

Westmere has a cluster of cafes, shops and specialist second-hand stores at the end of Garnet Rd, while Pt Chevalier has a mixed-bag shopping strip along Great North Rd and a few other shops on the peninsula. The area is well populated by cafes including Craft, Delicious, Malt and the Gypsy Tearoom at the West Lynn shops.

Leisure ★★★

The annual Grey Lynn Festival (held in Grey Lynn Park) attracts more than 40,000 people to its stalls and entertainment. Auckland Zoo, MOTAT and Western Springs are just down the road. Grey Lynn Park has a free toddler pool and sports grounds, and Coxs Bay Reserve has sports fields and a sea view.

Pt Chevalier Park at the end of the peninsula is a lovely open space with plenty of parking. The beach is accessed here or further back off Harbour View Rd and is pretty but tidal. The bottom of Raymond St is popular for launching windsurfers.

Real Estate
Trends

Westmere and Grey Lynn have experienced dramatic price gains recently. Grey Lynn because it's that bit closer to the city and is on Ponsonby's doorstep, Westmere because of its coastal views and proximity to Herne Bay. As the more affordable, spill-over location, Arch Hill has been in demand which has pushed prices up accordingly. Although most Arch Hill properties don't have off-street parking, this doesn't seem to deter the eager buyers ready to snap up any home that comes on the market.

As with all central city suburbs, demand will stay high and outstrip supply for the foreseeable future.

Rental and investment

This area has always been in huge demand by tenants because of the local nightlife and closeness to the city. It may not be so much a student zone these days but young city workers still love it.

Best streets

In Westmere, Rawene St and lower Garnet Rd. In Pt Chevalier, Harbour View Rd and Lynch St. In Grey Lynn, the upper reaches of Ariki St, Tutanekai St and Beaconsfield St. Popular in Arch Hill is Cooper St, which is preserved under heritage status.

Look Out ⊘

Under a new zone introduced in 2003, the look of the area may change and already has done to a certain degree along Great North Rd between Grey Lynn and Arch Hill. Zone 8 allows for developers to seek approval to erect multi-storey apartments within 2km of the CBD or close to certain surburban centres. Approval has to be granted, of course, but if you live close to the shops, be aware of what's happening over your back fence.

Why we live there

Film-maker Grant Lahood and singer Jackie Clark

When Grant and Jackie moved from Wellington some years ago, Grey Lynn was their choice of suburb. With their creative backgrounds, they typify the profile of the local residents.

Says Jackie: "The location is great. It's close enough to the city to still feel in touch with our wild youth [pre two children] when we used to go out a lot. It's a funky neighbourhood with a healthy mix of people. There are good schools, parks, and there are coffee places that are still a bit hokey. There are enough boutique shops to keep you interested but also Polynesian grocers and takeaways that sell everything from fish and chips to pizza. In 10 years time it might become too gentrified but it's good right now.

"Although we flirted for about 12 months with moving west for a bigger section, we can't seem to wean ourselves off the 'hood. We occasionally dip our toes into other parts of Auckland but really everything we need is here, including our work."

House prices

Cottage

Bedrooms	🛏🛏
Price	$400,000 plus

Villa or bungalow

Bedrooms	🛏🛏🛏
Price	$600,000 plus

Renovated houses

Bedrooms	🛏🛏🛏🛏
Price	from $700,000

Executive house close to the water

Price	$1 million plus

Rental prices

Flat or apartment

Bedroom	🛏
Price	$230 – $300/wk
Bedrooms	🛏🛏
Price	$300 – $450/wk

House

Bedrooms	🛏🛏🛏
Price	$435 – $520/wk
Bedrooms	🛏🛏🛏🛏
Price	$480 – $640/wk

Travel times

From Grey Lynn shops

CBD	off-peak 10 min
	peak 15 min

From Westmere shops

CBD	off-peak 10 min
	peak 20 min
North-western motorway	5 min
Airport	30 min
St Lukes mall	10 min

Pt Chevalier's shape creates a bit of a traffic bottle-neck. Beach-end properties are more expensive partly because of the alternative route to and from the city via Meola Rd. There are excellent bus services to the entire area, especially along the major arterial roads.

There'll be a few Waiheke Island residents rubbing their hands in glee. Not only do they get to live a lifestyle on a beautiful island with beaches, vineyards and cafes all on tap but they have been the out and out winners of the recent property boom. Property boom plus waterfront property mini boom plus a continuing nostalgia for baches and beach holidays has been a winning formula as well-off Aucklanders flock to part with more than $1 million for a slice of Waiheke paradise. The island is now also a big commuter suburb thanks to the ferry. Lying 90km northeast of Auckland is the rugged Great Barrier Island, 75% of which is conservation land. Rakino Island is near Waiheke, but has a much smaller population and more primitive facilities.

Who lives there?

While plenty of locals could still be described as left-leaning and green, Waiheke Island has become the residence of choice for many city workers. On the morning commuter ferry there's an eclectic mix of individuals and conversations can be lively. Some residents also own apartments and cars in the central city. Waiheke baches are being snapped up by wealthy professionals looking for something a bit different. During summer, the island's population rises to around 40,000.

All parts of the social spectrum seem to happily co-exist with each other. The diehard hippies have moved to Great Barrier or the Coromandel.

Waiheke has long been popular with artists and craftspeople. Now it's also a trendy haven for media and advertising personalities.

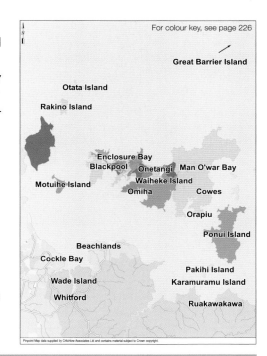

For colour key, see page 226

Pinpoint Map data supplied by Critchlow Associates Ltd and contains material subject to Crown copyright.

Population profile	Population in 2001 7,242	% Aged Under 15 years 20.05	% Aged over 65 Years 13.84
% European 86.12	% Maori 11.1	% Pacific Peoples 3.15	% Asian 2.03

There's high demand for properties from overseas buyers.

Great Barrier Island's population is mainly farming based. Its 1100 or so residents live clustered in scattered coastal settlements, Port Fitzroy and Okiwi in the north, Okupu and Tryphena in the southwest and Claris and Oruawharo (Medlands) in the east. The numbers swell in the summer.

Rakino Island's permanent population is tiny. Many wealthy urbanites are now seeking a slice of the island, however. Life on Rakino is for the hardy and adventurous, although this is less so now as the urbanites are bringing home comforts with them.

Typical dwellings

The classic Waiheke bach is becoming rare; many have been demolished to make way for more comfortable modern dwellings. You can still find some baches on the less-desirable southern side of the island.

Most houses are on large sections and while there are do-ups available, anything with a sea view sells fast and at a price. The new house styles vary, with mud brick, board and batten, barn style and Mediterranean stucco available. There are also a number of relocations from the mainland and plentiful supplies of modern Zincalume and creosote-coloured plywood.

This is not a place where you'd expect to find townhouses or apartment blocks although in a few places zoning has allowed for medium density housing. Palm Beach has a group of four designer homes and The Sands is a lock-up-and-leave apartment complex with an on-site manager at Onetangi.

Amenities
Schools ★★★

There is schooling on Waiheke Island for all ages and there are more primary schools proposed as the population expands. Many children commute to schools in the city and on the North Shore. For a full list, see page 272.

Shops ★★★

Waiheke Island's shops are now almost mainstream. The main block is in Oneroa with banks, restaurants, cafes, bookshops and more. There is a supermarket at Ostend, as well as numerous local shopping outlets and many arts and crafts stores.

Great Barrier has cafes, a pub and several stores. Rakino has nothing.

Leisure ★★★★★

In addition to the gorgeous white sand and pebble beaches, Waiheke Island is a great place for sea kayaking, horse riding, golf, fishing and diving, walks in the Forest and Bird reserve at Onetangi or at Whakenewha Park near Rocky Bay. Historical relics from World War II years, including tunnels and gun emplacements, can be explored.

Waiheke has become rightly famous for its vineyards during recent years.

Much of Great Barrier is covered with second generation native trees with pockets of regenerating native forest and remnants of kauri forest in the north. There are the remains of New Zealand's last whaling station, plus the Kaiarara Kauri Dam.

Real Estate
Trends

Back in the 1970s a young couple could

buy a good home on Waiheke for $15,000. These days you'd need a bit more cash. A two-bedroom Oneroa bach recently sold for more than $1 million. There are gated and exclusive clifftop estates which command prices of anywhere from $1 million to $4 million. You can still pick up a basic bach in the not so popular areas for around $300,000.

Sales on Waiheke haven't experienced the dip that affected many mainland areas recently and property on the island is still seen as a reasonably good investment.

The northern side of the island is premium because of the white-sand beaches, followed by the southern, then around Oneroa village and Blackpool. There are also some beautiful private baches only accessible by boat.

There's always a scrabble for bare land with few subdividable sites available. An 800m2 section is considered small here.

The new lifestyle blocks of up to 4ha are in great demand as hobby farms or vineyards, and with these estates come architecturally designed dwellings comparable to those in other Auckland waterfront locations.

Rakino Island has four residential areas, all surrounded by rural blocks of about 4ha. With the ever increasing demand for coastal and waterfront property, buyers have now turned their attention to Rakino. This has dramatically pushed up prices, with some coastal lifestyle blocks doubling in value in two years.

Rental and investment

Many renters pay the same as those on the outskirts of Auckland but prefer a 30-minute ferry trip to dealing with hours of traffic. Renting on Rakino is virtually non-existent and Great Barrier would be seasonal.

Why we live there

When winemaker John Dunleavy and his wife Deborah returned from overseas nearly 20 years ago, they wanted the perfect place to bring up a young family in a small caring community with open spaces and beaches not too far from Auckland city. "We love Waiheke. We first came here for a weekend back in 1983, fell in love with the island's beauty and went away with a deposit on a one-acre section at Palm Beach. It had 180-degree sea views and was only $15,000."

Now they are fully immersed in Waiheke Island's best known industry, establishing the Te Motu vineyard and more recently The Shed restaurant, in Onetangi valley.

Deb commutes to Auckland daily for her job as a production manager for a web-based training company. "We have the best of both worlds here – the city 35 minutes away for working, shopping, entertainment... and best of all the return to our island tranquillity, clean air, stunning beaches and a caring community full of an eclectic mix of people."

Best streets

On Waiheke Island, any beachfront roads like The Strand, Beach Parade, Palm Rd or Waikare Rd. There are no best streets on Great Barrier.

Travel times

From Waiheke Island

Onetangi to ferry terminal	15 min
Ferry to CBD	35 min
CBD to airport	1 hour bus trip from downtown Auckland

Ferries between Waiheke Island and the CBD run nearly hourly all day with extra sailings in peak times. Car ferries depart regularly from Half Moon Bay in Auckland and Kennedy Point on Waiheke. There are regular bus services around the island. Getting to Great Barrier involves a 30-minute flight. The ferry is seasonal. Rakino has regular ferry mail runs but no daily service.

Smart Buy ⊘

Although Waiheke Island is now as expensive as the mainland, the increasing demand for waterfront locations seems unlikely to change and the island's popularity as a permanent place to live shows no signs of slowing.

House prices

Waiheke Island

Do-up bach
Price $300,000 plus

Cottage with limited views
Bedrooms   🛏 🛏
Price $250,000 plus

Average house
Bedrooms   🛏 🛏 🛏
Price $400,000 – $600,000
With good sea views $500,000 plus

Renovated bach on the northern side
Bedrooms   🛏 🛏 🛏
Price $550 000 plus

Beachfront house
Bedrooms   🛏 🛏 🛏 🛏
Price $700,000 plus

Clifftop house in new estate
Price $1 million plus

Rakino Island
Sections $70,000 plus
Basic bach $150,000 plus
Coastal property $350,000 plus

Great Barrier Island
Entry level $200,000
Three-bedroom house $200,000 plus
Close to the water $400,000 plus

Rental prices

Flat
Bedroom   🛏
Price $195 – $330/wk
Bedrooms   🛏 🛏
Price $200 – $340/wk

House
Bedrooms   🛏 🛏
Price $230 – $300/wk
Bedrooms   🛏 🛏 🛏
Price $300 – $350/wk
Bedrooms   🛏 🛏 🛏 🛏
Price $400 – $600/wk

Kingsland used to be a grungy inner city haunt of students and their ilk, then it was seen as a cheaper alternative to Ponsonby and Grey Lynn. Those days are officially over. This is now the stamping ground of the modern incarnation of the yuppie. Market forces have seen demand grow but supply remain static ... and that always leads to price rises. Kingsland's tastefully groovy shops, galleries and cafes, narrow streets, villas and its closeness to the CBD are very alluring. Eden Terrace is an attractive mix of residential and commercial properties, an idiosyncratic, bohemian character and a number of student flats. The north-western motorway runs at the foot of these suburbs which is a plus or a minus, depending how far up the hill you can afford to live.

Who lives there?

This once less-than-desirable area is now humming to the sound of coffee machines, groovy urbanites, celebrities and the trendy cry of wee ones following in their parents' footsteps. Professionals have moved in, as traditional blue collar residents move out.

Western Springs has moved from a rental suburb to a thriving family area. The do-ups that renovators have purchased in the past are now ripe for re-sale and are being snapped up by willing buyers searching for pleasant homes, close to the city.

Gentrification of the whole region has been fuelled largely by returning ex-pats – supported by the exchange rate and with an eye for capital gains. The inner-city bohemian atmosphere has proved popular with gays. Some of the older Polynesian families

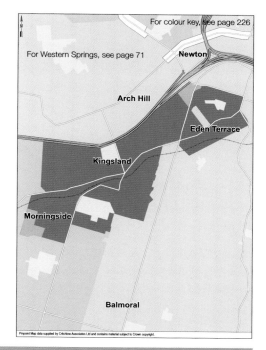

For colour key, see page 226

For Western Springs, see page 71

Newton

Arch Hill

Eden Terrace

Kingsland

Morningside

Balmoral

Pinpoint Map data supplied by Critchlow Associates Ltd and contains material subject to Crown copyright.

Population profile	Population in 2001 5,421	% Aged Under 15 years 13.61	% Aged over 65 Years 3.98
% European 65.52	% Maori 8.36	% Pacific Peoples 15.05	% Asian 9.96

remain, many living in homes owned for several generations.

Typical dwellings

These suburbs were established over time so there is a range of house styles, from turn-of-the-century villas and cottages through to California bungalows and townhouses. The majority of houses in Kingsland are villas.

Although many Western Springs sections are large – by inner city standards – subdivision opportunities are scarce.

There are a growing number of apartment complexes, such as those near the railway line in Morningside or further up New North Rd in Eden Terrace, with a few complexes still being completed.

The popularity of this area grows by the day, as more people want to live closer to the city and to transform that once run-down villa into their dream home. Scattered amongst the villas are the occasional replica dwellings and townhouses. There are some tatty blocks of flats, particularly down Don Croot St between Kingsland and Western Springs, but even this area is being slowly spruced up.

Kingsland is a protected heritage area under the council's district scheme.

Amenities

Schools ★★

The area doesn't have abundant schools, with only Kowhai Intermediate and Mt Albert Primary being located here. Neighbouring suburbs have plenty of options though.

For a full list, see page 272.

Shops ★★★★

There is a mix of trendy village-style shops in Kingsland and mega-mall style shopping

down the road at St Lukes. With Kingsland's boutique shops, restaurants and cafes appreciated by trendy types (and more than a few celebrities) from all over the city, it's often hard to find a car park on this stretch of New North Rd during dining hours. Practical service shops, such as Carters and Briscoes, are close by off Morningside Dr and there are supermarkets in Grey Lynn, St Lukes and Mt Eden.

Leisure ★★★★

Eden Park is, of course, a major draw card and Western Springs has outdoor concerts and annual festivals, and until recently, the speedway – although its eviction may not be a done deal. Western Springs Park with its huge central lake is a fabulous place for a family outing to ride bikes and feed the ducks. The zoo and Motat are right next to the park. Chamberlain Park Golf Course is along St Lukes Rd.

The area's parks also have skateboarding ramps, basketball hoops and rugby grounds.

Real Estate

Trends

Not long ago this area had abundant rentals, but these days owner-occupied properties are more the norm. Local DIY and garden stores do a roaring trade, with many residents happy to upgrade and modify what they have. A good example of the do-up potential is a housing development near the motorway. Originally owned by a Pacific Island trust, it was painted in garish, lollipop colours and had deteriorated to a very poor state. After being bought and restored by developers with sophisticated colour schemes, lockable gates and stainless steel appliances the units were sold individually as sought-after dwellings.

This area was definitely affected by the recent property boom, seeing mid $300,000 properties skyrocket into the $500,000s. The near-frenzy is only starting to taper off now.

Rental and investment

The ratio of rental homes has decreased, although there are still a number of purpose-built apartments and units, especially in the commercial end of Eden Terrace.

Best streets

First and Second Ave in Kingsland and Springfield Rd in Western Springs. Properties along Western Springs Rd, on the ridge overlooking Grey Lynn and Fowlds Park, now command $1 million plus.

House prices

	Bedrooms	Price
Unit	2	$280,000s – $380,000s
Cottage	2	$450,000 – $550,000
Bungalow or villa do-up	3	$400,000 plus
House	4	$550,000 plus

Rental prices

	Bedrooms	Price
Flat	2	$260 – $300/wk
Apartment or house	2	$300 – $350/wk
	3	$360 – $450/wk
	4	$425 – $550/wk

Travel times

From Kingsland shops

CBD	off-peak 5-7 min
	peak 15 min
CBD by train	15 min
North-western motorway	5 min
Airport	30 min
Westfield St Lukes mall	5 min

There's a good bus service, particularly along Great North Rd. Commuter trains stop at Kingsland station, right by the shops, and at Morningside. There are plans for a footbridge from the Kingsland station across busy Dominion Rd, primarily to help sports fans get to Eden Park but it will benefit all pedestrians.

Hanging tenaciously onto the skirts of its posher neighbour Remuera, this area can't help but be appealing. You may not be as handy to the CBD, but heading east for your major shopping is an option, the Eastern Bay beaches are a tumble down the hill, the motorway's just there, and it's just all very pleasant. Meadowbank has plenty of green space with the big Waiatarua Reserve and Remuera Golf Course rubbing shoulders. Ellerslie is a much older suburb with affordable villas and bungalows. St Johns – including the fashionable St Johns Park – is a more recent addition to the city's landscape. A notable St Johns landmark is the theological college with its parklike grounds. It provides tertiary education for both the Anglican and Methodist churches.

Who lives there?

Many families with school-age children buy in Meadowbank, turning their backs on the grammar zone fights that take place in Remuera next door. They might enrol their children in private schools and enjoy the extra disposable income saved on housing. If you want a stable area, friendly neighbours and a relaxed lifestyle, then Meadownbank's hard to beat. St Johns also attracts families. The whole area's more the domain of dual income families and is too expensive for most first-home buyers.

There's a wide multicultural mix as well, with many Asian migrants making these suburbs home, especially St Johns Park.

Typical dwellings

Meadowbank underwent a building boom

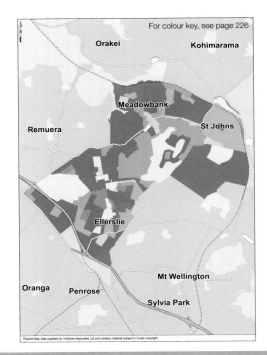

For colour key, see page 226

Population profile	Population in 2001 24,351	% Aged Under 15 years 17.51	% Aged over 65 Years 10.95
% European 71.75	% Maori 4.92	% Pacific Peoples 4.36	% Asian 18.60

some 20 to 30 years ago. As a result, many solid homes with generous living areas and double garaging were built on liberal, family-sized sections of about 600–800m2.

These, plus the mix of older established homes – including 1940s bungalows and many ex-state houses – and recent townhouses and developments, which blend well into the landscape, give the region a lived-in, friendly feel. The sense of spaciousness is one of the suburb's most attractive features. Generally, sections are fenced and tidy and not smack up against the neighbour.

St Johns includes many rental properties, while St Johns Park has large, modern, multi-bedroom family dwellings.

Ellerslie has some old villas as well as terrace housing complexes near the village. Ladies Mile and Pukerangi Cres still have some grand old merchants' houses.

Amenities
Schools ★★★

Meadowbank is not inundated with schools, however the local primary schools have solid reputations. And being on major bus routes makes travelling to nearby secondary schools easy. The private Michael Park and Rudolf Steiner School goes from kindergarten to high school levels.

For a full list see page 272.

Shops ★★★

Meadowbank is home to one of the best supermarkets in Auckland – the Foodtown nestled in the small Meadowbank mall. There's also easy access to Newmarket, Pakuranga/Howick and Botany Town Centre. Just around the corner on the Mt Wellington Highway there's a busy mega centre including The Warehouse, Noel Leemings, Rebel Sports, Briscoes, Plastic Box and an Ezibuy retail store.

Leisure ★★★

One of Meadowbank's great benefits is its easy access to the waterfront, with beaches and myriad water sports. Auckland Domain and One Tree Hill are just down the road. The big Waiatarua Reserve is popular with joggers and weekend strollers and Remuera Golf Course is well patronized (there's a long, long waiting list).

The impressive university sports fields and McDonald's tennis centre on Merton Rd are local assets. Ellerslie Racecourse is also here, and is the site of the a Sunday morning car fair. There's also a small par three golf course and driving range in the infield.

Real Estate
Trends

Meadowbank has often been seen as a cheaper alternative to Remuera, however, the price gap is narrowing. House prices here have increased dramatically during the recent property boom and even with a moderate softening in demand, prices remain stable. In Tahapa St a fibrolite, ex-state house on a good-sized section sold in early 2005 for $470,000.

St Johns Park has a lot of leasehold land owned by the St Johns Trust. Depending on the terms of the lease and ground rents, leaseholds make properties cheaper and more attractive.

Prices vary, from fairly high values in St Johns Park to three to four bedroom family homes in St Johns selling for the mid to late $200,000s and into the $300,000s.

Prices increase appreciably in St Johns Park, however. Surrounding the Remuera Golf Course and unfolding across former St Johns Trust land towards Meadowbank and Remuera, prices move from the late $400,000s through to upwards of $1 million.

Rental and investment

Investors are particularly attracted to St Johns with the high demand for rental accommodation in the suburb.

Best streets

Temple St is seen as Meadowbank's best. Ellerslie has no real standout streets. In St Johns and St Johns Park, anything near the golf course demands top dollar; also Panapa Dr, Coldham Cres and Charles Fox Pl.

House prices

Unit	
Bedrooms	🛏️ 🛏️
Price	$200,000 plus
Ex-state house	
Bedrooms	🛏️ 🛏️ 🛏️
Price	$350,000 plus
Newer house	
Bedrooms	🛏️ 🛏️ 🛏️ 🛏️
Price	$450,000 – $800,000
Property with golf course views	
Price	up to $1 million

Rental prices

Apartment/flat	
Bedroom	🛏️
Price	$190 – $250/wk
Bedrooms	🛏️ 🛏️
Price	$245 – $320/wk
House	
Bedrooms	🛏️ 🛏️
Price	$255 – $350/wk
Bedrooms	🛏️ 🛏️ 🛏️
Price	$330 – $450/wk
Bedrooms	🛏️ 🛏️ 🛏️ 🛏️
Price	$400 – $600/wk

Travel times

From Meadowbank	
CBD	off-peak 15 min
	peak 20 - 25 min
	By train 8 min
Southern motorway	5 min
Airport	30 min
Remuera shops	5 min
Newmarket shops	10 min
CBD by train from Ellerslie	14 min

Stagecoach Auckland and Howick & Eastern buses provide regular services, especially along main roads. The Tranz Metro train stops at Ellerslie and Meadowbank.

This suburb is a real melting pot – from well-off families in grand houses and tree-lined streets on the slopes of Mt Albert, to Asian students flatting near Unitec and relatively poor migrants renting in Owairaka. It's diverse, vibrant and cosmopolitan, with the sprawling Unitec campus on one boundary and the teeming St Lukes shopping mall on the other. Mt Albert was Auckland's second suburb – after Remuera – settled by well-to-do families in the late 1800s and early 1900s. St Lukes is less a suburb as home to the large mall. Locals debate just where it belongs - is it part of Morningside, Kingsland, Mt Eden or Mt Albert? Owairaka, at the Mt Roskill end of Mt Albert, is seen as the poor cousin of the area.

Who lives there?

Mt Albert is varied and culturally diverse. Residents include Polynesian families, Indians, Sri Lankans and other ethnic groups. There's a Somali community in Owairaka.

The beautiful and substantial bungalows and villas are home to many families attracted to the area by the larger sections and – until recently – moderate house prices. The area's a lot more "with-it" than many people previously realised and it's fairly close to the city. The past decade has seen a major transformation in the ethnic composition, with an influx of Asian students to local tertiary education institutes Unitec on Carrington Rd and the privately owned AIS St Helens on Asquith Ave.

The age composition of the area has also changed with more, younger families than

For colour key, see page 226

Point Chevalier

Western Springs

Morningside

St Lukes

Mt Albert

Sandringham

Owairaka

Wesley

New Windsor

Mt Roskill

Pinpoint Map data supplied by Critchlow Associates Ltd and contains material subject to Crown copyright.

Population profile	Population in 2001 18,591	% Aged Under 15 years 19.4	% Aged over 65 Years 9.29
% European 62.27	% Maori 6.99	% Pacific Peoples 11.46	% Asian 18.28

older retired people.

Mt Albert's Golden Triangle, on the mountain slopes with north-facing views, is definitely the place to live. Not only do you enjoy the best views, you are surrounded by elegant bungalows. Owners often move here from other sought-after suburbs. Gone are the days when Mt Albert was a stepping stone to Mt Eden, Remuera and beyond.

Typical dwellings

Many of the gracious homes built for some of the older family names in Auckland remain today. Most have been beautifully restored and renovated. There are also modern homes on half sites, units and ex-state houses.

St Lukes housing reflects the lifestyles of the inhabitants. Many locals live in townhouses and the abundant supply of smaller apartments, many of which are close to the mall.

Sought-after renovated villas and bungalows are available but tend to be small, with only two to three bedrooms.

Amenities
Schools ★★★★

The area is well served by schools. Gladstone School is very popular at primary level; many intermediate children attend Kowhai Intermediate in Kingsland, then co-ed Mt Albert Grammar caters for secondary pupils. For a full list, see page 272.

Shops ★★★★

Westfield St Lukes is a favourite shopping mall for many Aucklanders. It's now bigger and better, with cinemas and extended carparking. Around the corner, Briscoes and Carters are well patronised and across the road there's a collection of bulk retail style shops for appliances, bedding etc.

The Mt Albert shopping strip has undergone a major cultural renaissance during the past decade, with a significant Asian influence coming in. Noodle bars, Asian food supermarkets, internet cafes and souped-up late model cars are now common.

Leisure ★★★

The Philips Aquatic Centre in Alberton Ave is hugely popular, with everything from a wave pool and waterslide to baby pools.

Rocket Park in Wairere Ave is well used by young and old. And for great walking, you can't beat the volcanic slopes of Mt Albert.

Also in the area are many sports clubs and recreational facilities. Other green areas include Owairaka Park around the Mt Albert summit, Alan Wood Reserve, Unitec's landscaped grounds and many others. Eden Park is within walking distance from St Lukes for cricket and rugby matches.

Real Estate
Trends

The recently extended St Lukes mall and the commercial centre surrounding it has fuelled a demand for real estate in this area. New apartments are still being built, although there is a limited amount of land available. This area is especially popular with speculators and investors. The schools attract many families, who move on when their children reach secondary age or leave home.

Prices may not be at the heights of recent years, but they are probably sitting at about the right level. With the frenzied buying finished, buyers can take longer to decide what to buy. This neighbourhood has a range of prices, but without the extremes of some areas.

Rental and investment

For all the reasons mentioned earlier (students, immigrants etc), the rental market in this area is huge.

Best streets

Mt Albert's Golden Triangle has the most valuable residential properties in the area, including Allendale Rd, Stilwell Rd, Summit Dr and surrounding streets.

Smart Buy ⊘

House prices in areas with good schools and a reputation for being solid community suburbs, with good amenities, may ease off at times, but they'll never plummet. Also, look out for the mortgagee sales, where a few investors may have put too many eggs in one basket.

House prices

Unit or terrace house	
Bedrooms	🛏 🛏
Price	$260,000 – $350,000
Ex-state house	
Bedrooms	🛏 🛏
Price	$400,000s
Villa/bungalow	
Bedrooms	🛏 🛏 🛏
Price	$400,000s
Renovated villa/bungalow	
Price	$600,000
In the Golden Triangle	$1 million plus

Rental prices

Flat or apartment	
Bedroom	🛏
Price	$205 – $280/wk
Bedrooms	🛏 🛏
Price	$260 – $300/wk
House	
Bedrooms	🛏 🛏 🛏
Price	$360 – $450/wk
Bedrooms	🛏 🛏 🛏 🛏
Price	$420 – $600/wk

Travel times

CBD by car	off-peak 8 min
	peak 12 min
CBD by bus	peak 25 min
North-western motorway	5 min
Airport	30 min
St Lukes mall	5 min

Mt Albert has excellent public transport, with Stagecoach Auckland providing regular services, and the Tranz Metro commuter train running through Mt Albert on the Waitakere line.

Mt Eden is family-ville for the financially secure. The sort of place where you get run over by stroller-pushing mothers escorting their kids to school. The strollers are upmarket and all-terrain, the footpath equivalent of a 4WD. Nestled at the base of its namesake mountain, the suburb's other defining feature is its iconic village. It may not be the biggest suburban block of shops, but it has heaps of atmosphere, bustling with shoppers and with a hearty smattering of cafes (many with child-friendly sandpits and courtyards, of course). Balmoral and Sandringham now merge seamlessly into Mt Eden but will always been seen as the more affordable bits. A few minutes south and more elevated, Three Kings is yet more affordable, due mainly to pockets of State housing.

Who lives there?

The arty bohemian era that Mt Eden has been famed for is definitely passing – while some fondly remember it and indeed others yearn for it, raising families in desirable school zones has brought materialism and middle class values.

Although more ethnically and socio-economically diverse – therefore, possibly more interesting – than its neighbour Epsom, Mt Eden is still full of middle to upper-class families pursuing the quiet life.

It is seen by some as a "transient" suburb, with many families moving east to Epsom or Remuera when their children reach secondary school age.

Mt Eden is predominantly European, but with significant numbers of Asians and Indians. All the local primary schools appear

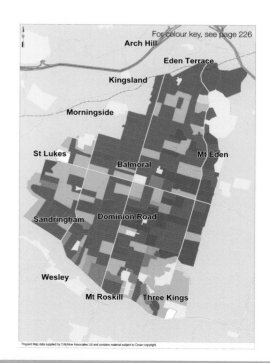

For colour key, see page 226

Pinpoint Map data supplied by Critchlow Associates Ltd and contains material subject to Crown copyright.

Population profile	Population in 2001 36,075	% Aged Under 15 years 19.53	% Aged over 65 Years 7.97
% European 66.15	% Maori 6.61	% Pacific Peoples 8.79	% Asian 18.99

to be bursting at the seams due to the district's numerous young families. As always, the Auckland Grammar zone is highly sought after by families with teenage boys.

In Three Kings the mix of residents is changing with new terrace housing blocks and infill housing being built. House prices are still relatively affordable here, compared to the suburbs closer to the city.

Cynics sometimes refer to Sandringham as a "poor man's Mt Eden". It's a highly cosmopolitan area with a wide mix of ethnic groups and nationalities and many young families.

Typical dwellings

Mt Eden has plenty of turn-of-the-century villas, interspersed with Californian bungalows and other period homes. There are fewer townhouses and infill developments than in nearby Epsom due to different local body rules in the past. To many Mt Eden residents, this is a definite plus. In Balmoral and Sandringham, the sections tend to be bigger and there are more bungalows.

Mt Eden has its share of older blocks of flats and one to two bedroom brick and tile units, plus terrace housing blocks. Some unattractive examples of long 1960s and 1970s single and double-storey blocks of flats sound a jarring note among streets of classic villas and bungalows.

The old state housing area of Three Kings is now a mix of owner-occupied housing and tenanted homes, with many ex-state homes getting trendy renovations. These solid houses are snapped up as soon as they hit the market and are attracting young working couples and professional singles to the area.

Amenities
Schools ★★★★

All the Mt Eden primary schools are highly regarded, as are Balmoral and Three Kings schools. As well as Auckland Grammar, co-ed Mt Roskill Grammar has a good reputation. Sandringham families are in zone for Mt Albert Grammar (co-ed) and Auckland Girls' Grammar.

For a full list, see page 272.

Shops ★★★★

There's plenty of shopping locally, with a range of shops at Eden Quarter including a well-stocked Foodtown. Mt Eden village has interesting specialty shops and boutiques.

Along Dominion Rd there are several Asian specialty groceries at Balmoral; Sandringham has Indian and Pakistani groceries and two halal butchers.

The Three Kings shopping centre includes a supermarket and a library.

Volcanoes of the world?

Mt Eden, Mt Albert, Mt Wellington, Three Kings, One Tree Hill... we proudly call them mountains, but on the worldwide scale of great volcanoes, they're really only hills. The fact that there are so many of them (about 50 volcanic features), however, makes them different. There is growing support to seek World Heritage status for the field. If the bid were successful the ancient volcanic field would join nearly 800 international treasures such as Egyptian pyramids and our own Mt Cook.

Auckland's volcanoes may be small in statue, but they're a big part of the tourist marketing. Regional authorities have even created "viewing protection planes" so that no large buildings obscure the views from key vantage points, which is why the Sky Tower wasn't allowed to be built on Symonds St, where it would have stolen Mt Eden's limelight.

These days, the mountains have been protected as parks and domains for our enjoyment. Before the mountains were protected, they were quarried for scoria to the extent that Three Kings, which was originally five peaks, is now just one. Mt Eden was formed 23,000 years ago; Rangitoto Island is the most recent volcano, formed some 600-700 years ago.

St Lukes mall is right next door in one direction and the busy Newmarket shopping precinct a few minutes down the road in the other direction.

Leisure ★★★★

As well as the Mt Eden Domain, the area has many smaller parks and reserves, including Edenvale Reserve, Potters Park and Centennial Park. In Three Kings, the quarry site has interesting walks up to the Three Kings Reserve, with great views from the top. The suburb is well catered for sports lovers too, with successful soccer and athletics clubs.

There is also Mt Eden Swimming Pool and Eden Park, the famed battleground for local and international rugby and cricket games.

Mt Eden village is well known for its cafes and restaurants which draw diners from all parts of the city. Dominion Rd and Sandringham Rd have a wide range of ethnic eateries.

At the city end of Mt Eden there's a cluster of quirky cafes and a few pubs.

Real Estate
Trends

Demand in Mt Eden is always strong and this has definitely fed through to the nearby areas. Houses in the grammar zone will always command premium prices. Some buyers are wealthy immigrants or ex-pats returning home. Young professional couples with high combined incomes and high debt tolerance also buy in the area.

Developers have been attracted to Three Kings and Balmoral for the do-ups still available there. Lately, there has been high demand for duplexes and smaller brick and tile properties as a way for younger people to gain a foothold in these suburbs.

Classic ex-state houses in Three Kings and Sandringham are in demand because of their relative affordability and for their reputaton as solid dwellings.

These areas were heavily influenced by the boom in recent years, but prices have now plateaued, with some seeing a slight drop. However, it is anticipated that this shift is temporary, and it hasn't really affected homes in the coveted grammar zone.

Rental and investment

The school zones will always attract a steady stream of renters. Not everyone who chooses to live in this desirable area can afford to buy.

Best streets

Anything in the grammar zones and the streets close to Mt Eden village. Fairview Rd and Woodside Rd have some big gracious houses, as do Horoeka Ave and Bellevue Rd at the northern end of Mt Eden.

In Sandringham, the roads nearest Mt Eden, especially north of Balmoral Rd, and those with more villas or bungalows than state houses. In Balmoral, the roads around the popular Maungawhau Primary are the most sought-after.

Smart Buy ⊘

You can't really lose in this part of Auckland, especially if you're buying in the grammar zone. Its location close to the city and other areas of Auckland means it will always be popular.

Three Kings is an up-and-coming area so may have good capital gain potential.

House prices

Unit
Bedroom 🛏
Price $150,000 – $200,000
Bedrooms 🛏 🛏
Price $200,000 plus
Bungalow/villa (outside grammar zone)
Bedrooms 🛏 🛏 🛏
Price $550,000 – $850,000
Bungalow/villa (in grammar zone)
Bedrooms 🛏 🛏 🛏
Price $800,000 plus
Large home by Mt Eden village
Price $1 million plus

Rental prices

Flat or apartment
Bedroom 🛏
Price $210 – $300/wk
Bedrooms 🛏 🛏
Price $275 – $390/wk
House
Bedrooms 🛏 🛏 🛏
price $400 – $490/wk
Bedrooms 🛏 🛏 🛏 🛏
Price $470 – $600/wk

Travel times

From Mt Eden village

CBD	off-peak 10 min
	peak 30 min
North-western motorway	10 min
Southern motorway	5 min
Airport	30 min
St Lukes mall	5 min

Stagecoach Auckland provides regular services to all these suburbs. Dominion Rd, Mt Eden Rd, Sandringham Rd and Balmoral Rd are all major bus corridors. Priority peak-hour bus lanes are making bus commuting into the city much quicker and more attractive to residents.

The cross proudly displayed on top of Mt Roskill at Christmas and Easter says it all – this is Bible country. But there's more to the area than a church on every corner. These are family-friendly suburbs with a great sense of community and God is worshipped more diversely these days with the big influx of migrants from various ethnic groups. Look more deeply into the solidly suburban streets of Hillsborough as you whip through on your way to the airport and you'll find some real estate gems hugging the Manukau Harbour coastline in leafy sections with great sea views. Nearby Waikowhai, which also prides itself on harbour views, has pretty much lost its separate identity and quietly merged with Hillsborough.

Who lives there?

Mt Roskill and Hillsborough have sizeable immigrant populations, with people from India, Korea, China and the Middle East. Families love the big rambling houses on decent-sized sections and are attracted to Mt Roskill Grammar's good reputation. Professional couples love the fact that you can commute just about anywhere from here. It's only 20 minutes, off peak, and about 40 minutes peak from the CBD, and is also handy to the airport, Manukau, Onehunga and West Auckland. And to top it all off, it's cheaper than most suburbs that are as handily placed.

Typical dwellings

Most houses in the area have been built with family living in mind. Mt Roskill and

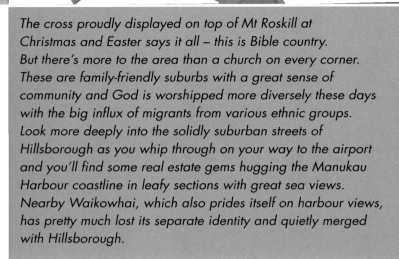

For colour key, see page 330

Wesley

Mt Roskill   Three Kings

Mt Roskill South

Hillsborough

Waikowhai

Pinpoint Map data supplied by Critchlow Associates Ltd and contains material subject to Crown copyright.

Population profile	Population in 2001 21,936	% Aged Under 15 years 20.9	% Aged over 65 Years 13.09
% European 50.56	% Maori 5.44	% Pacific Peoples 13.65	% Asian 30.06

Hillsborough were mostly developed in the 1950s and 1960s so there's a mix of weatherboard and brick-and-tile bungalows – salt of the earth suburban homes. Solid ex-state houses are also common.

There are also newer townhouses and infill housing, as the once quarter-acre sections are sliced up. However, it's not overly difficult to discover a full site, ready to be subdivided or enjoyed by the family.

Mt Roskill South is a subdivision developed since the 1980s, with executive-style homes.

Amenities
Schools ★★★★
Mt Roskill primary, intermediate and grammar school share the same big rambling grounds – an unusual configuration but a big plus for siblings walking younger kids to school. Lynfield College, the other local secondary school, isn't as high-profile as Mt Roskill, but is still well-regarded.

For a full list, see page 378.

Shops ★★
Three Kings Plaza has a range of shops, a supermarket and a library. Only minutes away there's Royal Oak, Mt Eden, Mt Roskill shops on Dominion Rd, Lynfield and Blockhouse Bay shopping centres, the huge DressSmart outlet centre at Onehunga – and who can forget that megalithic merchandising mecca, Westfield St Lukes.

Leisure ★★★
Parks and reserves are plentiful, with approximately 12ha of land dedicated to green belts and sports grounds, including Keith Hay Park, the War Memorial Park and Winstone Park. The area is a walker's

paradise, and a golfer's dream – there are three local golf courses. There are two muddy and tidal beaches, so not great for swimming, but fine for boaties and windsurfers.

For fitness enthusiasts there's the Lynfield Recreation Centre (YMCA) and Cameron Pool (Roskill Aquasport). Local sports clubs include the New Zealand Hockey Federation, the Eden Roskill District Cricket Club, as well as clubs for bowling, rugby, soccer and tennis. With the area's multinational composition, there is more culinary variety in Mt Roskill than before, including many ethnic food outlets.

Real Estate
Trends
Trends here tend to follow school zones, so when homes formerly in the high-profile Mt Roskill school zone suddenly became part of Lynfield College zone, prices dropped. This was especially so in Mt Roskill South and parts of Hillsborough, which tend to have better homes and in some cases sea views.

Properties are always in demand, however, as the area is very much favoured by families. There has also been increased

demand from renters who now want to buy.

Land is available in the form of half sites. Subdivision continues as a trend, with larger, four-bedroom townhouses on half sites proving popular with immigrant families.

Although the proposed motorway extension has negatively effected some properties close to the route, many people believe that when it's finished, this 4km stretch of road will be a blessing.

Rental and investment

With rental demand slowing and interest rates continuing to climb, rental properties are becoming harder to fill. Some landlords are lowering their prices just to keep the property occupied, even if they aren't making as good a return.

Best streets

In Hillsborough, streets near the sea. In Mt Roskill, Stamford Park Rd and Oakdale Rd.

Smart Buy ⊘

The motorway extension may be a pain while it's being built, but when it's completed, the new 4km route from the Queenstown Rd interchange will link up with the Avondale extension to the northwestern motorway. It should make life much easier for cross-town commuters. And it's not just about cars – there will be a cycleway along the southern side of the extension and bridges over Hayr Rd and May Rd. If you can live through the mayhem, the area will be a lot more accessible to all areas of Auckland.

The area is still reasonably priced, and if you buy in the Mt Roskill Grammar zone you should do well.

House prices

Unit
Bedrooms	🛏 🛏
Price	$200,000 plus

Bungalow
Bedrooms	🛏 🛏 🛏
Price	$325,000 – $375,000

Top-end Mt Roskill townhouse
Price	$450,000 plus

Hillsborough brick and tile
Bedrooms	🛏 🛏 🛏
Price	$400,000 plus

Large Hillsborough house
Price	$450,000 plus
With sea views	$1 million

Rental prices

Flat
Bedroom	🛏
Price	$200 – $250/wk

House
Bedrooms	🛏 🛏
Price	$310 – $330/wk
Bedrooms	🛏 🛏 🛏
Price	$370 – $395/wk
Bedrooms	🛏 🛏 🛏 🛏
Price	$400 – $540/wk

Travel times

From Mt Roskill shops

CBD	off-peak 15-20 min
	peak 30-40min
Airport	10-15 min
St Lukes mall	10 min
Royal Oak shops	10 min

Hillsborough is handy for residents wanting to get to the airport, but otherwise it's a bit land-locked. Mt Roskill residents rely on major arterial routes such as Dominion Rd and Mt Albert Rd. The area is well served by Stagecoach buses and peak time bus lanes are improving travel times.

Onehunga may be far from the centre of Auckland but it's one of its oldest suburbs. Dating from the 1840s, it's chock full of elegant colonial villas and quaint workers' cottages on the slopes overlooking the Manukau Harbour and the port. Many are on large sections. Although the area became run-down during the years, more recently Onehunga has been discovered by young urban professional homeowners brandishing paintbrushes and hammers. Onehunga's location has many pluses – it's close to One Tree Hill, handy to the airport, and not too far from the CBD either. Oranga has been viewed as a more rugged version of Onehunga, although it's also being spruced up now. Penrose and Te Papapa are mostly industrial and commercial.

Who lives there?

Onehunga's attractive location and its generally larger sections makes the area appealing to families, but many professional single people and couples also live here.

Traditionally Onehunga is solidly working class and has been home to many Maori and Polynesian families over the years, many of whom still live there. A wide range of ethnic groups is represented – more than 50 different nationalities are currently enrolled at Penrose High School.

Typical buyers into the suburb include young local couples seeking their first home do-up and migrants from Asia – as well as from Europe and South Africa.

Typical dwellings

Many of Onehunga's earliest homes were

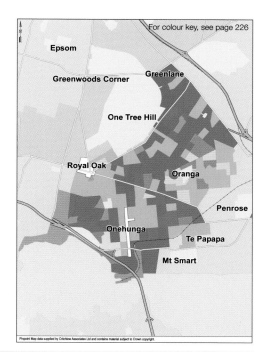

For colour key, see page 226

Epsom
Greenwoods Corner
Greenlane
One Tree Hill
Royal Oak
Oranga
Penrose
Onehunga
Te Papapa
Mt Smart

Pinpoint Map data supplied by Critchlow Associates Ltd and contains material subject to Crown copyright.

Population profile	Population in 2001 25,890	% Aged Under 15 years 20.03	% Aged over 65 Years 10.76
% European 61.45	% Maori 8.9	% Pacific Peoples 17.46	% Asian 14.77

built by, and for, soldiers looking to settle with their families on their own patch of land. This suburb is still full of the classic villas, bungalows and worker's cottages that are in demand by large numbers of house buyers in the greater Auckland market.

While many of the older homes have already been renovated, there are still a few untouched vintage houses just waiting to devour a renovator's every spare dollar. There is also a range of more modern housing, including 1950s brick and tile bungalows and many contemporary brick and tile or plaster and tile family homes. Weatherboard state houses and ex-state houses are plentiful, as well as stucco duplexes. There are a number of historic properties, including the one-time residence of Governor Grey, in Symonds St. Infill housing is common and larger properties are now harder to find.

There are also a number of one to two bedroom apartments which have been built predominantly on industrial land during the past five to 10 years.

Amenities
Schools ★★★
Local schools include Onehunga Primary School and Te Papapa School. For secondary students there's Onehunga High School and Penrose High School.

For a full list, see page 272.

Shops ★★★★
Onehunga Mall is a lively place thanks to a clever revamp in early 1990s. The local shopping embraces an assortment of retail and service stores, banks and increasingly trendy restaurants. The huge Dressmart outlet centre attracts shoppers from throughout Auckland for its fashion bargains.

Leisure ★★★
Open spaces include One Tree Hill Domain and Cornwall Park as well as Jellicoe Park and Waikaraka Park and the motorway-edged Onehunga Wharf. Waikaraka Park cemetery is steeped in history, and there are a number of heritage walks in the area.

Sporting facilities include the Onehunga War Memorial Pool and the Manukau Cruising Club, as well as clubs catering for bowling, soccer, rugby, squash and rowing.

There are some excellent ethnic restaurants in Onehunga as well as artistic and cultural facilities and a modern library.

Real Estate
Trends
The recent over-excited Auckland property market, combined with immigration and favourable economic activity, has seen a shortage of properties here – both for sale and rental. The real estate market continues to progress in Onehunga and prices certainly haven't fallen lately.

Terrace houses have been popular with Asian couples and families, either to rent or

buy. Houses are more expensive nearer to One Tree Hill; the lower parts of Onehunga are close to busy roads and industrial areas.

It's hard to estimate prices as the area is changing constantly. For an average family home, expect to pay $400,000 to $600,000.

Rental and investment
Older character homes are popular as rentals, but also attracting the punters are the newer townhouses close to the suburb's shopping hub.

Best streets
Mariri and Huapai Rds, the western end of Grey St and Arthur St and Quadrant Rd.

Smart Buy ⊘
For years this area has been tipped as one to watch. With the motorway extensions and the new eastern arterial, access has greatly improved. Although good buys are getting harder to find they are still around. Prices have eased off, if only slightly, and with Onehunga being a trendy alternative for young couples looking for their first villa or bungalow, the area still holds promise.

House prices

Unit	
Bedroom	🛏
Price	$150,000 plus
Bedrooms	🛏 🛏
Price	$200,000 plus
Old worker's cottage	
Price	$300,000 plus
Villa or bungalow on half site	
Bedrooms	🛏 🛏 🛏
Price	$350,000 plus
Renovated villa or bungalow on full site	
Price	$500,000 plus
New townhouse close to One Tree Hill	
Price	$550,000 plus

Rental prices

Flat	
Bedroom	🛏
Price	$190 – $220/wk
Bedrooms	🛏 🛏
Price	$250 – $290/wk
House	
Bedrooms	🛏 🛏 🛏
Price	$340 – $400/wk
Bedrooms	🛏 🛏 🛏 🛏
Price	$400 – $500/wk

Travel times

CBD	off-peak 15-20 min
	peak 1 hour
Airport	10 min
Royal Oak shops	2 min
Southern motorway	5 min

Stagecoach Auckland provides regular services to Onehunga, with many buses intersecting at this point from different parts of the city.

If you take a map of greater Auckland and stick a pin in the middle, it will land on One Tree Hill. One of Auckland's iconic landmarks, One Tree Hill – or Maungakiekie – used to be defined by its lone pine until the tree was attacked by a Maori activist and had to be removed. The summit provides some of the best views in Auckland and is surrounded by beautiful parkland. The Royal Oak roundabout is like the centre of a compass – you can go north to Epsom, east to Onehunga, west to Mt Albert or south, although not directly, to the airport. Greenlane is sandwiched between the motorway and Cornwall Park, and has suffered an image problem due to an abundance of car dealerships. It's close to, but traditionally much cheaper than, both Epsom and Remuera.

Who lives there?

Traditionally, Royal Oak is a suburb for families with teenaged children. There is a genuine mix of residents however, with older people also finding the flat terrain easy to get around. The population is predominantly Pakeha/Euro-pean and tends to be second or third home buyers. Families with young kids use One Tree Hill as a stepping-stone to Epsom when their children reach secondary school age. Also moving into the area are ex-Pakuranga and Howick residents who are tired of traffic delays and would rather spend more time with their families. Many young professionals like its central location.

Typical dwellings

Established in the 1930s when neighbouring Onehunga with its thriving port became

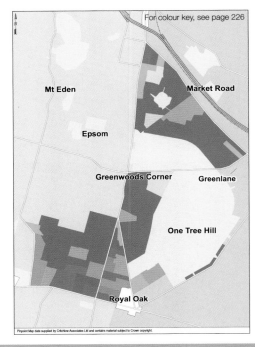

For colour key, see page 226

Mt Eden

Market Road

Epsom

Greenwoods Corner

Greenlane

One Tree Hill

Royal Oak

Pinpoint Map data supplied by Critchlow Associates Ltd and contains material subject to Crown copyright.

Population profile	Population in 2001 11,271	% Aged Under 15 years 19.11	% Aged over 65 Years 12.86
% European 70.91	% Maori 4.07	% Pacific Peoples 3.09	% Asian 23.02

crowded, One Tree Hill and Royal Oak have many period bungalows, now often on half sites. Royal Oak and Greenlane have a large assortment of bungalows through to the modern plaster or brick-and-tile homes popular with developers in the 1990s. There are a few townhouses on Manukau Rd, but no high-rises. There are some big bungalows still on large sections nearer to Onehunga. Greenlane has some grand houses in the streets that hug Cornwall Park.

There are still many state houses as well as brick and tile units, concentrated in streets like Te Rama Rd. There has been a general increase in townhouses throughout the area, due to infill housing.

Amenities
Schools ★★★

There is a good range of schools. Cornwall Park School and Royal Oak Primary are well regarded primary schools. If you're not in the Auckland Grammar – Epsom Girls' Grammar zones, other local secondary schools are the co-ed Catholic Marcellin College, Onehunga High School or Penrose High.

For a full list, see page 272.

Shops ★★★

Royal Oak is a thriving shopping hub for locals. The mall has Whitcoulls, Paper Plus, Pak 'N Save, Hugh Wrights and Plastic Box, as well as various clothing and specialty stores. Several new cafes and restaurants, including many ethnic ones, have opened locally in the past five or six years.

Nearby Greenwoods Corner has an interesting stretch of shops and cafes, and Newmarket is less than 10 minutes' drive north along Manukau Rd.

Leisure ★★★

The area's biggest recreation asset is Cornwall Park and One Tree Hill Domain. This expanse of country amid suburbia is too precious to ignore, with lambs gamboling on the green hillside, chickens strolling in the sun and huge groves of historic trees. Auckland City Council is nurturing seedlings to replace the "one tree" on top of the mountain, that fell victim to a chainsaw protest a few years ago.

Cornwall Park has recreational areas, barbecues, a restaurant, an information centre and a working farm families can walk through. On the One Tree Hill Domain side of the mountain there's a planetarium and a popular playground.

At peak times the park can be busier than Queen Street, with bumper-to-bumper power walkers pushing designer buggies or being dragged along by over-zealous canines. But if you get off the beaten track there's plenty of peace to be found in this beautiful place.

Other attractions of these suburbs include nearby Alexandra Park and also Ericsson Stadium, where hope springs eternal for the New Zealand Warriors.

Real Estate
Trends

The steady rise in sales in recent times has impacted on One Tree Hill, particularly in the areas bordering Epsom.

The Auckland and Epsom Girls grammar zones comes very much into play in Greenlane, with the $100,000 (at least) price differential between in-zone and out-of-zone properties. The possible emergence of a new secondary school on the former Auckland College of Education campus in Epsom would no doubt affect prices.

Local Hero: Cornwall Park's Acacia Cottage, Huia Lodge and Garden Cafe

Clustered together into what seems like Auckland's pretty English quarter, these three buildings are a tiny bit of colonial history. Built in 1841 in downtown Auckland, Acacia Cottage was moved here in 1920. Huia Lodge was officially opened in 1903, and is a cute, gingerbread-cottage-like piece of Queen Anne Revival architecture. Having housed successive park caretakers, and kiosk managers, it's now an information centre.

The kiosk, which began in 1908 as an open-sided pavilion for serving refreshments, is now both an ice-cream pick-up point and a genteel indoor-outdoor dining and cafe space. Its elegant, traditional feel seems more Christchurch than Auckland.

Rental and investment

The rental market is strong, with a tidy two-bedroom unit renting at around $280 a week while some larger properties command as much as $790 a week.

Best streets

Maungakiekie Ave and Wapiti Ave in Greenlane, Haydn Ave, Raurenga Ave and Lewin Rd in Royal Oak and Kowhatu Rd and Irirangi Rd in One Tree Hill.

House prices

Unit	
Bedrooms	🛏 🛏
Price	$250,000 plus
Bungalow on half site	
Bedrooms	🛏 🛏 🛏
Price	$400,000 plus
Bungalow on full site	
Bedrooms	🛏 🛏 🛏 🛏
Price	$500,000 plus
Townhouse	
Bedrooms	🛏 🛏 🛏 🛏
Price	$575,000 – $625,000
Large character house bordering park	
Price $1 million plus (many are leasehold)	

Rental prices

Flat	
Bedroom	🛏
Price	$195 – $250/wk
Bedrooms	🛏 🛏
Price	$250 – $300/wk
House	
Bedrooms	🛏 🛏 🛏
Price	$350 – $450/wk
Bedrooms	🛏 🛏 🛏 🛏
Price	$440 – $$650/wk
Bedrooms	🛏 🛏 🛏 🛏 🛏
Price	$680 – $790/wk

Travel times

From Royal Oak	
CBD	off-peak 10-20 min
	peak 30 min
North-western motorway	4-5 min
Southern motorway	4 min
Airport	15 min
St Lukes mall	10 min

There's a regular Stagecoach bus service to these suburbs and the roundabout points drivers in all directions.

Panmure is more than just its infamous roundabout, where entering and exiting is always a challenge. It's a diverse suburb with a bustling main street encompassing a distinct part of Auckland's geography next to the Tamaki River. Some parts have views of notable landmarks, and it has varied housing types to satisfy an assortment of tastes and requirements. Mt Wellington is one of those Auckland suburbs that many people know of, but few know anything about. The suburb itself is an eclectic mix of modern townhouses, family dwellings and state housing (much of it former) but also reveals a delightfully surprising range of older character villas and bungalows – many in original condition, just waiting for keen renovators to move in and get to work.

Who lives there?

A variety of people choose to live in Panmure, including many first-home buyers. Migrants from a huge range of countries also live here, attracted by the lower prices, choice of rentals and closeness to major employment areas in Mt Wellington and further south. The massive Sylvia Park development will also provide thousands of local jobs. The recently developed townhouses and terrace blocks around the Panmure Lagoon and near the shopping centre have attracted young professional couples seeking reasonably priced modern accommodation.

Despite this, it's still a working to middle-class area that acts as a gateway to the eastern suburbs. In Panmure and Tamaki, the University of Auckland's Tamaki campus attracts students and lecturing staff.

For colour key, see page 226

Tamaki

Panmure

Mt Wellington

Sylvia Park

Southdown

Westfield

Pinpoint Map data supplied by Critchlow Associates Ltd and contains material subject to Crown copyright.

Population profile	Population in 2001 26,049	% Aged Under 15 years 23.62	% Aged over 65 Years 8.81
% European 45.02	% Maori 16.01	% Pacific Peoples 24.42	% Asian 18.93

Many local residents are either state housing tenants or renters.

On the flip side, there are some very expensive homes, owned by captains of industry, peppered throughout the suburb, especially near the estuary. Mt Wellington is sometimes perceived as beneath Ellerslie in desirability. It's seen as an affordable option for younger professionals who work in the CBD. Good deals are available and there is a range of large family homes on big sections.

Typical dwellings

The types of houses in Panmure are as diverse as the suburb itself. There are turn-of-the-century villas and renovated bungalows, but the houses are predominantly 1960s and 1970s family homes and state houses. Numerous state houses have been sold by the Government in recent times, although this has slowed with current government policy.

With its many sizeable sections (between 600m2 and 950m2), these are ideal suburbs for families. Big executive-style houses can be found along the Tamaki River, and on the hill heading towards Pakuranga.

Amenities
Schools ★★★

The majority of schools in the area are public, interspersed with a few specialist schools, such as the special needs Somerville School. For a full list, see page 272.

Shops ★★★

Panmure's main street is full of shops and is a bustling place at any time of the day. Major retail outlets are also dotted along the Mt Wellington Highway and near the corner of the Ellerslie Panmure Highway is a bulk retail area with all the usual outlets, including a superstore Harvey Norman.

The bulldozers have now flattened the buildings on the old army barracks land next to the southern motorway at Sylvia Park in Mt Wellington, and a massive 24ha, $1 billion retail, office, entertainment, educational, residential and community project has begun. It'll be a huge boon to the area.

Leisure ★★★

The popular Lagoon Gymnasium (formerly Swimarama) is well patronised and the lagoon itself is host to many maritime activities as well as a pleasant walking environment.

The landmark of Mt Wellington provides panoramic views of Auckland and its harbours. This spot is popular with both visitors and locals, offering a reasonably flat and easy stroll at the summit. Other views from the summit include the impressive arrays of local amenities, starting with the superbly landscaped university playing fields for rugby, cricket, tennis, netball and soccer on Merton Rd.

A miniature train runs in Peterson Reserve

next to Waipuna Lodge on Sundays.

Panmure's main drag has plenty of eateries including the well-regarded Chinese vegetarian restaurant The Authentic.

Real Estate
Trends

One of the remarkable aspects of Panmure is the enormous variation in real estate prices. Most of the properties are at the mid to lower end of the market but there are some on the Tamaki River banks – especially at the boat-yard end – worth more than $1 million.

The market for investors remains buoyant in Panmure with plenty of keenly contested rental properties on the market. A number of recent apartment developments have added to the wide array of properties available and are being bought by either landlords or owner-occupiers.

The burgeoning interest in Panmure is fuelled by its affordability and good access to water – the Panmure Basin, Tamaki River and estuary. Also, it's closeness to the CBD, the eastern bays and eastern suburbs is also a plus point.

Plans for the old Mt Wellington quarry site have been many and varied but the current one is for high density housing.

Rental and investment

Aside from the Housing New Zealand property in Tamaki, rental properties in the area are popular with students and staff of the university. Rents have increased significantly during recent years.

Best streets

Bridge St in Panmure; Marine Lane in Mt Wellington and Dunkirk Rd in Tamaki.

House prices

Unit	
Bedroom	🛏
Price	$169,000 – $189,000
Bedrooms	🛏 🛏
Price	$189,000 – $289,000
House	
Bedrooms	🛏 🛏 🛏
Price	$300,000 plus
New executive townhouse	
Price	$500,000 plus
Waterfront property	
Price	$1 million plus

Rental prices

Flat	
Bedroom	🛏
Price	$175 – $195/wk
Bedrooms	🛏 🛏
Price	$230 – $260/wk
Apartment	
Bedrooms	🛏 🛏
Price	$310 – $320/wk
Bedrooms	🛏 🛏 🛏
Price	$340 – $380/wk
House	
Bedrooms	🛏 🛏 🛏
Price	$300 – $350/wk
Bedrooms	🛏 🛏 🛏 🛏
Price	$350 – $415/wk

Travel times

From Panmure roundabout

CBD	off-peak 13 min
	peak 20 – 25 min
Southern motorway	5 – 7 min
Airport	25 min

The Tranz Metro train stops at Tamaki and Panmure railway stations. The area is also well served by Stagecoach buses in some parts and Howick and Eastern Buses elsewhere.

Good things come in small packages, so they say – and Parnell is certainly one of them. For a small place it has a huge impact on the city's culture and property values. With a quiet confidence it knows it has some of the city's most beautiful old houses and the best boutique shopping and cafe strip – mention Ponsonby as a near contender and the locals will utter a genteel titter or two. Newmarket is a very different story – big, glitzy shops stretch as far as the eye can see beckoning a multitude of shoppers on their retail missions, whether it's the roadside shops or the big improved Two Double Seven mall. Although there have been some prosperous residential real estate developments in Newmarket in recent years, all those shops don't leave much room for housing.

Who lives there?

Parnell attracts all kinds of residents. Its handy location is a huge selling point. Being only a few minutes' drive from the city and Newmarket – on fine days it's a pleasant walk – makes it popular with professionals and retired people as well as students.

There are many old Auckland families in Parnell, who have lived here for generations. The suburb has been an established centre for the artistic intelligentsia; and – as with Ponsonby and other inner city suburbs – many residents are categorised as bobo, or bourgeois bohemians. Artists, writers and interior designers also live in Parnell, but they're not the starving in the garret variety.

Many families with secondary school-age children live here – it's mostly in zone for Auckland Grammar and Epsom Girls'

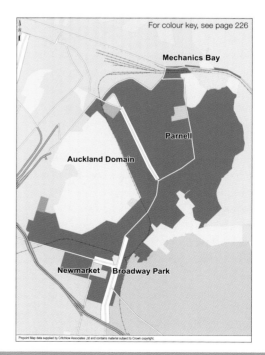

For colour key, see page 226

Mechanics Bay

Parnell

Auckland Domain

Newmarket   Broadway Park

Pinpoint Map data supplied by Critchlow Associates Ltd and contains material subject to Crown copyright.

Population profile	Population in 2001 7,593	% Aged Under 15 years 10.27	% Aged over 65 Years 8.06
% European 81.59	% Maori 4.27	% Pacific Peoples 1.82	% Asian 8.85

Grammar and is close to many private schools.

As with other wealthy suburbs, ex-pats returning with wallets full of overseas currencies have found relocation fairly effortless. Buyers into Parnell are mainly Pakeha and Europeans although a few Asians have also settled here. By comparison, Newmarket attracts more Chinese buyers; it is a cosmopolitan professional area with lots of business people. A number of older couple whose children have left home also live in the suburb.

Typical dwellings

Parnell boasts some of Auckland's grandest old homes, including Historic Places Trust houses, and is brimming with turn-of-the-century villas and bungalows. However, modern architecture has also made a subtle mark here, with sleek townhouses tucked behind older houses. The suburb has many units and apartments, which are currently in high demand. Although many of the sections are small and neighbouring houses are only a stone's throw away, Parnell oozes atmosphere. Many Parnell houses have spectacular sea views of Rangitoto Island through to the harbour bridge.

While Newmarket has fewer houses than Parnell, there are numerous 1840s worker's cottages. These tend to be too small for family living, but are attractive for singles and childless professional couples. The Broadway Park development, with its arrangement of terraced homes, duplexes and mid to high-rise apartments also serves this sector.

Amenities
Schools ★★★

There is a primary school in Parnell and another in Newmarket, plus the private Junior College of New Zealand. Parts of the area are in zone for Auckland Grammar School and Epsom Girls' Grammar School.

For a full list, see page 272.

Shops ★★★★★

Gracing the shopping strip on Parnell Rise are most of the leading fashion houses, art galleries and some of Auckland's best restaurants and trendiest cafes. With its cobbled paving and heritage buildings, the area mixes chic retail with a village atmosphere.

It is a great place to while away an afternoon or a whole day. Be prepared to watch the credit card bend, however, as the offerings are not bargain basement.

Newmarket's shopping strip is busier and more commercial, with a mix of boutique retail and chain stores, and a high number of overseas visitors. The big Two Double Seven mall at one end was recently revamped and extended.

Leisure ★★★★★

There are plenty of open spaces – the Auckland Domain, Parnell Rose Gardens and Dove-Myer Robinson Park, and a number of smaller reserves. Newmarket Park has undergone a major upgrade.

Both the Auckland Museum and the Auckland Cathedral are major centres of cultural activity. Parnell library is located in the former Foundation for the Blind building. Newmarket has two large cinema complexes.

There are three tennis clubs, including the ASB Bank Tennis Centre and public swimming at the refurbished Parnell Baths and the Olympic Pool & Fitness Centre.

Real Estate
Trends

Trends in Auckland's property market tend to start in Parnell so it's a place to watch for changes in activity. It traditionally hasn't been a place for first-home buyers although the now abundant supply of purpose-built and trendy apartments do offer more choice for high-earning younger folk.

In Newmarket, there are many new luxury high-rise apartments on the skyline, full of 50-somethings looking for inner-city excitement now their children have decamped. The lock-up-and-leave-style accommodation makes travelling easy and being close to restaurants, shops and movies allows for extensive entertaining. These apartment complexes are also prominent in Parnell, on Parnell Rise, Gladstone Rd and further down St Stephens Ave.

The larger modern townhouses are also popular with this age group, who may not be ready to completely lose the backyard. These homes allow for a lap pool, extensive decking and terraces and designer gardens. However, you have to be fairly well-heeled as some sell for more than $4 million, with the average apartment into the millions.

Rental and investment

There are a lot of people who want to live in this exclusive area, but don't have enough money to buy here. This continues to fuel the rental market.

Best streets

The lower end of St Stephens Ave and the streets that run off it, such as Bridgewater Rd, Crescent Rd and Judge St.

Local hero: Parnell Baths

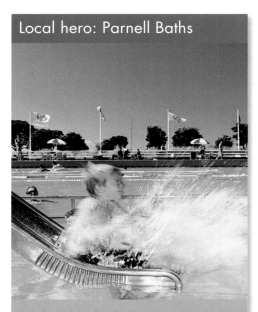

The historic Parnell Baths, on Auckland's waterfront, are one of the city's unique features. The 60m salt water pools reopened in January 2003 following a $4.2 million upgrade. The facility is a great place for the whole family, with new features including a partially heated children's pool with water toys and a water playground. Three hot pools designed for toddlers, children and adults keep swimmers of all ages warm on cooler days. There are qualified attendants on duty at all times, lounging chairs and an all-weather cafe serving up ice-creams and healthy snacks.

Originally opened in 1914, the Parnell Baths were redeveloped in the 1950s in the Modernist style. A striking abstract mosaic mural of swimmers adorns the changing room walls. According to architecture lecturer Peter Shaw, the baths are one of the great Modernist icons of New Zealand architecture.

House prices

Apartment

Bedroom	🛏
Price	$300,000 plus
Bedrooms	🛏 🛏
Price	$400,000 plus

New apartment

Price	$650,000 – $1 million plus

Broadway Park, terrace house

Price	$500,000 plus
Stand-alone house	around $1 million

Renovated character home on half site

Price	$600,000 plus
Full site	$800,000 plus

Large townhouse

Bedrooms	🛏 🛏 🛏 🛏
Price	$2 million plus

Rental prices

Flat/apartment

Bedroom	🛏
Price	$240 – $350/wk
Bedrooms	🛏 🛏
Price	$330 – $460/wk

House

Bedrooms	🛏 🛏
Price	$500 – $700/wk
Bedrooms	🛏 🛏 🛏
Price	$560 – $790/wk

Travel times

From Parnell Rise

CBD	off-peak 5 min
	peak 15 min
	15 min walk
Motorways south and west	3 min
Airport	25 min
Remuera	5 min

From Newmarket

Britomart CBD by train	10 min

Ponsonby revels in its profile as the absolute soul of Auckland's vibrant, multicultural cosmopolitanism. It's a unique part of the city, where professional sportspeople, media celebrities, patrons of the arts, captains of industry and icons of Auckland's gay subculture rub shoulders in Ponsonby Rd's trendy cafes. There's no shortage of people clamouring to live here, on the fun side of town. Herne Bay has been high class for a long time now, thanks to its fabulous harbour views, grand old homes and gracious leafy streets. St Marys Bay generally has better views than Herne Bay, but smaller sections, and running beneath it is one of New Zealand's busiest stretches of motorway. Freemans Bay has great city views, but a reputation for losing the sun early in the day.

Who lives there?

Rightly or wrongly, the label "chardonnay socialist" has been attached to Ponsonby residents. They're an eclectic mix of all ages and sexes – and families do live here as well. It's a melting pot for all cultures, ethnicities and lifestyles with a large gay community. While it's true the area has a warm social conscience and an appetite for all that is trendy, there's also an obvious hankering for the finer things in life. The term "bobo" – bohemian bourgeois – is used to describe this neighbourhood, with its concentration of advertising and media types, creatives and assorted ex-hippies-made-good.

Originally a blue-collar and Polynesian area, Ponsonby was a 1960s student mecca. The drift back to the city and away from traffic jams has seen a steady gentrification

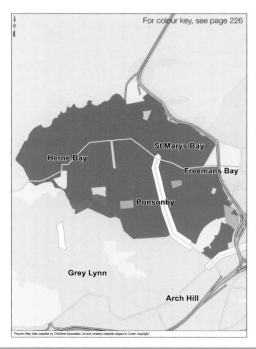

For colour key, see page 226

St Marys Bay
Herne Bay
Freemans Bay
Ponsonby
Grey Lynn
Arch Hill

Pinpoint Map data supplied by Critchlow Associates Ltd and contains material subject to Crown copyright.

Population profile	Population in 2001 14,415	% Aged Under 15 years 14.19	% Aged over 65 Years 7.62
% European 82.39	% Maori 6.66	% Pacific Peoples 8.14	% Asian 4.79

of the scruffy old villas and bungalows.

As with nearby suburbs, there has been a noticeable inward drift of eastern suburbs, attracted by the more cosmopolitan atmosphere. All the western inner-city suburbs appeal to a mix of double income professional couples (with or without children), singles and gays. Very few Asian migrants buy into Ponsonby – mainly due to the higher upkeep required for older homes.

The demographics of St Marys Bay also reflects the assortment of residences. Inhabitants range from prosperous single yuppies and dinkies through to one and two child families. A sizeable number of the apartments have been bought with pink dollars.

Typical dwellings

Where demand exceeds supply, prices tend to rise – and Ponsonby is a good example of this. Villas and bungalows are snapped up as soon as they come on the market, irrespective of their state of repair. Although pure do-ups are becoming rare, there is still some renovating potential here.

Herne Bay has larger villas and more stately homes. Section sizes in St Marys Bay and Freemans Bay are typically 300m2, while Herne Bay's average is 500-600m2. Small section sizes mean many Ponsonby, St Marys Bay and Freemans Bay properties don't have off-street parking.

Proportionally there are not as many $1 million plus homes in Freemans Bay as in St Marys Bay – the quality of the homes in general tends to be more variable. Where St Marys Bay is almost exclusively residential, Freemans Bay is mixed use. There's more apartment construction in Freemans Bay.

Amenities
Schools ★★★

The area is well served by primary schools, but there's a dearth of secondary schools. Zones include Auckland Girls Grammar and Western Springs College but many of the moneyed residents send their kids to private schools across town – or move out to buy in Auckland Grammar zone when their sons reach high school age. There are two Catholic secondary schools.

For a full list, see page 272.

Shops ★★★★★

This area is famous for its shopping. Ponsonby and Jervois Rds are lined with trendy specialty stores selling designer clothing, homewares and jewellery. Local icons such as Ponsonby Pies and Atomic Cafe enjoy patronage from locals and visitors alike and there are plenty of restaurants catering to all tastes and styles. Ponsonby Rd has its own website www.ponsonbyroad.com.

There are fairly new supermarkets in Richmond Rd and College Hill and plenty of

Protecting our housing heritage

Ponsonby, one of Auckland's earliest inner-city suburbs, has buildings dating back 150 years, including Ponsonby and Jervois Rd commercial facades and the jumble of homes that line residential streets off the main thoroughfares.

Wander down a side street such as Renall St, and you'll see house exteriors that have been lovingly preserved. The first houses in Ponsonby were workers' cottages built in areas such as Freeman's Bay while more substantial homes were built for the wealthier in St Mary's Bay. Ponsonby boomed in the 1870s and 1880s with many ornate homes being built.

Dwellings that have survived the wear and tear of time are now zealously protected by the Auckland City Council's through its Residential 1 zoning, which means homeowners must maintain their home in keeping with the character and history of the area. This includes renovations and additions. Adding a modern necessity such as a garage needs careful consideration because its design mustn't detract from the house or street. Even paintwork should reflect the age of the house. Exteriors are the main concern - nobody will be denied a designer kitchen.

bakeries, flower and fruit shops. Downtown Auckland, Newmarket shops and St Lukes malls are all fairly close by.

Leisure ★★★★

Many local parks, including Victoria Park, Western Park, Grey Lynn Park and Cox's Bay, are great places to relax and get some fresh air. The famous local rugby club sharing the suburb's name now plays just down the road in Western Springs – and residents enjoy being close to the zoo, MOTAT and Western Springs Park as well.

The historic Pt Erin Baths are well frequented, as are a collection of little beaches along the waterfront.

Local sports clubs include bowling, yachting, rugby, soccer, snooker, tennis, petanque and squash.

However, if we're being frank, the most popular leisure activity in this part of town is people watching while sipping a trim latte.

Real Estate
Trends

Inner city suburbs continue to see steady demand and growth. Talk of "plateauing" and bursting bubbles doesn't yet ring true in this part of town. While there may be some softening, few commentators predict a plummeting of prices.

This area will always attract buyers, due to its closeness to the city, colourful residents and fabulous cafe culture. Young people are buying apartments in droves, or if there's enough cash, smaller cottages and villas, and many families hanker to live in the large homes in Herne Bay or St Marys Bay.

These suburbs have been greatly affected by the recent property boom, with prices skyrocketing. Now that the market is quieter, some higher-end properties are sitting unsold for longer, with some lowering their price (albeit only slightly) to meet the market. You won't get much change from $1 million for a fairly modest home on a decent section.

Rental and investment

This area is always popular with renters and prices tend to remain fairly constant.

Best streets

Marine Pde, Sarsfield St and Argyle St in Herne Bay; Vermont St, O'Neill St and Summer St in Ponsonby. Dunedin St, Hackett St and London St in St Marys Bay, and Arthur St, Paget St and Hepburn St in Freemans Bay.

Ask anyone in New Zealand what "Remuera" means to them and, chances are, their answer will have something to do with being rich. The suburb's traditional make-up is changing, however. The younger generations of its blue-blood families are less likely to stay and taking their place is a steady stream of new money wanting a slice of the top suburb status. Although Remuera faces some competition in the top property-price bracket from Herne Bay and coastal North Shore, being in the Auckland Grammar and Epsom Girls' Grammar zone will always give "Remmers" a competitive advantage. The area's traditional style (protected in part by zoning legislation), mature trees, old churches and stately family homes are always an attraction for its well-shod, well-spoken, Merc-driving residents.

Who lives there?

It's no secret that Remuera is home to the medium-to-high socioeconomic bracket. Nowadays it's a mix of the nouveau riche and multi-generational moneyed families. It has long been established as the residential area of choice for captains of business and industry and their families. Much of the country's old money is housed within these impressive villas and bungalows, although inter-generational loyalty to the suburb does seem to be dying off.

As Remuera is within the Auckland Grammar School zone and close to a number of private schools, it is popular with well-heeled, education-conscious families seeking a nice suburban home. School zoning is a definite attraction for large numbers of affluent migrant families. There

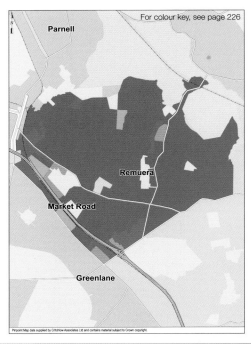

For colour key, see page 226

Parnell

Remuera

Market Road

Greenlane

Pinpoint Map data supplied by Critchlow Associates Ltd and contains material subject to Crown copyright.

Population profile	Population in 2001 18,660	% Aged Under 15 years 19.98	% Aged over 65 Years 12.28
% European 81.74	% Maori 2.17	% Pacific Peoples 1.53	% Asian 12.68

are also numerous retired people living in apartments so they can be near to their grandchildren and the shops.

The suburb retains a youthful balance, with a large number of professional people aged under 40 trying to establish a foothold. For couples on a high joint income, the area's excellent resale prospects make a big mortgage look like a good bet. A large number of expats choose to return to Remuera, and their British pounds and US dollars make the area affordable.

Typical dwellings

Remuera has some of the largest old homes in Auckland and a few are still on extensive grounds. Heritage zones protect the character of certain streets – parts of Bassett Rd, Arney Rd, Portland Rd and Seaview Rd are special-character zones in the district plan.

During the past decade, contemporary, minimalist designer homes and luxury medium-rise apartments have taken pride of place along the suburb's north-facing slopes and ridge, adding to the selection of housing styles available. The slightly less desirable southern slopes are filled with many renovated character villas and bungalows.

The undulating geography of the suburb means that views of the city, the Hauraki Gulf and One Tree Hill are common. Nearly every pocket of land has been filled, with many older houses being relocated to make way for new, high qualtiy developments – we're not talking ticky-tacky here.

Amenities
Schools ★★★★★

The public schools are are top quality and there are a number of private schools close by, including St Kentigern and Kings prep schools and Baradene College. The suburb is in zone for both Epsom Girls' and Auckland Grammar Schools (boys only). Diocesan School for Girls and St Cuthbert's are both nearby in neighbouring Epsom and Junior College is in Parnell.

For a full list, see page 272.

Shops ★★★

Remuera's popular shopping strip is dominated by banks, antique shops, real estate agents, boutique clothes stores and cafes. A great place for the locals to catch up, it is regularly humming despite being so close to the thriving shopping mecca of Newmarket.But after the sun goes down, there is no one to be seen. In the words of one local: "By 9pm, you would think everybody has died."

Further down the road, the old Remuera Village is wall-to-wall restaurants, so it's a little livelier after dark. There's a cluster of cafes and designer shops in Benson Rd too.

Leisure ★★★

Bordered by Newmarket, Orakei, Meadowbank and Epsom, Remuera is home to numerous parks and reserves.

Proudly poised overlooking its residents is Mt Hobson, where walking tracks offer a challenging workout.

There are numerous sports clubs in or near Remuera, including cycling, lawn and court tennis, bowling, squash, badminton, netball and football. Remuera Golf Club is actually located in neighbouring Meadowbank. Ellerslie Racecourse is nearby.

Remuera has a grand old library, at least three medical centres and two hospitals nearby. The beginning of Remuera Rd is New Zealand's medical specialists' mile, the local equivalent of Harley St.

Three popular retirement homes are St Vincent's, Remuera Gardens and the Remuera Life Care Retirement Village. Local fare includes a handful of restaurants and cafes, many of which are frequented on a weekly basis by locals.

Travel times

CBD by car	off-peak 10 – 15 min
	peak 25 – 45 min
CBD by bus	30 – 40 min
Britomart CBD by train	10 min
Southern motorway	1– 5 min
North-western motorway	10 min
Airport	30 min
Newmarket	5 min

Stagecoach Auckland provides a regular bus service, plus the area is serviced by the Tranz Metro commuter train service on the Papakura route.

Real Estate
Trends

Remuera Rd has traditionally been a dividing line, with homes on the side of the street known as the "northern slopes" being worth much more than the other side. On the southern side, Armadale Rd, from the motorway back, has more bungalows. Relatively speaking, it has been the cheaper end of Remuera. Tired bungalows are of little

value in Remuera, but the land on which they sit is at a premium. The comfortable mix of traditional and contemporary is testament to the changing face of Remuera. This suburb will continue to be a destination of choice for many years to come.

You still need a bit of money to obtain a 524, 520 or 529 telephone number and you won't find much for under $700,000. Even something very tired on a "bad street" could set you back upwards of $800,000. Large family homes are always in demand and don't last long on the market, especially if they have been renovated.

Rental and investment

The eastern suburbs rental market can only be described as chaotic, with many people looking for an address in the grammar zones.

Best streets

All the streets north of Remuera Rd are desirable. Of special note are Victoria Ave, Arney Cres, Arney Rd, Eastbourne Rd, Waiata Ave, the upper part of Portland Rd, Seaview Rd and Westbourne Rd.

Why we live there

Cardiologist Warwick Jaffe and family

Cardiologist Warwick Jaffe, his wife Megan and their two children Samuel and Elliot moved to Remuera more than three years ago. Having lived in Epsom and Mt Eden, where they found the infill housing and traffic congestion of those suburbs frustrating, Remuera was a logical option being close to work and school. "The move has been most successful and we are extremely happy living here," says Warwick.

Finding the village atmosphere welcoming and friendly, the couple felt they had a wide choice of excellent schools, both public and private. "The boys currently attend King's School and we are very much part of the King's 'family'. As our two boys move to secondary school, we are zoned for some of the best schools in Auckland."

Minutes to work, the CBD, Parnell, Newmarket, and only eight minutes to St Heliers, the family also enjoy the local shopping at Remuera and Newmarket, the restaurants in Parnell (especially Cibo), the viaduct and Ponsonby.

House prices

Cottage
Bedrooms	🛏️ 🛏️
Price	$450,000 – $$500,000

New apartment
Bedrooms	🛏️ 🛏️
Price	$500,000 plus
Bedrooms	🛏️ 🛏️ 🛏️
Price	$800,000 plus

Older townhouse
Price	$500,000 plus

New townhouse
Price	$900,000 plus

Do-up on a half site
Bedrooms	🛏️ 🛏️ 🛏️
Price	$600,000 plus
Bedrooms	🛏️ 🛏️ 🛏️ 🛏️
Price	$800,000 plus

Renovated bungalow
Price	$1 million plus

New mansion
Bedrooms	🛏️ 🛏️ 🛏️ 🛏️
Price	$2 million plus

Rental prices

Flat or apartment
Bedroom	🛏️
Price	$250 – $470/wk
Bedrooms	🛏️ 🛏️
Price	$345 – $500/wk
Bedrooms	🛏️ 🛏️ 🛏️
Price	$355 – $630/wk

House
Bedrooms	🛏️ 🛏️
Price	$425 – $450/wk
Bedrooms	🛏️ 🛏️ 🛏️
Price	$410 – $550/wk
Bedrooms	🛏️ 🛏️ 🛏️ 🛏️
Price	$540 – $750/wk
Bedrooms	🛏️ 🛏️ 🛏️ 🛏️ 🛏️
Price	$550 – $745/wk

West

Dominated by the moody, bush-clad Waitakere Ranges and a dramatic wild coastline, west Auckland has a character quite unlike the region's other areas. Its residents are independent thinkers and creative – this is home to a film and TV industry, top comedians and one of our best-known fashion designers. This was the first city in New Zealand to declare itself nuclear free and its greenie reputation is well-established. Waitakere City is an "eco city", which means it strives to do everything from producing less rubbish and planting more trees to containing urban sprawl and reducing traffic accidents.

West Auckland never seems to stand still. Its population is young and forward-thinking. Current initiatives include updated transport centres, new libraries, lobbying

for an international airport at Whenuapai, new civic centres and a campus linked to the wine industry. It's a major centre of tourism, arts and culture, and the landscape includes everything from gentrified lifestyle blocks, fabulous native bush gardens and architecturally designed homes.

People here are both down-to-earth and idealistic; they can laugh at themselves and the "Westie" label (supposedly all about fast cars, a hippy-ish outlook and black jeans); and they're becoming more ethnically diverse.

West Auckland was shaped by rapid post-war expansion, and is now a series of town centres. Henderson is its undisputed CBD,

rain dripped native bush
pounding surf beaches
black jeans and big dogs
green, green, green

and a vibrant retail and civic centre. Areas of industrial land add to the mix and further out you'll find orchards, market gardens, viticulture, rich farmland and majestic black-sand beaches surging with pounding surf. The area has always had a strong industrial base, beginning with timber and flax milling, and kauri gum digging, followed by brick works and pottery industries. During the 1970s, New Zealanders ate their dinners off the heavy crockery produced by the now defunct Crown Lynn factories in New Lynn.

Back in 1902 Assid Corban helped to kick-start west Auckland's wine industry. Viticulture is becoming an ever-more significant industry here with much of the activity now based at Kumeu.

At the weekend, many Aucklanders head to west Auckland's beaches or bush for walks, picnics, scenic driving, gannet-watching, fishing, boating or to experience the notorious west coast rips. Surfers come from throughout the city to catch the wild waves. The fabulous 10,000ha Centennial Memorial Park includes a large chunk of the Waitakere Ranges and some of the beaches.

AUCKLAND

WEST

Where else can you walk from town to your lifestyle block but in Helensville? Set in the rolling rural Kaipara River valley, Helensville is catching the eye of lifestylers who've been priced out of Kumeu and Huapai. Once conservative and isolated, Helensville is now a mix of go-ahead town and heritage charm. One born-and-fled, now-returned resident couldn't believe the change: "I drove out from Auckland, saw this huge signpost, 'Helensville', and I thought, oh my, we are on the map!" Nearby Parakai is benefiting from the spin-off in residential interest and the community of Shelly Beach is a gem on the South Head Peninsula, with lifestyle blocks and horticultural land. Kaukapakapa township is the hub of the surrounding rural area.

Who lives there?

Lifestylers, artists, self-confessed eccentrics, families and elderly people come together happily in a community that expresses the best of what small-town New Zealand is all about. The children of born-and-bred locals generally stay and raise their own families. Others leave and come back with renewed enthusiasm for the easy sophistication it now has compared with 20 or 30 years ago. Newcomers from West Auckland and the North Shore will happily get into their cars for the commute to Auckland, when not long ago they'd baulk at struggling through urban motorways and traffic lights. As one puts it: "It takes my friends the same time to get from Titirangi to Dominion Rd as it takes me to get from Helensville, 35 minutes – and my drive is much better than theirs."

For colour key, see page 226

Tauhoa Hoteo

Mangakura

South Kaipara Head

South Head Glorit

Lake Ototoa Araparera

Kakanui

Waioneke Makarau

Shelly Beach

Kanohi

Motukuru Island Kaukapakapa

Parkhurst Loch Norrie

Parakai

Helensville

Ohirangi

Wharepapa

Rewiti

Huapai

Pinpoint Map data supplied by Critchlow Associates Ltd and contains material subject to Crown copyright.

Population profile	Population in 2001 6,819	% Aged Under 15 years 25.34	% Aged over 65 Years 8.84
% European 83.99	% Maori 15.35	% Pacific Peoples 3.52	% Asian 1.54

Typical dwellings

Helensville is best known for its villas, whether they're simple square fronts or more ornate return-verandah versions. Those in the township are originals; out in the back blocks there are some relocated villas trucked off sections in Auckland's inner-city suburbs. Auckland buyers widen their eyes in delight when they hear the price tags, considering what a similar home might cost in Mt Eden or Devonport.

Other homes include weatherboard houses of all shapes, sizes, styles and conditions. Helensville also has its brick and tile contributions – in this case, the very smart and sought-after Amberly Heights homes on elevated sections close to Kaipara College.

Parakai's older housing stock includes basic family homes on typical quarter acre sections and smaller stand-alone two-bedroom houses on much smaller plots. The new brick and tile homes being built on the 70-site River Valley estate behind Palm Springs pools are bringing choice and a modern look to the township. Construction of a 177-unit retirement village in the new residential development is to start shortly. In the Parakai shopping area, a two-storey retail block of six, with first floor accommodation, is under way, with a second block of four units under consideration.

South Head is largely lifestyle blocks. Kaukapakapa is a mix of lifestyle blocks and large farms.

Amenities

Schools ★★

There are primary schools in Helensville, Parakai, South Head and Kaukapakapa. Secondary school-aged children come into Kaipara College, Helensville from a wide rural catchment area.

For a full list, see page 272.

Shops ★★

Helensville's busy little shopping strip now includes a Woolworths supermarket.

As well as the usual furnishing, gifts, craft, appliance and chemist shops, there are a number of antique and collectables shops including the Lock Stock and Barrel and the ground floor of The Old Post Office. Art galleries include the well known Muddy Creek Art Gallery, Artspace and Arts of the Kaipara. Parakai's shops include a grocery store.

Leisure ★★★

Parakai is famous for its thermal pools that attract locals, tourists and elderly people who like to soothe their aching joints in its waters. Aquatic Park has two hydroslides that are something of a local landmark as well as an indoor and outdoor pool. Palm Springs across the road has two outdoor pools.

Woodhill Forest has trails for motorbikes, mountain bikes and horses. It's popular for orienteering and tramping.

Entertainer Jools Topp

Jools Topp is one half of the hilarious Topp Twins. While twin sister Lynda is something of a townie, Jools is anything but. "I never have been and I never will," she declares. Jools' patch is 6.8ha of rolling pasture on the outskirts of Helensville which is also home to her horses, cows, chooks, dogs and cats. It's close enough to Auckland for her gigs and the airport is only 1 hour 10 minutes away. "It can take that long to get from Ponsonby to Newmarket!"

She loves Helensville for its sense of openness and the riverside location that will keep it that way. She doesn't worry about the possibility of some day waking up to acres of rolling brick and tile sprawl. "You can't stop progress, nobody can, but I think Helensville will still be a small town with all its old charm for a long time yet. Most people living here have realised that there's sense in slowing down a bit. They're getting away from the idea that life is only about rushing about making money."

For a different kind of walk there's the Helensville Riverside Heritage Walkway, and there are many gardens open for visits during the year as well.

The Helensville Showgrounds host an annual A&P show. Boating is popular along the Kaipara River.

Helensville's eateries include the Cafe Regent in the art deco Regent Cinema building, Cafe Upper Crust, the Ginger Crunch Cafe at the railway station and the Art Stop cafe. Kaukapakapa has its hotel restaurant and cafe. Parakai has Black Pete's Bar and Grill. At Shelly Beach South Head the Shelly Beach Store has takeaways and cafe-style food.

More upmarket dining is a 10-minute drive to Kumeu. The Macnut Macadamia Farm Cafe is at South Head.

For golfers, there's the Helensville Golf Club and a course at South Head which has fantastic views of the Kaipara Harbour.

Real Estate
Trends

Demand for Helensville villas far exceeds supply, even once buyers have got over the common misconception that there are plenty to choose from for less than $100,000. Real estate agents say estimating villa prices is difficult because so few of the larger restored ones come onto the market.

Helensville is especially popular for buyers from West Auckland, the Hibiscus Coast and Whangaparaoa wanting to both downsize and escape traffic lights. The new brick and tile homes are popular with families and older people downsizing from rural lifestyle blocks. High prices for semi-rural lifestyle blocks around Kumeu are pushing city buyers further out to Helensville's fringes. As a result

Travel times

From Helensville

CBD	off-peak 45 min
	peak 60 min plus
Parakai	5 min
Kumeu/Huapai	12 min
Muriwai	20 min
South Head	25 min

Ritchies Coachlines runs buses six days a week between Helensville and Auckland's CBD. There is mounting public pressure for the Auckland to Waitakere passenger rail service to be extended to Helensville. In the meantime some locals drive to Waitakere, then commute by rail from there.

large rural properties are progressively being cut down into appealing 1ha blocks and into little subdivisions that must include their own sewerage system because of the lack of a reticulated system.

In Parakai $300,000 is big money and it's the new brick and tile homes that are picking up the $300,000 plus sales. Older homes are slow to move throughout Parakai.

In Kaukapakapa there's very little land under $400,000 now, with lifestyle blocks from 1 to 4ha fetching upwards of $500,000.

Best streets

Rimmer Rd in Helensville for its lifestyle blocks; Garfield St in town for its quaint villas. Fordyce Rd in Parakai.

Rental and investment

Rents have nudged upwards in recent years as investors and lifestylers have spotted the potential in both a quieter lifestyle and a return on a lot less money than it costs to buy elsewhere in the region.

House prices

Helensville

House
Bedrooms (2)
Price $200,000 – $230,000

Villa do-up
Bedrooms (3)
Price $250,000 – $380,000

Renovated villa
Price $400,000 plus

Villa on lifestyle block
Bedrooms (3)
Price $500,000 – 600,000

New house
Bedrooms (4)
Price $300,000 – $350,000

Parakai

Basic house
Bedrooms (2)
Price $175,000 – $185,000
Bedrooms (3)
Price $220,000 – $250,000

Newer house
Bedrooms (3)
Price $320,000 – $340,000

Villa on 800m2
Bedrooms (3)
Price $350,000 – $400,000

Rental prices

House
Bedrooms (2)
Price $220 – $250/wk
Bedrooms (3)
Price $250 – $300/wk

Brick and tile house
Bedrooms (4)
Price $280 – $350/wk

4ha lifestyle block with large house
Price $350 – $450/wk

Henderson is a big suburb going big places. It's heartland West Auckland, and the thriving CBD of Waitakere City. Progress on many fronts make it the envy of other big centres. There's a new civic centre and a "baby Britomart" transport centre underway. Waitakere Hospital has new status as a general hospital with expanded surgical facilities.

There's a Henderson Vineyards Business Campus planned for Lincoln, and Henderson's potential as a film and television precinct based around the studios in Henderson Valley Rd is being promoted off-shore. Te Atatu Peninsula has shaken off its image as the poor cousin of Te Atatu South. It boasts new houses by the water and a commute into the city without a single traffic light.

Who lives there?

About 160 years young, Henderson was where Yugoslav migrants brought their horticultural skills in the days when the countryside was a vista of orderly vineyards and orchards. There are still strong multi-generational links throughout Henderson. Children raised here will often be drawn back to raise their own children. Nowadays, Chinese, Korean and Indian migrants, as well as those from Eastern Europe and South Africa, contribute to Henderson's vibrant cosmopolitan flavour.

This is largely solid working-class territory, with some more moneyed folk in the prestigious estates of Henderson Heights and along the eastern coast of Te Atatu Peninsula. It has its share of oldies, some of whom live in Waitakere Gardens retirement complex

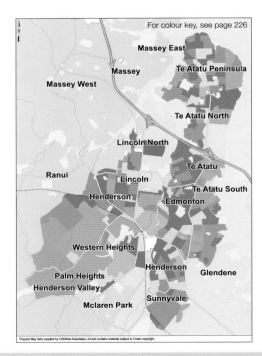

For colour key, see page 226

Pinpoint Map data supplied by Critchlow Associates Ltd and contains material subject to Crown copyright.

Population profile	Population in 2001 50,013	% Aged Under 15 years 23.72	% Aged over 65 Years 10.95
% European 64.54	% Maori 14.97	% Pacific Peoples 14.46	% Asian 11.61

in the centre of town. The peninsula continues to be hugely popular with city (Auckland and Henderson) commuters, young families and affluent buyers. Te Atatu South's popularity as a family suburb is assured because it's near the motorway on-ramp and sections are large.

Typical dwellings

Henderson's houses are synonymous with the famous "Dally palaces", built by Croatian migrants from Dalmatia during the 1970s. They were big with brick cladding, tiled roofs and basement garages. White wrought-iron balustrades defined the front steps and there were often rose gardens across the front. Now these are a popular second stop for young homeowners trading up from group-home-style first homes in the likes of Lincoln and Te Atatu North. A big plus in their favour is their generous 600-700m2 sites, which can't be subdivided.

Brick continues to be the cladding material of choice, as the developers who've moved into the old vineyards and orchards have created enclaves of prestigious homes. In the likes of Burgundy Park, Western Heights and Palm Heights, streets have mouthwatering

names, such as Chardonnay, Semillon, Cognac and Shiraz – a nod to Henderson's famous wine-making heritage.

Amenities
Schools ★★★

Abundant primary schools serve these areas Summerfield School opened in 2001 with a predetermined enrolment zone. Unitec's Waitakere campus is in the heart of Henderson, and the Bible College of New Zealand is near the motorway end of Lincoln Rd. For a full list, see page 272.

Shops ★★★★

The WestCity Mall in the heart of Henderson's busy shopping precinct has grown in size and sophistication to reflect the tastes of the wide West Auckland area. At the Corban Estate Arts Centre a Pacific cultural market is held on the first Saturday of every month. Lincoln Rd has several retail centres, boasting just about every big-name store. Local shops are dotted throughout the suburbs. Every little village within Henderson has its own amenities, often including a library, Plunket rooms and a community centre. The Palomino Shopping Centre at Sturges Rd, for example, is just the right number of well-heeled steps away from the homes of the Burgundy Park estate.

Leisure ★★★

At the city end of Henderson Valley Rd, Opanuku Reserve offers a restful playground area for weary parents. For those keen to broaden the mind and stretch the legs there's the International Walkway of Trees that runs alongside the Henderson Creek off Central Park. The 7.2ha Kiwi Valley complex in

Henderson Valley Rd includes farm tours, an equestrian centre, a stunt school that services the film industry, and Old MacDonald's travelling farmyard.

The West Wave Aquatic Centre is in the heart of Henderson. The new Waitakere Trusts Stadium is located on Central Park Dr, and a new library is planned as part of the redevelopment of the Trading Place area of Henderson's CBD.

On the Te Atatu Peninsula, there are plans to develop the 80ha of water's edge land looking across to Auckland city into a "people's park" which will link up with the peninsula walkway. The Jack Pringle skate park is part of the village green; in Te Atatu South there's the Lloyd Morgan Lions Park. Boating buffs get the best views from the Te Atatu's Taikata Sailing Club at the tip of the peninsula.

For eateries try Moka on Great North Rd, as well as the wide range of Indian, Asian and Middle Eastern restaurants along the main shopping route. At the Kiwi Valley complex there's the Last Straw Cafe. Te Atatu has its Peninsula Palms Cafe, the Compass Point Cafe and Connections family restaurant.

Real Estate
Trends

With rising median prices and a shortage of housing stock on their books, real estate agents report keen competition across all price ranges. Many first-home buyers have grown up here, travelled, then returned. "Once a Westie, always a Westie," says one. Families move from other suburbs of Auckland in search of a home close to the lush native bush of the Waitakere Ranges and the fabulous West Coast beaches. Asian

migrants are continuing their influx. There's far less land available for building on, with lifestyle buyers having to look as far north as Helensville if they want no near neighbours. Te Atatu continues to pull in the investors who have watched its potential unfold over recent years. Te Atatu Peninsula is often touted as "the next Pt Chevalier". Peninsula prices are, therefore, on the up, with the $1 million ceiling burst by a 340m2 home with views but no water access. Among the peninsula's traditional first-entry group housing stock there is far less available for under $300,000 than there was two years ago. Waimanu Bay sections can fetch $600,000 plus, which translates into healthy capital gains for investors who on-sell instead of building.

Rentals and investment

Big variances in rental prices reflect the wide range of housing stock, from the ex-group houses in older areas to flash new homes.

Best streets

Burgundy Park Ave in Henderson Heights, Frank Evans Pl in Henderson and Waikura Dr, Spinnaker Dr and Karemoana Dr on the Te Atatu Peninsula.

Why I live there

Entertainer
Pio Terei

Pio, his wife Debbie and their three children share their 1.6ha West Auckland property with calves, chooks and a few sheep. Pio has lived here for more than 10 years and says he'd never swap the lifestyle. "It's rural, it's ideal for bringing up children and it's close to wonderful shopping and restaurants. We've got cafes and vineyards and we're just over the hill from Piha." Based from home, Pio can juggle appointments to avoid peak-hour traffic.

Look Out ①

Don't move here unless you're prepared to be a proud "Westie". People here love the term, saying all that negative stuff about black jeans, loud Holdens and crushed velvet is outdated and just, well, nonsense. As one Westie says. "I mean, where do these people come from who are negative about Westies? They need to get over it. It's time to be positive. Being a Westie is something special. It's just because they aren't called Northies or Southies or Easties – Westie is our label and we just love it."

House prices

Unit
Bedrooms 🛏 🛏
Price $250,000 – $280,000

House
Bedrooms 🛏 🛏 🛏
Price $240,000 – $300,000
(add $50,000 for Te Atatu Peninsula)

Better quality house
Bedrooms 🛏 🛏 🛏 🛏
Price $370,000 – $450,000

Executive house
Bedrooms 🛏 🛏 🛏 🛏
Price $600,000 – $800,000
With views $900,000 plus

Rental prices

House
Bedrooms 🛏 🛏
Price $250 – $300/wk
Bedrooms 🛏 🛏 🛏
Price $260 – $320/wk
Bedrooms 🛏 🛏 🛏 🛏
Price $420 – $540/wk

Travel times

CBD	off-peak 10-15 min
	peak 25-40 min
West Coast beaches	20 min
Airport	30 min

A train line and good bus services run through Waitakere City. Henderson and its environs are well served with access routes to the north-western motorway via either Lincoln Rd or Te Atatu Rd. A train ride to the CBD takes about the same time as a motorway trip.

Beneath the sleepy and bucolic romanticism of this semi-rural part of Auckland lies a veritable hotbed – of property price increases. This area led the mainland charge during the recent property boom. The area supports everyone from horticulturalists and viticulturalists to hobby farmers and we-really-take-it-seriously lifestylers. Part of the appeal is that suburban-style sections have hit the market so you can have the country lifestyle without having to feed livestock. Ten years ago, no one thought anything of the local chap who'd chug along the main road to the dairy in his tractor. Now, that main road is a bustling arterial route for the four-wheel-drive monsters that are the wheels of choice for Kumeu's "now" generation.

Who lives there?

Kumeu/Huapai has lots to offer, including a community with a spirited mix of all ages and interests. This is rural living at its best, with country farming areas serviced by a wide range of retailers at the townships.

Well-established professionals are significant buyers, arriving in their shiny four-wheel-drives with their young children, and a passion for the lifestyle rather than the land's productive appeal. The area is popular for the self-employed working from home and those who can vary their commuting times. For anyone who decides to really go rural, there are large tracts of land in Dairy Flat and Taupaki.

Typical dwellings

With new subdivisions being built and palatial homes dotting the rolling landscape

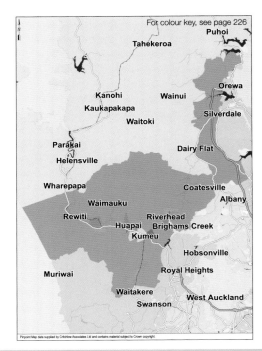

For colour key, see page 226

Puhoi
Tahekeroa
Orewa
Kanohi Wainui
Kaukapakapa
Silverdale
Waitoki
Parakai Dairy Flat
Helensville
Wharepapa Coatesville
Waimauku Albany
Rewiti Riverhead
Huapai Brighams Creek
Kumeu
Hobsonville
Muriwai Royal Heights
Waitakere
Swanson West Auckland

Pinpoint Map data supplied by Critchlow Associates Ltd and contains material subject to Crown copyright.

Population profile	Population in 2001 14,748	% Aged Under 15 years 24.13	% Aged over 60 Years 8.18
% European 90.01	% Maori 6.81	% Pacific Peoples 1.75	% Asian 2.58

of lifestyle blocks, the flavour of the wider area is continuing to change. Among the older housing stock, there are original farmhouses and small cottages, plus villas relocated from city suburbs.

New subdivisions include Freshfields and Cloverfields at Waimauku, where large houses are taking shape. Tucked among the horticultural countryside, the best homes include tennis courts, pools and stables.

Amenities
Schools ★★★

Here you'll rediscover everything that's great about rural schools, including "ag days" when children show off their pets and produce. There are four primary schools but older children have to travel to Takapuna or Henderson for secondary schooling. For a full list, see page 272.

Shops ★★★

There's energetic commercial and retail expansion going on in Kumeu. Huapai and Kumeu each have their own shopping areas with plenty of parking in a forecourt off the main road. The sprawling array of shops

sell everything from envelopes to antiques. There's a library at Huapai and Plunket rooms at Kumeu. For more substantial shopping, the Westgate shopping centre is about 10 minutes drive away.

Leisure ★★★★

Kumeu's enviable choice of leisure activities reflects a location that's close to both rural and suburban facilities. Woodhill and Riverhead forests offer ideal terrain for motor-cycling, orienteering and horse riding. Rimmers Rd, near Muriwai Beach has motorcycle tracks. In Kumeu/Huapai proper, sporting facilities include golf, squash and tennis courts and a driving range. For moviegoers, there are theatres at Westgate. There are several restaurants tucked among the vineyards, including River Mill, Allely House, Gracehill Vineyard Restaurant, Settlers Lodge, The Hunting Lodge and the Soljans Estate restaurant. For top cafe fodder, try Carriages restaurant, Blossoms Cafe or Misada, or visit the stylish BeesOnline honey centre and cafe complex.

Real Estate
Trends

A shortage of properties and abundance of inquiries are keeping prices buoyant, but without the panic buying of recent years. Now buyers are a little more cautious. There's continued strong interest from overseas, including British and South African migrants although the bulk of buyers are local, including those trading up and down within the immediate Kumeu/Huapai area, and those preferring a move into "town" from their large farm holdings.

All 26 units in the new Parkview Retirement

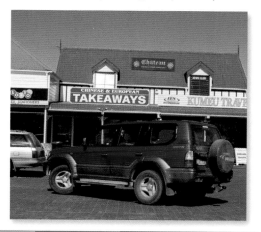

Village have long sold, with demand for as many again if they were ever to be built.

Across the board, there have been strong price increases. As quickly as subdivisions have been developed, sections have been sold and then on-sold before construction has begun. Lifestylers have been willing to pay as much for a 1ha block as for a non-subdivisible 4ha block, but there are signs that this is changing.

Rental and investment

Most demand for rental property comes from families waiting to buy or in the process of building homes. Riverhead is popular with those trying out real rural living.

Best streets

Matua Rd and Sunny Cres in Huapai; Pomona Rd in Kumeu; Solan Estate, Freshfields and Cloverfields in Waimauku.

Local Hero: the Kumeu showgrounds

After 83 years, the annual Kumeu Show continues to get bigger and brighter. Entrants for the traditional agricultural and horticultural show come from throughout the North Island for the March competitions, and to enjoy the famous village camaraderie. Equestrian events include show jumping, 500 trade sites showcase associated agricultural businesses, and stalls sell crafts. The volunteer Kumeu A&H Society owns the 34ha showgrounds, which are also used for annual events including a hot-rod show, the Kumeu Wine and Food Festival, and a folk festival.

House prices

Older house	
Bedrooms	🛏 🛏 🛏
Price	$375,000 – $400,000
Executive house	
Bedrooms	🛏 🛏 🛏 🛏
Price	$500,000 – $550,000
1ha bare land	
Price	$450,000 – $500,000
With house	$800,000 – $1 million
4ha bare land	
Price	$600,000 – $800,000
With older house	$650,000 plus

Rental prices

House	
Bedrooms	🛏 🛏
Price	$250 – $320/wk
Bedrooms	🛏 🛏 🛏
Price	$320 – $350/wk
Bedrooms	🛏 🛏 🛏 🛏
Price	$400 – $450/wk

Travel times

CBD	off-peak 40 min
	peak 1hr
Westgate shopping centre	15 min
Auckland Airport	off-peak 45 min
	peak 90 min
Muriwai Beach	15 min

As rare as emeralds

The grass really must be greener on the other side. As increasing numbers of citysiders cash up their suburban holdings for a patch in the country, the amount of true rural land around Auckland is becoming increasingly scarce.

Certainly you've got to travel further afield to get to it. Acreages of homes are replacing acreages of productive horticultural and farming land that was once easy to see around the fringes of the city. Now keen lifestylers who've been priced out of the semi-rural areas closest to suburbia (think Kumeu, Whitford, Waimauku) are having to move ever outwards to places like Helensville for their green pastures.

The landscape beyond Albany and Dairy Flat is increasingly dotted with palatial executive homes on big blocks of land. Coatesville hasn't been dubbed "rural Remuera" for nothing. Where once rural real estate agents could drive clients round for two days to show them a choice of acreages for their dollar, now they're lucky if they've "the odd block here and there" to show clients.

Town planners have had to address the residential/rural balance within rural areas. Within Dairy Flat, the 63-section Goodlands Estate is a cluster subdivision within the "countryside living" zone of the Rodney District Council. The proposed new district scheme will include "farm park" designation – essentially low-density developments where new homes are sprinkled throughout the farmscape with the balance of land held in common ownership, much like the body corporate concept of city apartments.

In the meantime the rural/residential boundaries are continually shifting and the prices are altering accordingly. Adding to the pressure is the fact that a lot of rural land is being landbanked by investors and developers who foresee a time when zoning will change and smaller sections will be allowed where currently 4ha minimums are the standard.

Land on Albany's fringes has doubled in price during the past couple of years. Even more affordable options at Kaukapakapa have increased from between $150,000 and $180,000 for a 1ha to 2ha block to more than $300,000.

Dairy Flat has far fewer big rural blocks (20ha) than even two years ago but that doesn't stop the queue of buyers when one does come onto the market. Much of the rural land here has now been subdivided into the more popular 2ha to 4ha blocks.

If, after all that, you're still interested, these prices will give you an idea of property values.

Dairy Flat

4ha block	$900,000 – $1.6 million
4ha with a small house	$1 million –$1.5 million
Goodlands Estate houses on 1500m2	$800,000 plus
20ha of non-subdividable land	$1 million plus
20ha with subdivision potential	$3.2 million plus
1 to 2ha in Riverhead/Coatesville	$2 million – $3 million.

New Lynn is solid suburbia from its heart to its heights, from the older established areas to stylish homes in the newer subdivisions. New Lynn's big focus is its signature mall but it has a lot else going for it including its flat topography which happily suits its loyal older residents and pram-pushing parents. Status is important within New Lynn where locals like to make sure you know exactly where they live.

Glen Eden is shucking off its backwater status thanks to the enviable energies of forward-thinking locals. They have revitalised its playhouse theatre, smartened up its RSA, acquired an excellent library and put in a railway station café. Don't get Glen Eden confused with Glendene - that's a newer area which sprouted during the 1960s and 1970s.

Who lives there?

First home buyers, long-term elderly residents and migrant families from throughout Asia make up the loyal locals.

Glen Eden continues to be a traditional first home buying area, and used as a stepping stone to the more desirable neighbouring Green Bay and Titirangi. In some cases, the boundaries are blurred with Golf Rd very definitely a New Lynn address but more commonly aligned with Green Bay. Families who settle long term do so for the popular primary and intermediate schooling, the local shopping and the closeness to rail transport. Glendene's young parents were often raised in the west and are now buying the newer houses. Older houses attract investor interest.

Kelston is a family suburb famous for its secondary schooling. It too has homes in

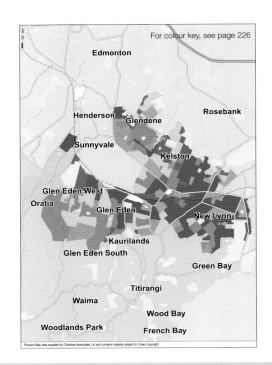

For colour key, see page 226

Edmonton
Henderson
Glendene
Rosebank
Sunnyvale
Kelston
Glen Eden West
Oratia
Glen Eden
New Lynn
Kaurilands
Glen Eden South
Green Bay
Titirangi
Waima
Wood Bay
Woodlands Park
French Bay

Pinpoint Map data supplied by Critchlow Associates Ltd and contains material subject to Crown copyright.

Population profile	Population in 2001 42,216	% Aged Under 15 years 23.94	% Aged over 65 Years 9.77
% European 58.91	% Maori 12.49	% Pacific Peoples 18.80	% Asian 14.83

long-term family ownership, including some of the enviable water's edge homes largely unseen from the street.

New Lynn and its environs is real New Zealand, without pretence and elitist overtones. It's heartland stuff with families of all ages and stages working hard to make an honest living, commuting to work and supporting their local shops and services. The elderly out here do the same. They have lived here most of their lives and such loyalties go with them until the end.

Typical dwellings

Older homes on large sections are common to all these suburbs, built in the days when weatherboard and corrugated iron were the building materials of choice for affordable homes. These properties have been snapped up for their subdivision potential and the result is a wide choice of modern brick and tile infill housing.

Glen Eden and Kelston both have a wide range of housing including the odd original farmhouse, some Art Deco homes, post-war bungalows and the more recent weatherboard styles. Glen Eden also has both new terrace housing and older group housing.

In New Lynn, the Ambrico Pl and Crown Condominium complexes are now an established part of the streetscape. In Glen Eden there are smaller townhouses around Albionvale Rd.

Amenities
Schools ★★★★

Kelston has primary and intermediate schools, the separate boys and girls high schools and the Kelston Deaf Education Centre. Children from Glen Eden's primary

and intermediate schools and Glendene primary schools usually travel to Kelston for secondary schooling. Kelston Boys High School is well-known for its rugby prowess.

For a full list, see page 272.

Shops ★★★★

Each community has its own shopping centre, including the expanded Kelston Shopping Centre, the Glenmall in Glen Eden and the Glendene village shops at the roundabout. The Lynn Mall Shopping Centre is the hub of the wider area with more than 120 shops. On Tuesday and Thursday mornings before the mall shops open, supervised "mall walks" take participants away from bad weather and potholes and within easy reach of post-exercise coffee stops. Towards Titirangi, the old Ford premises on the corner of Great North Rd and Titirangi Rd is earmarked for development as a bulk retail centre.

Leisure ★★★

Waitakere City has an enviable list of neighbourhood parks in line with its aim of having a quality walk within 10 minutes walk of every residence. Glen Eden has Ceramco Park, the Clarence Reserve and Virgo Common. Kelston has the Kelman Park as well as the Cobham Reserve and Archibald Park. New Lynn's pride is the 2ha Manawa wetland reserve created from a defunct clay quarry. Using a series of interconnecting ponds to improve water quality, the Waitakere City Council has transformed the wetland reserve into a recreational amenity for both people and wildlife to enjoy.

The New Lynn Community Centre in Totara Ave is the first large new facility in Waitakere City to have artistic concepts intergrated into its design and construction.

Glen Eden has its famous Glenora Rugby League Club, the swimming centre at Parrs Park and the Ceramco Park Functions Centre. Glen Eden's refurbished RSA is further evidence of the energy that locals have put into improving their local amenities.

Both New Lynn and Glen Eden have a large selection of ethnic eateries that reflect their multi-cultural communities including Asian and Mediterranean. Kelston has the Arum cafe at Palmers Gardenworld. For fine dining, locals tend to head to Titirangi and Henderson.

Real Estate
Trends

Once the poor relation of neighbouring suburbs, New Lynn has become a sought-after area especially with first home buyers who feel out-priced elsewhere. Within New Lynn there is continued strong interest from developers in all properties with subdivision potential.

In Glen Eden weatherboard homes are popular for families irrespective of size.

New Lynn's apartment and terrace houses are popular with the wide mix of Asian nationalities that are settling here.

Manhattan Heights' substantial 1970s homes and Glendene homes continue to appeal if they've been well maintained and modernised. Kelston's appeal is greatest among families and they'll stay put here for years which makes any of it's water's edge properties quite hard to secure for newcomers. Prices rise as you get closer to Titirangi and Green Bay, where homes are also of higher quality – think granite kitchen benches rather than laminate.

Glen Eden has pockets of lower cost housing in the area around Solar Rd, with the highest prices being paid for the older, more established homes.

Rental and investment

On the figures below, add a premium of $20 or $30 a week for a four-bedroom house if it has significant extras such as a third bathroom and garaging for more than two vehicles. For Glen Eden and Kelston, $10 to $20 a week less across the board is the best indicator.

Best streets

Ryehill Cl and De Val Dr in New Lynn. Konini Rd and Pleasant Rd in Glen Eden. All of Manhattan Heights in Glendene. Anything on the water's edge in Kelston.

Why I live there

Waitakere City Mayor Bob Harvey

Glen Eden has been Bob Harvey's home for more than 36 years. For him it epitomises the best of community living with its new library and its refurbished playhouse theatre. He sings the praises of the local shops for their wonderful service. "There's Sudan Hairdressing with its art and style that makes it one of the best in Auckland. The local fish shop is fantastic. The mall is modern, clean and a real treat. You can stop at the railway station café. It's a community that's alive and thriving and it's all just 15 minutes from my favourite beaches, the bach at Karekare and the world's only subtropical rainforest next to a metropolis. I like it."

Smart Buy ⊘

There are still a reasonable number of subdividable properties, which make good buying. Purchasers aren't put off by having to seek neighbours' approvals for resource consents either - if they believe they can subdivide their property then they're buying them for their capital investment.

House prices

Older house
Bedrooms
Price $280,000 – $330,000
Modern house
Bedrooms
Price $380,000 – $430,000
Executive house
Bedrooms
Price $450,000 – $550,000

Rental prices

House or unit
Bedrooms
Price $240 – $270/wk
House
Bedrooms
Price $290 – $340/wk
Bedrooms
Price $340 – $360/wk

Travel times

CBD	off peak 15 min
	peak 40 min
Airport	off peak 20 min
	peak 40 min
Henderson	off peak 10 min
	peak 15 min

The New Lynn transport centre is next door to the New Lynn Railway station and from there Stagecoach runs buses to both the CBD and West Auckland. Services also run from New Lynn to Otahuhu, Panmure and Manukau City. Rail services run through New Lynn from West Auckland to the CBD with connections on to the southern line to Papakura and Pukekohe and the south-eastern line through Orakei to Glen Innes.

Swanson's enviable location in the foothills of the Waitakere Ranges defines its identity. These hills are home to Swanson's creative folk – probably the very ones who used to live in Titirangi before it became too upmarket and crowded. The restfulness of the bush and the availability of good-sized blocks of land are a lure for families wanting a more laidback semi-rural lifestyle, and good access to beaches and countryside. They're happy progressive people who put energy and time back to the community. Waitakere township has a similar style plus all of the charm of a country town. Massey North folk like to call themselves Westgate, an area which is considered to be a bit more progressive and urban.

Who lives there?

Swanson's vibrant community reflects the alternative lifestylers who live there – both the hippie types and those seeking a less crowded alternative to the city. Ranui has a solid mix of Maori and Pacific Islanders and an equally solid mix of first home buyers and renters. Waitakere is popular with larger families and their gaggle of farm animals and pets, for the down-to-earth lifestyle it offers. They are very community spirited. An example is The Swanson Railway Cafe, established by energetic locals who bought the land and moved the old Avondale rail station building to the site.

Typical dwellings

Swanson has a mix of older weatherboard homes and some newer development of brick and tile houses. Ranui's Pooks Rd and

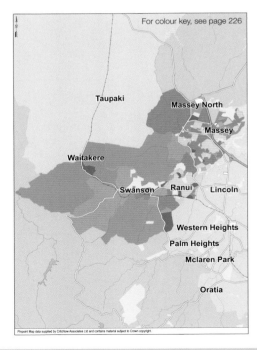

For colour key, see page 226

Taupaki
Massey North
Massey
Waitakere
Swanson   Ranui   Lincoln
Western Heights
Palm Heights
Mclaren Park
Oratia

Pinpoint Map data supplied by Critchlow Associates Ltd and contains material subject to Crown copyright.

Population Profile	Population in 2001 31,485	% Aged Under 15 years 27.59	% Aged over 65 Years 6.03
% European 64.7	% Maori 15.46	% Pacific Peoples 18.11	% Asian 7.37

Coroglen Garden developments have settled happily into the landscape. They're a stylish complement to Ranui's original weatherboard homes and the flush of group homes built during the 1960s. Anything larger than three bedrooms is the exception.

In Waitakere, section sizes range from residential on 1012m2, semi-rural on 1350m2 and rural on large acreages. Massey North, around the Westgate area, has the Rush Creek development built by Fletcher Homes and Universal Homes' Stonegate enclave. Massey's upmarket homes include those in Royal Heights which have views across the Waitemata Harbour.

Amenities
Schools ★★★★

The area is well served by primary schools. Secondary school-age children travel by train to high schools in Henderson, Massey and Avondale. For a full list, see page 272.

Shops ★★★

There's retailing for every lifestyle here. Swanson has its car boot sales, and plant, produce and craft market. Waitakere township has its dairy. Royal Heights Mall in Royal Rd includes the well-known Swiss Butchery. The Westgate shopping centre is the retail focal point for Massey.

Leisure ★★★

The Massey Leisure Centre is a fine example of the Waitakere City Council's artistic input into community facilities. Artists were commissioned to incorporate Massey's past and present flavours into its themes and materials – in everything from the carpets to the palm mosaic and the children's play sculpture.

The Auckland Outdoor Health Club in Ranui is a private naturists' (as in nudists) club set in parklike grounds.

The Signal Gallery in Swanson showcases the work of local artists and artisans.

Golf courses include the Waitakere Golf Club, the Massey Golf Club and the Redwood Park Golf Club in Swanson. There are pony clubs in Massey and Waitakere township. Massey also has archery and athletics clubs.

At the foot of the Waitakere Ranges is Crystal Mountain gallery which houses the country's largest selection of crystals and minerals from around the world.

The Swanson Station Cafe is the top stop in Swanson for all commuters, rail or car.

Three top restaurants in the Waitakere Ranges include the Waitakere Park Lodge, The Nikau Club and the Tuscan-influenced Devines. There are several eateries in the Westgate shopping centre.

Real Estate
Trends

As the rural areas of Kumeu and Taupaki are now priced beyond the reach of many, interest has turned to the similarly natured Swanson and Waitakere. Which means prices are holding strong here. Recent sales include $1 million for a 4ha Waitakere property and $735,000 for a six-bedroom house with a two-bedroom secondary dwelling.

During the busiest days of the recent property boom, Ranui saw many a tussle between first home buyers and rental investors. Many large sections have been either subdivided or a minor rental unit added. Ranui is one of the last areas in Auckland to go up in price and amongst the first to drop off.

Massey is attracting a lot of second-home buyers in the middle income bracket.

Rental and investment

The rental stock is almost exclusively three-bedroom homes. Waitakere township rarely has rental properties available. The narrow band of rentals in Ranui reflects the socio-economic status of the renters.

Best streets

Christian Rd, Swanson; White Heron Dr and Petrel Pl in Royal Heights.

Why I live there

Landscape architect Gudrun Fischer

For German-born Gudrun Fischer and her husband Eile, owning a home on a bush block in the Waitakere Ranges comes with a responsibility to protect it for future generations. "I'm passionate about that," says Gudrun, who runs her Outdoor Design business from home. Her office looks out through the bush. "When I come back from visiting clients I can draw the curtain of the bush around me and leave all the hustle and bustle behind. It is such a privilege to live here. This place is not something I own to do what I wish. It is our duty to guard it and keep it unspoilt."

House prices

House (deduct $50,000 for Ranui)

Bedrooms	🛏 🛏
Price	$230,000 – $250,000
Bedrooms	🛏 🛏 🛏
Price	$280,000 – $320,000
Bedrooms	🛏 🛏 🛏 🛏
Price	$320,000 – $380,000

2ha to 4ha lifestyle block

Price	$600,000 plus

Rental prices

House or unit

Bedrooms	🛏 🛏
Price	$240 – $270/wk
Bedrooms	🛏 🛏 🛏
Price	$280 – $330/wk

Better-quality house

Bedrooms	🛏 🛏 🛏
Price	$350 – $375/wk

Travel times

From Westgate

CBD	off peak 25 min
	peak 40 min
North Shore	20 min
Airport	45 min

Waitakere town is the last train stop on the line from the CBD. Buses run from Massey, Ranui and Swanson to the CBD.

Smart Buy ✓

If you have a hankering for the rural life but don't want to pay through the nose, the land around Waitakere township is for you. It's about as rural as you can get, reasonably close to town and you'll be among truly community-spirited people. And as Auckland spreads, land values can't help but grow.

Trees are to Titirangi as coffee is to Ponsonby. Everyone in Titirangi loves them, from the tree-hugging Greenpeace member hippies who disappear up their long winding driveways to the cafe set and young families who embrace the bush for its restful vistas and cool canopy. Beyond Titirangi, the little bays that hug the Manukau Harbour coastline out to the heads offer the same lifestyle appeal but with an even more secluded feeling and sea views thrown in.

Oratia, with its big flat sections and views back to the city, is one of the best-kept secrets of these parts. Some of Titirangi's low-lying neighbours like to piggy-back on the suburb's status but don't be fooled. If they're not living in the bush, then they're not true Titirangi-ites.

Who lives there?

Alternative lifestylers and commuting professionals and every philosophy in between is represented here. Titirangi has it all except thankfully the slash-and-burn mentality that has seen whole suburbs elsewhere sprouting row after row of brick-and-tile homes

There's continuing interest from British migrants and even holiday-makers who become so smitten with the bush, the village and its lifestyle that they move here. One real estate agency reports 27% of its sales during six months to UK buyers, attracted to the absence of cheek-by-jowl housing. Green Bay is one of Auckland's most affordable family suburbs and has a core of elderly who can move to Pinesong Retirement Village in Titirangi when their needs change.

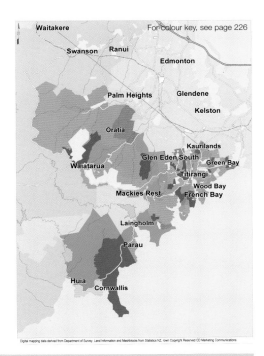

For colour key, see page 226

Digital mapping data derived from Department of Survey. Land Information and Meshblocks from Statistics NZ, rown Copyright Reserved CD Marketing Communications

Population profile	Population in 2001 24,120	% Aged Under 15 years 24.07	% Aged over 65 Years 8.67
% European 87.82	% Maori 7.25	% Pacific Peoples 3.96	% Asian 4.17

Typical dwellings

A Titirangi house is all about timber. Homes are perched on poles, clad in weatherboard and finished inside with cathedral-style beamed ceilings and tongue-and-groove pan-elling. The 1960s and 1970s style that de-fined Titirangi's development has found new favour. Building extensions have to conform to strict Waitakere City Council regulations to protect existing trees.

In Oratia cottages and weatherboard bungalows grace the large sections. Several small enclaves of new housing give a broader choice for home buyers.

Baches and cottages are among Laing-holm's housing stock, and appeal to first-home buyers.

Green Bay has a mix of units, group housing stock and larger, well-appointed houses to suit all tastes, needs and financial bottom lines.

Amenities
Schools ★★★★

This area is well-served by schools, especially Green Bay. For a full list, see page 272.

Shops ★★★★

Titirangi's quaint shopping village has cafes spilling outdoors, stone walls and cobbles. There are plenty of restaurants and cafes including the Hardware Cafe. Lopdell house, the public art gallery, includes a German/Italian bakery. For a real sense of community, rub shoulders with the early birds to peruse the 100 stalls that make up the Titirangi Village market on the last Sunday of every month. There is art, craft and collectables, but pre-cious little parking because of its popularity.

Leisure ★★★★

Aside from the stunning Waitakere Ranges Regional Park, there are numerous small neighbourhood green areas. There's also the coast with many attractive bays and beaches. Titirangi has numerous groups catering for arts and crafts, as well as Lopdell House Gallery, and a number of sporting facilities and clubs. The Titirangi Golf Club is near Green Bay.

Real Estate
Trends

Oratia has almost overtaken Titirangi in appeal, both for its affordability and the ease of flat land over Titirangi's bush-clad hills. Oratia has rated within Auckland's top 10 suburbs for capital gain during the past 12 months. Buyer interest is as much from the western suburbs of Glen Eden, Titirangi and Green Bay as from overseas. Oratia's generous 2000m2 to 4000m2 properties are the drawcard as are those with views back to the city. Serviced sections with some bush have also come on to the market.

Within Titirangi, sales at the higher end, $500,000 to $600,000, have slowed in line with the wider Auckland market. Entry level into Titirangi is $400,000 plus which makes

it a popular starting point for Dinks – the affluent "double income no kids" profile. Individual prices in this heavily wooded area are affected by factors like access to sun or availability of off-street parking.

Laingholm and the coastal areas around Huia are popular for first home buyers. Anything priced at the low end of the range is quickly snapped up.

Rental and investment

There's a growing rental market here despite the scarcity of listings. In Titirangi, home-owners will rent out their homes while on an extended overseas holiday or on business transfer out of Auckland. As with sales, many factors determine the rental return including the degree that surrounding bush may compromise views or sunshine.

Best streets

South Titirangi Rd and Kohu Rd in Titirangi. Cliff View Dr in Green Bay; Carter Rd in Oratia.

Local Hero: the bush

The thing that defines Titirangi most in the mind of all Aucklanders is its bush. Protected by local by-law, you can only clear as much as you need for a house site. The one-ness with nature, the birdlife and the cool green-dappled shade is offset by lack of views and sun for some properties … but then Titirangi residents don't mind.

Legislation is currently planned to make the Waitakere Ranges and foothills a national heritage area, which would protect them from too much development by putting a lower limit on section size and requiring that any development be in scale and with the character of a bush or rural nature. For current residents, it means that the character that attracted them to Titirangi in the first place – the lack of cheek-by-jowl living – will be preserved. Some landowners are opposed and some people predict a rush of subdivision applications before the draft bill becomes law. The heritage area also includes about 17,000ha of forest and coastal areas owned by the Crown and the Auckland Regional Council.

If you want to get out and experience the bush, there's a hugely popular walk within easy reach of the village, starting at the Woodlands Park water treatment station. It used to be a bush maintenance track, which gets referred to as the pipeline road. On your street maps it's marked as the Exhibition Dr walkway. One hour 15 minutes is a reasonable estimate for the return walk. Don't bother rushing – that's not what bush-walking is about.

House prices

Titirangi

<u>House</u>
Bedrooms   🛏🛏🛏 (3)
Price $400,000 – $450,000
(add $100,000 for good views)

<u>Executive houses</u>
Bedrooms   🛏🛏🛏🛏 (4)
Price $600,000 – $800,000

Oratia

<u>Cottages</u>
Bedrooms   🛏🛏 (2)
Price $300,000 – $360,000

<u>House</u>
Bedrooms   🛏🛏🛏 (3)
Price $400,000 – $450,000
Bedrooms   🛏🛏🛏🛏 (4)
Price $600,000 – $650,000

<u>Serviced sections with bush</u>
Price $280,000 – $330,000

Green Bay

<u>Unit</u>
Bedrooms   🛏🛏 (2)
Price $200,000 – $250,000

<u>House</u>
Bedrooms   🛏🛏🛏 (3)
Price $320,000 – $370,000

<u>Executive house</u>
Bedrooms   🛏🛏🛏🛏 (4)
Price $450,000 – $600,000

Laingholm

<u>Cottage</u>
Bedrooms   🛏🛏 (2)
Price $280,000 – $300,000

<u>House with sea views</u>
Bedrooms   🛏🛏🛏 (3)
Price $300,000 – $380,000

<u>Executive house</u>
Bedrooms   🛏🛏🛏🛏 (4)
Price $450,000 – $500,00

Rental prices

<u>House or unit</u>
Bedrooms   🛏🛏 (2)
Price $230 – $300/wk
Bedrooms   🛏🛏🛏 (3)
Price $320 – $350/wk

<u>Executive house</u>
Bedrooms   🛏🛏🛏🛏 (4)
Price $400 – $450/wk
(drop about $20 for Laingholm and Huia)

Travel times

<u>From Titirangi village</u>

CBD	off peak 35 min peak 1 hour plus
North-western motorway	15 min
Airport	40 min
Lynmall shopping centre	10 min

The nearest train link is Glen Eden. Stagecoach buses serve most of the main streets of Titirangi.

Smart Buy ⊘

A bach or cottage down Laingholm way is good buying, especially for rental investors. It's an area one letting agent describes as having "the best quality tenants" looking for long-term rentals.

Wild and rugged, the beaches to the west of Auckland have a strong reputation linked to raw beauty, rolling surf and black sands. It's an inspiring place, drawing holidaymakers and an increasing number of city escapees to savour its disconnection with all that's stressful about suburbia. Its soleful beauty has helped put this part of New Zealand smack on the world map. Karekare's beach was the back-drop for the 1993 movie The Piano and Xena has had her starring moments here. Piha is the most exclusive neighbourhood and the only settlement with houses right on the beach. Muriwai appeals for its accessibility to Auckland. The mystical remoteness of Bethells Beach, Anawhata and Karekare just helps to increase their appeal and feeling of exclusivity.

Who lives there?

The West Coast beaches are not for the faint hearted – the drive to Piha alone needs to be undertaken with respect for the terrain, and a good gearbox. It's also not the place for faux lifestylers who think they can transplant their city house designs on the landscape. As one real estate agent put so eloquently: "Start talking like that at a party out here and the music would stop all on its own."

For the increasing number of citysiders choosing to relocate and commute, it's out with the "black and bling" and in with bare feet and no threads of pretence. There's anecdotal talk of wealthy people cashing up their more expensive Coromandel beach houses for baches in Piha. For the middle-aged affluent, it's about revisiting the surfie haunts of their teenage years with their own

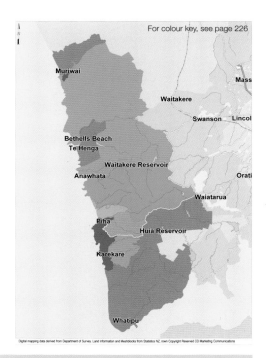

For colour key, see page 226

Muriwai
Mass
Waitakere
Swanson   Lincol
Bethells Beach
Te Henga
Waitakere Reservoir
Anawhata   Orati
Waiatarua
Piha
Huia Reservoir
Karekare
Whatipu

Digital mapping data derived from Department of Survey, Land Information and Meshblocks from Statistics NZ. rown Copyright Reserved CD Marketing Communications

Population profile	Population in 2001 6,894	% Aged Under 15 years 24.76	% Aged over 60 Years 5.87
% European 88.99	% Maori 8.96	% Pacific Peoples 2.61	% Asian 1.65

kids. The aged population in these suburbs tend to move closer to medical facilities in town. Migrants, including many English, add to the rich character of the settlements. The 30-40 minute commute to Auckland city makes Murawai and Piha popular with business people.

Piha has a concentration of affluent people with the dosh for a spare home ... and for the props to enjoy their entertainment and water sports. Surf the waves, surf the internet - they do it all.

Typical dwellings

It's a heartening sight to the see rustic baches tucked into the bush alongside stylish new homes. As these areas become more popular with permanent residents, many baches are getting the full makeover treatment. New houses are usually sympathetically designed for the surroundings. This is given bureaucratic weight by the ever tightening regulations regarding subdividing land (you virtually can't do it) and the removal of trees (only enough to make space for the dwelling). City values and city design don't cut it here. As one long-time resident put it: "It'd

be an insult to build a big fence out here."

These settlements are small. Piha has some 700 titles; Anawhata has about 30 houses, some relying on solar and wind power. Karekare has its 4ha blocks but comparatively few properties with sea views. Up the coast, Muriwai has a colourful diversity of houses from baches to mansions and every style and price tag imaginable.

Amenities
Schools ★

Piha has a thriving pre-school, but children bus to primary schools and secondary schools in suburbs closer to town.

From Muriwai children bus to Waimauku. The Lone Kauri Community School at Karekare is officially part of Oratia Primary School. For a full list, see page 272.

Shops ★

The general store is what these communities are all about. They sell all sorts of household wares and food stuffs, freshly baked cakes (at Piha's store) and display notices about local services and where to find the best bed and breakfast overnighter.

Supermarkets are at the nearest major suburb – for those at Muriwai Beach it's Kumeu, for Piha it's Henderson.

Leisure ★★★★

Rolling surf waves, stunning beaches, rocks to fish from, freshwater lakes, waterfalls, hills to hang-glide from and miles of bush walks – if the outdoors is your thing, this is heaven.

Both Piha and Murawai have surf clubs and there are golf courses on the way to Bethells (Waitakere Golf Club) and Murawai.

Murawai has an off road motorcycle track and Woodhill Forest is close for off-road or mountain-biking. Murawai is popular for horse-riding and the famous gannet colony at the beach has made the area popular amongst tourists.

Piha has a private saltwater lagoon. The locals will tell you how to get there.

In March each year, weather permitting, the Karekare Volunteer Fire Brigade runs its beach races. Piha and Muriwai both have community libraries.

Posh nosh means a trip towards town. Both the Piha RSA and the Piha Surf Club put on good meals throughout the year and there are deli foods and German-style pastries available at the Piha Store and good take-aways at the Muriwai Lodge Store. WUZ's café at Muriwai Beach is well-known for its seaside breakfasts.

During summer, a Ponsonby-class pie cart parks up at Bethells Beach.

Real Estate
Trends

Overseas buyers have been swooping on these fabulous beaches in recent years but now the balance is swinging back to a more even split between those migrating from Britain and the US to those migrating from the pent-up lifestyles of inner-city suburbs.

Competition for properties is still hot because comparatively few come onto the market. Since property in Piha hit the $1 million mark two years ago, prices appear to have stablised. New homes are slowly replacing old baches and with construction costing, in one case, close to $2 million the potential for a multi-million dollar sale is on the cards. There are few properties left

for subdivision which pushes the exclusivity index up even higher.

Muriwai isn't fetching Piha prices, yet. Top sales have been in December 2004 when a Richard Priest designed house sold for $890,000 and $1 million for a 5ha block with a relocated home. Both were bought by ex-pat Kiwis.

Views are everything - Muriwai buyers would rather buy a bach with views for $550,000 than a big four-bedroom home with none for $400,000. A recent $545,000 sale for a four-bedroom home is top dollar for a home without a view.

Land will always be at a premium in Muriwai, but two new, and rare, developments are generating interest. One is a package of four 1500m2 clifftop sections with $500,000 to $600,000 sales tags. And the Taiapa Lifestyle Estate on the Waimauku/Muriwai border has sites from 1ha to 8ha selling for $350,000-plus.

An old Anawhata bach sold for more than $1 million in 2004 but listings are rare. Karekare is obviously where all the artists go. One property sold recently for $350,000 - by an artist, to an artist with a backup offer from another artist in the wings.

Rental and investment

Rental property is eagerly sought after throughout these beachside communities. Not surprisingly, rental lists become more plentiful after the Christmas break although there's no clear seasonal trend with supply and demand varying throughout the year.

Best streets

Oaia Rd and Ngatira Rd at Muriwai Beach; Marine Pde and Garden Rd at Piha; Tasman

House prices
Piha beach
Bach
Bedrooms   🛏️ 🛏️
Price   high $400,000s
Bach on the beach
Bedrooms   🛏️ 🛏️
Price $1m – $1.75m
Designer house
Bedrooms   🛏️ 🛏️ 🛏️ 🛏️
Price $700,000 plus

Muriwai
Bach
Bedrooms   🛏️ 🛏️
Price $240,000 – $260,000
With sea views $500,000 – $550,000
Modern house
Bedrooms   🛏️ 🛏️ 🛏️ 🛏️
Price $530,000 – $545,000
Clifftop $800,000 – $900,000

Karekare
Bach
Bedrooms   🛏️ 🛏️
Price $390,000
House near beach
Bedrooms   🛏️ 🛏️
Price $470,000 – $500,000
With sea views $750,000 – $800,000

Bethells beach
Bach
Bedroom   🛏️
Price $320,000 – $340,000
House
Bedrooms   🛏️ 🛏️
Price $350,000 – $380,000

Rental prices
Piha / Muriwai
Bach
Bedrooms   🛏️ 🛏️
Price $230 – $240/wk
(add $50 for better quality house)

House
Bedrooms   🛏️ 🛏️ 🛏️
Price $320 – $420/wk
Bedrooms   🛏️ 🛏️ 🛏️ 🛏️
Price $450/wk

Travel times
From Piha
CBD   off peak 40 min
   peak 65 min
Henderson Centre   35 min
From Muriwai
CBD   off peak 30 min
Westgate shopping centre   15 min

Public transport is non-existent in Piha and Murawai; it's either yours or the neighbour's car or the bike. Then again this is the sort of place where locals will happily help out.

Smart Buy ✓
A bach is the one to aspire too out here, whether it's high profile on the beach or something uniquely Kiwi that no-one can see in the bush. Prices are pushing them out of the reach of many buyers, but it you're lucky enough to be able to buy one you'll be onto a lifestyle and an investment winner.

...ding Hobsonville, Whenuapai and Herald Island

This used to be a disparate group of suburbs – the shiny new West Harbour, the hippy Herald Island and the airforce base of Whenuapai. Now this area at the top of the Waitemata Harbour is happily morphing into a unified spot with lots of lifestyle choice. It's a sort of edge-of-suburbia living with sea views and with market garden stalls, plant nurseries and a fabulous marina. West Harbour's elegant enclaves of large brick and tile homes have aged nicely. Whenuapai is one of Auckland's best-kept secrets, with some of our finest waterfront properties hidden beyond its mature trees. In Hobsonville, rural properties along Scott Rd offer prestigious buying and while they're still pretty rustic, the baches of Herald Island are being joined by new designer houses.

Who lives there?

This is lifestyle territory and suburbia for the affluent and upwardly mobile. Serious money is needed to enjoy quality homes here, whether they're the upmarket new houses of West Harbour or hidden from view on the water's edge at Whenuapai. As moves to get state and private secondary schooling in place inch towards firm decisions, more families will no doubt be attracted to the area.

Typical dwellings

There's a great contrast between the duplex dwellings and wire fences that define housing owned by the airforce, and the elegant executive houses of West Harbour's finest enclaves. Just a stone's throw from airforce land, Scott Rd's mix of homes includes some stunning water's edge properties.

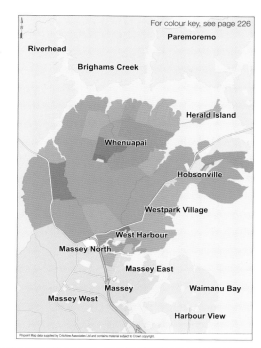

For colour key, see page 226

Riverhead
Paremoremo
Brighams Creek
Herald Island
Whenuapai
Hobsonville
Westpark Village
West Harbour
Massey North
Massey East
Massey
Waimanu Bay
Massey West
Harbour View

Pinpoint Map data supplied by Critchlow Associates Ltd and contains material subject to Crown copyright

Population profile	Population in 2001 16,062	% Aged Under 15 years 25.35	% Aged over 65 Years 5.96
% European 73.91	% Maori 9.76	% Pacific Peoples 7.99	% Asian 12.61

Whenuapai has million-dollar homes with harbour views hidden from sight on Pohutukawa Rd. Nearby Totara Rd has million-dollar houses on lifestyle blocks and quality family homes on the water's edge.

Herald Island's charm is its mix of old and newer homes and bachy cottages.

West Harbour houses are maintained with immense pride by their owners. The Cove development includes a mix of 35 terrace townhouses and two stand-alone homes, with a further 10 planned.

Amenities
Schools ★★★

There's no local secondary school. Ex-airforce land has been bought for a state secondary, but a decision on its future is not likely until early 2006. Plans for a private secondary school to be known as Sutherland College in Brighams Creek Rd are with the council for resource consent. In the meantime, older children bus to secondary schools in Takapuna, Te Atatu and Henderson. For a full list, see page 272.

Shops ★★★

Westgate is the retail centre of choice here (see overleaf). Local shops in Hobsonville, West Harbour and Whenuapai cater for most needs. There's a full range of marine-related services at the 600-berth Westpark Marina, and plans for expansion.

Leisure ★★★★

Stroll through Westpark Marina for boating eye-candy or take the coastal walkway from the marina to enjoy the water views. Throughout West Harbour there are playgrounds and parks, including Luckens

Reserve which meanders down to the water. At the Hobsonville end of Upper Harbour Dr, there's a vintage car display at the Monterey Park Motor Museum. Sports facilities include the Hobsonville Bowling Club and the Belvedere Tennis Club. Eating is a feast of choice here, and includes the new cafe Peas in a Pod.

Real Estate
Trends

In West Harbour, the best properties near the water's edge have had their own mini-boom.

Whenuapai sales suffered with talk of the air force base becoming a commercial airport. Plans were shelved but local councils are now pushing for a reconsideration.

Conversely, the construction of a second Greenhithe bridge to speed access to the North Shore has helped values. There's considerable Asian interest in rural blocks here, with a new trend towards consortiums of buyers purchasing rural land that may someday be able to be subdivided for residential development (land banking).

Top prices are nudging $3 million for water's edge land along Scott Rd in Hobsonville. One owner turned down $6 million for a 4ha block of land, so it's anybody's guess what the larger 4.8ha blocks are worth.

High prices are being reached in Whenuapai's lifestyle belt, too. As a general rule there's nothing on the water's edge for less than $1.8 million, whether it's bare land or has a house. On West Harbour's esplanade strip, sales tags read $1.5 million and more.

Rental and investment

There's a limit to what renters will pay, and $650 a week appears to be about it.

Best streets

Mansion Court and Courtneys in West Harbour; Scott Rd in Hobsonville; Pohutukawa Rd and Totara Rd in Whenuapai.

Local Hero: Westgate shopping centre

Coming from Auckland city, you'll see it on the left at the top of the north-western motorway. Westgate shopping centre is geographically more allied to Massey North but West Harbour people claim it as their own. As shopping centres go, Westgate is a biggie, with more than 40,000m2 of retail space designed around a (free) central carpark. In 2004, an outlet mall with 12 retailers was added. This year will see a Main Street reconfiguration to the central layout, and extra space for retail and banking outlets.

House prices

Basic house	
Bedrooms	🛏 🛏 🛏
Price	$300,000 – $350,000
Newer house	$400,000 – $600,000

Executive house with views	
Bedrooms	🛏 🛏 🛏 🛏
Price	$1 million plus

Lifestyle block with older house	
Price	$800,000 – $1 million plus

Lifestyle block on the water with new house
$1.7 million – $2.7 million

Rental prices

House	
Bedrooms	🛏 🛏 🛏
Price	$300 – $350/wk

Townhouse	
Bedrooms	🛏 🛏 🛏
Price	$400 – $425/wk

Executive house	
Bedrooms	🛏 🛏 🛏 🛏
Price	$600 – $650/wk

Travel times

CBD	off-peak 25 min
	peak 60 min plus
Westgate/north-western motorway	5 min
Takapuna	30 min
Glenfield Mall	20 min

Commuters have a choice of two routes to Auckland city – via Upper Harbour Dr and through the North Shore, or down the north-western motorway. There is keen interest in the proposed Upper Harbour Expressway. Linking Albany to Westgate, it is seen as a positive solution to traffic problems.

Ritchies Coachlines runs buses to the city and buses from New Lynn to Takapuna travel through West Harbour. There are also services through Hobsonville.

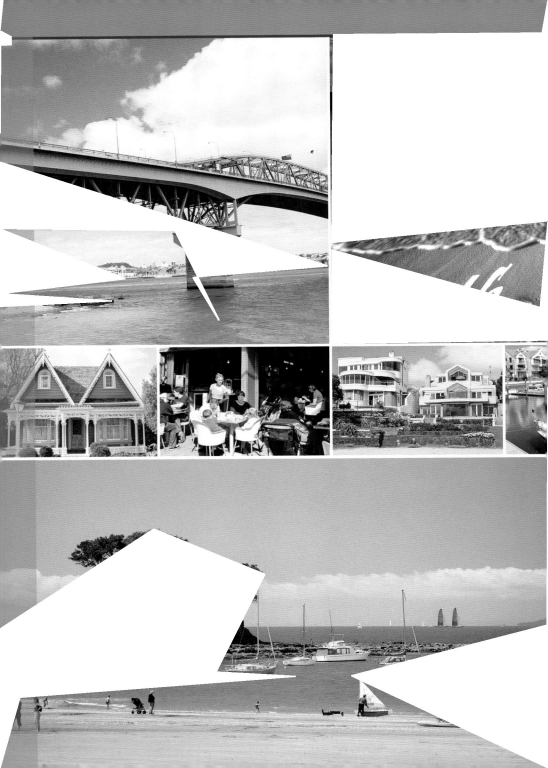

The North Shore is synonymous with golden beaches, water sports and big shopping malls. It evokes a sense of lifestyle potential, epitomised by the stunning million-dollar beachfront and cliff-top mansions of Takapuna and Milford's Golden Mile. Even those living in deepest suburbia are within easy reach of the beaches. The shore has a reputation for being a very white, middle-class city, a safe secure place to bring up children, with great amenities and schooling. Around 70% of schools on the shore are decile eight or above and it was a coup for the area when Massey University established its gracious campus at Albany.

Whatever the attraction, new residents are pouring in, particularly to Albany, which is the fastest growing area of the North Shore.

Albany's expanding commercial and retail area has predictably brought extensive new housing into the area. It's also being credited with raising the profile of the upper East Coast Bays, which have traditionally been the poor relation of the suburbs nearer Takapuna. North Shore's amenities have developed along with the population. Sporting facilities, leisure centres and shopping complexes have all grown rapidly across the city, many touted as the biggest and best in greater Auckland. A lesser known attraction is the shore's green areas. There are 454 reserves covering 1579ha.

Real estate values reflect this diversity. Multi-million dollar waterfront properties aside,

sun-kissed sands
rangitoto island's silhouette
family-friendly
schools aplenty

there are plenty of suburbs packed with modest first homes. Recently, the shore has sprouted an abundance of new subdivisions and terrace housing, as well as more infill housing.

Devonport was the first area of the shore to be populated by Europeans. Settlements grew as paddle steamer ferry services began plying their way across the Waitemata Harbour into areas such as Bayswater, Takapuna, Northcote and Birkenhead. When the Harbour Bridge opened in 1959 the North Shore woke up with a start! Within 10 years housing developments were sprouting up everywhere – note the proliferation of 1970s homes in most suburbs. Families were planned for and industry boomed.

The northern motorway extension is doing to Orewa and the Whangaparaoa Peninsula what the Harbour Bridge did to the more southern suburbs.

The main thorn in the side of North Shore-ites is the gruelling peak hour traffic which crawls along the main arterial routes, as well as the motorway. Moves are afoot to improve this, however, with new busways being built.

Like a runaway train, Albany seems unstoppable. Its development as the undisputed commercial, retail and light industrial CBD of the North Shore continues unabated. There's barely any land that hasn't already been earmarked for spec housing. Albany and Greenhithe are a picture of contrasts. Sure, Albany village is still quaint, saved by the new motorway north heading off in another direction, but most of it's shiny and new. Greenhithe has kept its rural charm. There are new houses and roads but this bush-clad waterside spot remains idyllic. Brookfields and Northwood, are more established, while North Harbour is predominantly commercial. Paremoremo has its share of big lifestyle properties ... and a maximum security prison.

Who lives there?

Albany and Greenhithe have a broad population base, ranging from urban professionals to lifestylers. Some students of Massey University's Albany campus live locally. There are the the semi-retired and hip singles, both looking for lock-up-and-leave style living.

Brookfields Park and Northwood are hugely popular with ordinary families Albany's two private schools, Kristin and Pinehurst, are a major draw-card for those with more money. Affluent owners in Paremoremo don't seem bothered about living near Her Majesty's tenants at the prison.

Typical dwellings

Again, there's a broad range, from the modest weatherboard houses near the old

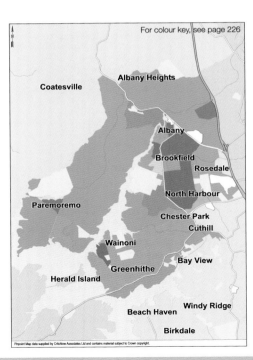

For colour key, see page 226

Coatesville
Albany Heights
Albany
Brookfield
Rosedale
North Harbour
Paremoremo
Chester Park
Cuthill
Wainoni
Bay View
Greenhithe
Herald Island
Windy Ridge
Beach Haven
Birkdale

Pinpoint Map data supplied by Critchlow Associates Ltd and contains material subject to Crown copyright.

Population profile	Population in 2001 11,634	% Aged Under 15 years 24.29	% Aged over 65 Years 5.65
% European 84.01	% Maori 7.14	% Pacific Peoples 1.88	% Asian 8.38

village to swanky new houses in the many developments. Brookfield Park and Northwood are laden with brick-and-tile houses on sections of about 600m2. Bushlands has a much wider range of styles, including stucco, brick-and-tile, small and large homes, and home-and-income options, reflecting its development some 10 years ago. The largest homes are those in the prestigious The Oaks and Oak Manor. There are townhouses in Schnapper Rock Rd and The Avenue.

Greenhithe has a mix of rural and upmarket residential properties, all sitting on a minimum of 1200m2 land. Universal Homes has a mix of some 50 townhouses and duplex homes in its Greenbough development and its Aintree Heights development features 50 standalone gracious country homes. Oteha Valley Rd has terrace houses and Universal Homes has 108 more townhouse and duplex dwellings in the pipeline at Atherton Heights. A second 50-site development off Oteha Valley Rd will bring both spec homes and owner's own design-and-build homes to the local landscape.

Paremoremo has million-dollar homes on lifestyle blocks.

Amenities
Schools ★★★

Huge population growth has been matched by good schooling. In 2005 Albany Junior School on the corner of Appleby Rd and Albany Highway opened to Year 7 students. It'll grow one year at a time, eventually catering for Year 7 to 10 students. Oteha Valley Rd's new primary school opened in 2004 and Greenhithe's second primary school is being built in Kyle Rd, due to open in February 2006.

Aside from the private schools of Kristin and Pinehurst, older pupils travel out of the area for secondary schooling. For a full list, see page 272.

Shops ★★★

In a very short time, Albany has become a shopper's dream. Not only is there the Mega Centre selling everything imaginable, but Westfield is to build a mega mall here. Plans include a retail and entertainment centre with 80 to 90 shops and a multiplex cinema. It'll open in 2007. Greenhithe's shops include a bakery, a takeaway and a local garage – all part of its rural appeal.

Leisure ★★★★

Despite the burgeoning subdivisions, there are plenty of reserves in the area, including Lucas Creek Reserve, Wainono Park and the Albany Scenic Reserve. Lucas Creek is great for those who love canoes and rafts – you can paddle down to the harbour. There's lots of bush-covered land in behind Rosedale and throughout Greenhithe.

A special spot is the Wharf Reserve, a tiny reserve just off the Albany Highway where you can hear native birds by the creek.

Horses are part of the rural scene, with pony clubs and equine centres aplenty. For golfers, the North Shore Golf Club borders Albany Highway. Each community has the usual sports grounds and clubs, including tennis and soccer. Albany locals have all of Glenfield's amenities at their doorstep and the Millennium Institute of Sport complex at Mairangi Bay. Up the road by the Silverdale motorway exit there's this country's first indoor snow facility (Snowplanet) as well. Eateries in Albany Village include The

Wine Box Cafe and the highly acclaimed Totara Restaurant that's in a purpose-built building reminiscent of an old schoolhouse. The new boutique cafe Collins House is a welcome first for Greenhithe. There is also the Malthouse (Greenhithe Tavern) and the Purple Rain Brasserie.

Real Estate
Trends

With a ready student market and long-term capital gain in mind, ex-pat Kiwis are buying investment properties in Albany. Affordable townhouses and homes in the middle price brackets are eagerly sought by campus academic staff. New four-bedroom homes on 1200 - 1500m2 sites have broken the $1 million ceiling. Newer houses in the Bass Rd area are fetching $500,000 to $600,000.

Greenhithe always has a steady attraction; also for English and South African buyers who see the big houses on large sections as good value for money. Water views command top dollar in Greenhithe because so much of the land bordering the upper harbour is reserve land. There's some movement away from Greenhithe among buyers who don't like the new motorway by Wainoni Park.

Prices in rural Albany have doubled during the past two years making lifestylers move beyond Paremoremo towards Coatesville. More affordable land is as far out as Kaukapakapa.

Rental and investment

The highlight of an Albany landlord's year is the seasonal influx of tertiary students at the end of the summer holidays. A variety of apartments are available at a range of rents. Greenhithe attracts few renters because of the traffic bottlenecks and the disruption caused by motorway and bridge construction.

Best streets

Oak Manor Dr (aka Millionaires Row) in Albany; Vanderbilt Pde in Brookfield; Sycracuse Pl in Northwood; Rame Rd and Kingfisher Gr in Greenhithe and the new homes in Kitiwake Dr.

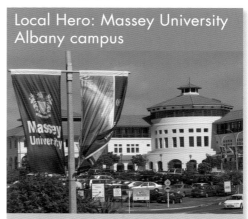

Local Hero: Massey University Albany campus

The distinctive Spanish-mission style of Massey University's Albany campus has given Albany a landmark that promises to get better with age, nestled as it is against a backdrop of bush. Six buildings make up the 10-year-old campus (with two currently being built). Facilities at the former Otehe Rohe campus are linked to the new buildings by public walkways. In its entirety, the Massey campus has more than 6500 students, 350 staff and 20 bachelor programmes from business and social sciences to design, fine arts and music. It carries out world-class research in the field of molecular ecology and gives a great deal back to the community with amenities like a new recreation centre, and functions such as a popular public lecture series and a music series.

Travel times

CBD	off-peak 20 min
	peak 1 hour plus
Harbour Bridge	15 min
Airport	60 min
North Shore Hospital	15 - 20 min

Regular buses service Albany, with some stopping at Takapuna. Others are express so go straight through to the CBD. The new Upper Harbour Bridge is being built alongside the existing Greenhithe Bridge. as part of a wider transport plan for the area that will see the bridge join up with the Albany Expressway via a 5km Greenhithe deviation due for completion in two years.

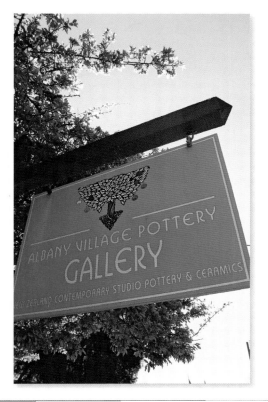

House prices

Albany

Older or terrace house

Bedrooms	
Price	$360,000 – $420,000

Newer house

Bedrooms	
Price	$450,000 – $700,000

New executive house

Bedrooms	
Price:	$850,000 – $1 million plus

Semi-rural 1ha to 2ha blocks

Price	$600,000 – $800,000

Greenhithe

1200m2 section

Price	$400,000 – $450,000

Older house on 1300 – 1500m2

Bedrooms	
Price	$650,000 – $850,000
With water views	$750,000 – $1 million

New townhouse/duplex

Bedrooms	
Price	$449,000 – $525,000

New house

Bedrooms	
Price	$618,000 – $650,000

Rental prices

Albany

Apartment

Bedrooms	
Price	$280/wk

Newer house

Bedrooms	
Price	$480 – $500/wk

Greenhithe

House

Bedrooms	
Price	$410/wk
Bedrooms	
Price	$430 – $440/wk

The thing that people first loved about this place is the thing that's fuelling its resurgence in popularity. Once upon a time, Beach Haven and Birkdale were holiday destinations then they fell heavily from favour – real estate agents wouldn't even include their names in advertisements. North Shore snobs likened the area to the Bronx in New York, but now they're waking up to the fact that coastal Beach Haven is one of the last places in Auckland where you can buy water's edge property for less than $700,000 – for the time being. There's more coastline here than in any other Auckland suburb, lots of Titirangi-style bush and harbour views across the upper Waitemata Harbour to Hobsonville and beyond.

Who lives there?

Singles, couples and first-home buyers are among the broad mix of people here. Some rent while others have bought ex-state houses and begun the renovation treadmill that is Auckland's rite-of-passage into home ownership. There's significant interest among smart singles looking for a modest investment near to the city and – thanks to the Kaipatiki Bridge – to Glenfield and Albany.

There's a steady influx of buyers and families from other parts of the North Shore, especially the East Coast Bays. On the back of deliciously persuasive real estate marketing, they're trading morning sunrises over Rangitoto Island for homes with land and bush around them – and cash to spare.

Interest from British buyers is steady because of the bush-clad coastline.

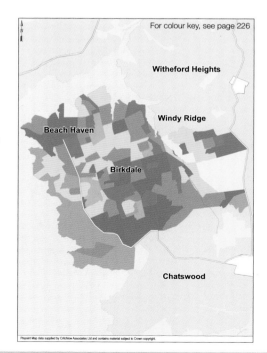

For colour key, see page 226

Witheford Heights

Windy Ridge

Beach Haven

Birkdale

Chatswood

Pinpoint Map data supplied by Critchlow Associates Ltd and contains material subject to Crown copyright.

Population profile	Population in 2001 18,603	% Aged Under 15 years 24.35	% Aged over 65 Years 7.76
% European 74.07	% Maori 14.06	% Pacific Peoples 9.19	% Asian 8.40

Typical dwellings

Baches in original condition and those that have been souped up into impressive family homes dot the streets. There's quite a bit of infill housing. There are many Reidbuilt homes built in the 1960s and 1970s for the first-home market. Apartments include mews-style apartments and a new block of 15 in Beach Haven Rd.

On the harbour side of Rangatira Rd, townhouses with sea views sit at the back of just about every original home.

Amenities
Schools ★★★★

Families have a wide choice of schools. Birkenhead College is a Goodman Fielder School of the Year winner and has a strong reputation in sport (orienteering and hockey) as well as music, drama and arts. For a full list, see page 272 .

Shops ★★★

Birkdale and Beach Haven each have local shops. Beach Haven's little retail area is about to be given a facelift and more retail space. The opening of the Kaipatiki Bridge link from Beach Haven to Glenfield has created a direct route to the Glenfield Mall.

In the other direction there's mall shopping, a Countdown supermarket and The Warehouse in Birkenhead, as well as strip shopping along Mokoia Rd.

Leisure ★★★

For leisure activities, Shepherd's Park has sports grounds, tennis and squash facilities. For fresh-air fiends, there's also a recently completed coastal walkway and parks and reserves to wander through.

Beach Haven's best-known eatery is the Au Bon Coin, which offers courtyard dining beneath a big pohutukawa tree. For those needing to eat and rush, there is an Asian bakery, a takeaway and a pizza shop.

Real Estate
Trends

Buyers are coming from further affield as they appreciate the lifestyle appeal and value for money of coastal properties here. It only takes a few renovations to really lift the area. A big part of the attraction is that this is a destination rather than a through-route afflicted with noisy traffic.

There are still sizeable properties with subdivision potential. Steady movement at the top end of the coastal market is having a flow-on effect. That magical $1 million figure was recently reached with the sale of a property and adjoining site but it's certainly not yet typical.

Waterfront houses will fetch $150,000 to $200,000 more than homes with only water views. Water's edge properties have nearly doubled in value during the past few years. Buyers with $450,000 to $550,000 will get a good family home.

Rental and investments

Renters here want long-term accommodation. A nice home here will cost as much to rent as the most basic home in Takapuna.

Best streets

Water's edge Brigantine Pl and Aeroview Dr in Beach Haven; Valkyria Pl in Island Bay; Rosecamp Rd in Mariner's Cove; Gatman Pl in Birkdale; Tramway Rd and Japonica Dr in Beach Haven.

Why we live there

"King of the Castle" Ron Reid

Ron Reid wasn't joking when he decided to build "something that no-one else in the street has" on his Verbena Rd, Birkdale property. Inspired by a picture of an English castle, he drew up plans for the five-bedroom, three-storey Lymington Castle. It stands on "two or three acres" of land that was part of an 100-acre dairy farm bought by Ron's father-in-law in 1919. One of the founders of Reidbuilt Homes, Ron hand-cut the Hinuera stone for the castle. New stone was delivered in eight-tonne truckloads twice a year, and Ron can't remember how long his DIY project took but he thinks it stretched from the 1950s into the 1970s. All he remembers of the completion date was pulling on his beret to keep the stone dust out of his hair, tucking his ruler into his pocket and heading out to cut more stone – until his wife reminded him that he'd finished the project the previous day!

House prices

House on half site
Bedrooms	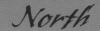
Price	$260,000 – $280,000

House on half site with sea views
Bedrooms	
Price	$275,000 – 325,000

On full site with sea views
Price	$450,000 – $520,000

Renovated coastal house
Bedrooms	
Price	$600,000 – $800,000

Rental prices

Mews-style apartment
Price	$340 – $360/wk

House
Bedrooms	
Price	$320 – $360/wk
Bedrooms	
Price	$340 – $390/wk
With sea views	$400 – $450/wk

Travel times

From Birkdale

CBD	peak 45 - 60 min
	off-peak 20 min
Birkenhead shops	5 min
Glenfield mall	5 min
North Shore Hospital	15 - 20 min
Airport	45 min

Peak-hour priority lanes for buses and car-poolers cut the driving time to the city by a third. Birkenhead Transport is based at Verrans Corner and its buses loop the area before heading into the city through Birkenhead. It takes less than five minutes to get from Beach Haven to the Glenfield mall over the new Kaipatiki Bridge.

Belmont and Bayswater are very much more than streets off the main drag between Takapuna and Devonport. When you're squashed between two illustrious neighbours, something's gotta happen, and happen it has. Its average little houses on their flat, wide streets are being spruced up. This area is just the ticket for family life. Shops and beaches are handy, there's boating down at the Bayswater marina, coastal walks and schools nearby. Five minutes' drive in either direction gets the theatre/restaurant goers to whatever their cultural urges desire. Bayswater Pt has wonderful views across to the city; Belmont's eastern shoreline has the same golden sands and Rangitoto Island views as Cheltenham and Takapuna. Beat that!

Who lives there?

These suburbs are a good healthy mix of all sorts of people, from retirees who have lived here for yonks, young aspiring families who perhaps can't afford Devonport yet, and sophisticated young professionals getting into the home ownership market. There's the sort of good cultural diversity you get when an area such as this has its grounding in solid blue-collar workers. With such a mix, community spirit is alive and well.

With the area on the up and up, that lively mix is likely to start skewing towards those who have more money.

Typical dwellings

Belmont and Bayswater were established long after Devonport so the housing stock includes everything from all decades after the

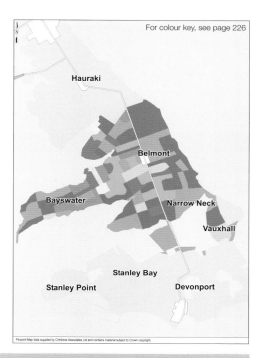

For colour key, see page 226

Hauraki

Belmont

Bayswater

Narrow Neck

Vauxhall

Stanley Bay

Stanley Point

Devonport

Pinpoint Map data supplied by Critchlow Associates Ltd and contains material subject to Crown copyright.

Population profile	Population in 2001 9,015	% Aged Under 15 years 21.76	% Aged over 65 Years 13.91
% European 87.05	% Maori 9.35	% Pacific Peoples 2.56	% Asian 4.99

1920s – bungalows, 1930s art deco stucco homes, 1950s ex-state houses, 1960s brick and tile units and 70s weatherboard houses. Of course, 21st century renovations are giving all of the above a new improved twist. And wouldn't you know it, state housing is tucked in there too. Something for everyone.

The state houses on Lake Rd driving into Belmont aren't an indication of the flavour of the area. The best homes are tucked off the side streets and along the water's edge on both coastlines.

With homes built originally on large 900m2-plus sections, this area has attracted its share of infill housing which at least gives choice to prospective purchasers.

Amenities

Schools ★★★★

This area is well served with local primaries that are a flat walk away and close, but not too close, to the busy main roads. Belmont lays claim to the intermediate school which feeds into Takapuna Grammar School, which is further along Lake Rd towards Takapuna.

For a full list, see page 272.

Shops ★★★

Belmont's busy shopping precinct includes several hairdressers, a bakery, a shoe repair shop, the recycled clothing boutique Enygma and the art supplies/gallery shop Palette. There's a chemist and a medical centre with the closest supermarkets being New World stores at Hauraki Corner and another one in Devonport.

Leisure ★★★

Boating and outdoor activities are right on your doorstep, whether it's sailing, other activities run by the Takapuna Boating Club at Bayswater or just meandering down to the Bayswater marina to oggle at the big yachts. Bayswater boat ramp is a mecca for windsurfers who zip up and down this part of the harbour on a brisk and breezy day.

Outdoor jaunts include beach walks along the beautiful sands of Narrow Neck beach where there's a playground and a shop. Some 5ha of former naval land at Takapuna Head is being developed into public open space by the North Shore City Council. On the opposite side of the peninsula there are reserve walks amongst the mangroves and mudflats. If the wetlands appeal, then try the boardwalk off the Kawerau Reserve for a change.

Eateries include Thai, Italian and Indian plus excellent cafe food at Vanilla, the popular cafe in the Belmont Shopping Centre that's easily spotted by the traffic lights travelling south to Devonport. What more proof do you need that this is a family patch than the McDonalds and Pizza Hutt fast food outlets in the heart of this patch of suburbia?

Real Estate
Trends

Belmont and Bayswater always have a healthy trade of families either selling to trade up to Devonport or Takapuna, or "empty nesters" cashing up the equity in their expensive houses after the kids have left home ... but not necessarily losing their quality of life or their ferry access to the city.

Throughout this area many larger properties are still being subdivided, with true 1930s Californian bungalows on large sites fetching the premium prices. Lake Rd divides Belmont (seaside) and Bayswater (harbourside) and has become a physical price demarcation – houses on the seaward side get a $100,000 premium.

Rental and investment

Because of its physical in-between-ness, it's hard to attract tenants here, even with the ferry services from Bayswater to the city and Devonport. Rents are, therefore, a little lower than you would assume.

House prices

Renovated ex-state house
Bedrooms		🛏 🛏
Price	$300,000 – $400,000	
Bedrooms		🛏 🛏 🛏
Price	$430,000 – $500,000	

Brick and tile unit
Bedrooms		🛏 🛏
Price	$250,000 – $380,000	

Modern house
Bedrooms		🛏 🛏 🛏 🛏
Price	$630,000 – $700,000	

Seaward executive house
Bedrooms		🛏 🛏 🛏 🛏
Price	$850,000 – $1 million plus	

Rental prices

Brick and tile unit
Bedrooms		🛏 🛏
Price	$230 – $340/wk	

Tidy modern house
Bedrooms		🛏 🛏 🛏
Price	$380 – $520/wk	

Townhouse
Bedrooms		🛏 🛏 🛏 🛏
Price	$500 – $580/wk	

Travel times

CBD	off peak 10-15 min
	peak 40-50 min
North Shore Hospital	10 min
Hauraki corner	5 min
Devonport	10 min
Airport	45-60 min

There's a regular Stagecoach bus service into Takapuna and the CBD. Urban Express runs a Monday to Saturday bus service into the CBD via Takapuna. Best of all, there's the Bayswater ferry service that leaves from the wharf by the marina.

Devonport is pretty unique – a combination of classy historic town and seaside village, with a bit of arty bohemian thrown in. This suburb is the iconic, historic face of the North Shore – and its future is well assured, thanks to the passion of many of its residents who are behind every initiative to keep Devonport true to its Victorian heritage. Devonport is also steeped in maritime history, with the New Zealand Navy base at Stanley Bay and gun emplacements on North Head and Mt Victoria. You're never far from either the sea or the village here, but you're a long way from the noise of the motorway and the high rises that now typify the seaside suburbs on the city side of the harbour. And you can forget commuting hassles with a gentle harbour ferry ride to the CBD.

Who lives there?

Arty, creative types have always favoured Devonport for its peaceful atmosphere, its beautiful coastline and its historical charm. It's also highly popular among young professionals and families with school-age children, often relocating from overseas or other parts of New Zealand, who want a sophisticated, user-friendly community to get comfortable in.

Typical dwellings

Devonport boasts many elegant, picturesque Victorian and Edwardian villas and cottages, large and small, along the water's edge and down the little streets beyond the village. It's the North Shore's largest collection of villas. Inconspicuously dotted among the older houses are a smaller number of 60s brick-and-tile units and homes.

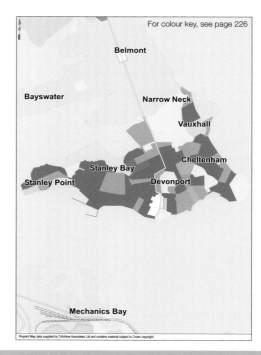

For colour key, see page 226

Belmont
Bayswater
Narrow Neck
Vauxhall
Cheltenham
Stanley Bay
Stanley Point
Devonport
Mechanics Bay

Pinpoint Map data supplied by Critchlow Associates Ltd and contains material subject to Crown copyright.

Population profile	Population in 2001 7,374	% Aged under 15 years 21.2	% Aged over 65 Years 10.78
% European 92.76	% Maori 5.53	% Pacific Peoples 1.91	% Asian 2.03

Devonport's heritage character is strongly supported by the North Shore City Council and zoning regulations require renovations to enhance the historical flavour of individual buildings, the immediate neighbourhood and the wider suburb. Street facades pre -1930 can't generally be altered and rear additions and alterations must be done using sympathetic materials. But inside, you can do what you wish.

There are few apartment blocks - and that's considered a big attraction compared with the likes of Mission Bay or Kohimarama.

Amenities
Schools ★★★★

Quality schooling is one of the attractions of this area. Primary schools throughout the area feed into Belmont Intermediate. Students then move onto Takapuna Grammar School in Lake Rd, which is the only secondary school in the area and, incidentally, one of the oldest high schools on the North Shore. For a full list, see page 272.

Shops ★★★★

Shopping here is more than just filling your basket, it's about relaxing and enjoying the village charm that sets Devonport apart from other suburbs. Most shops still have their

original facades, including the grand old Esplanade pub at the bottom of the main street. Once you've dealt with the supermarket list at New World (discreetly tucked down a side street), there are all the little galleries, boutique-style shops and bookshops to distract you on the way home.

Leisure ★★★★★

There's plenty of scope to enjoy the outdoors here, whether it's lazing on one of the beautiful beaches or climbing North Head or Mt Victoria to take in the harbour and city views. As if the North Head tunnels aren't enough of an outing on their own, the local Real Theatre Company has used them as a theatre venue! Tranquil Cheltenham Beach has huge pohutukawa trees and a fabulous view of Rangitoto Island. Water sports are popular here, with five boat ramps around the Devonport shoreline. Tennis, cricket and bowls are also well catered for.

If looking at all the beautiful old homes makes you want to know more about local history, the hour-long Old Devonport Walk is well worth the time and effort. There's also a museum at the naval base.

Devonport is well supplied with restaurants and other eateries, including Manuka, the Stone Oven Bakery and Cafe and the award winning Ice It Cafe in Church St.

Real Estate
Trends

Devonport central is a place many North Shore homeowners aspire to; some will move four or five times before they reach their chosen street. Most of the North Shore's east coast bays coastline was developed post -1960, after the harbour bridge opened, so Devonport is one of the few suburbs on the shore featuring villas, along with Northcote and Birkenhead Pts. Buyers tend to come from the shore, from other parts of New Zealand or from overseas – not so much from the city side of the harbour.

Devonport central is now fetching premium prices, pushed up by returning ex-pat Kiwis and British migrants. Prices of $800,000 to $1 million-plus are not uncommon; no more than five minutes' walk to both ferry and

village are key factors. In Stanley Pt, homes on large properties go for $900,000-plus.

Unlike other seaside suburbs, sea views are not the determining factor for price. In a suburb with a villa heritage dating back to the days when cars were a novelty, off-street parking and garaging are top selling features.

House quality rather than number of bedrooms also affects price. A top quality three-bedroom home can fall into the same price bracket as a four/five bedroom home needing work.

Rental and investment

The same factors apply to rental returns: water views aren't as big a deal as off-street parking and garaging.

Overseas tenants generally pay the higher rentals, especially the Brits - the exchange rate is favourable enough for them to pay a six- to 12-month rental until they decided where they will buy.

Best streets

Jubilee Ave in Cheltenham; the peninsula end of Stanley Pt Rd and First and Second Ave in Stanley Pt.

Local Hero: the Domain trees

Planted some 50 years ago, these elegant London plane trees have been allowed to express themselves rather than be pruned annually to little more than a trunk stump with a technique known as pollarding. Devonport's graceful specimens are protected under the North Shore City Council's tree and bush protection regulations, which means maintenance work can't be carried out without council permission. As beautiful as they are, they haven't yet made it onto the Schedule of Notable Trees, which would mean they're documented on the district plan.

Look Out ⓘ

If slick, minimalist architecture is your thing, this isn't the place for you. Extensive "renovations" that have seen brand new homes arise from the rubble of near-complete demolition have attracted the wrath of concerned locals, keen to protect the suburb's historic character. They want the council to close the loopholes and more tightly define the difference between a renovation and a demolition/rebuild.

House prices

Unit

Bedrooms	🛏 🛏
Price	$250,000 – $300,000

House

Bedrooms	🛏 🛏 🛏
Price	$680,000 – $750,000

Premium house

Bedrooms	🛏 🛏 🛏
Price	$700,000 – $850,000

Premium house on large site

Price	$800,000 – $1 million

Rental prices

Unit

Bedrooms	🛏 🛏
Price	$200 – $280/wk

Villa or house

Bedrooms	🛏 🛏 🛏
Price	$480 – $550/wk
Bedrooms	🛏 🛏 🛏 🛏
Price	$580 – $800/wk

Travel times

From Devonport

CBD	off-peak 20 min
	peak 1 hour plus
CBD by ferry	12 min
Northern motorway	off-peak 15 min
	peak 45 min
Takapuna shops	10 min
Airport	off-peak 45 min
	peak extremely variable

The ferry is the saving grace for Devonport commuters, with some 30 sailings every week day. There's also a Stagecoach bus service that runs into the city. People who love this place don't see the one-road in, one-road out as a nightmare. To them, it makes Devonport a destination rather than a noisy, transit suburb.

The times are a-changing in Glenfield. Developed through the 1960s and 1970s, Glenfield has shaken off its old image as a boring, unsophisticated "nappy valley" for young families. It's still a family-friendly place, but it's boring no longer. Those who move into Glenfield tend to stay long term or trade up within the area. They're also showing their confidence by investing in start-up businesses or hanging on to that first home as an investment. It has often been said that Glenfield's demographic typifies heartland New Zealand. These days, Glenfield has its share of the latest looks in housing developments just like other suburbs, with terrace housing and big executive homes on the fringes. It's giving buyers much wider choice and giving Glenfield a much higher profile beyond the North Shore.

Who lives there?

Glenfield has now lost many traditional first home buyers. People moving here now are more likely to be second home buyers. The number of local trade vehicles confirms the perception that this is hearty self-employment area, with residents who give a lot back to their community.

Newer housing developments are attracting professionals from within and from outside Glenfield. Some, including residents of Glendhu Rd, think of themselves as living in Albany rather than Glenfield.

Typical dwellings

There's huge choice in Glenfield, from the well-known traditional group houses with their rectangular design and aluminium joinery/Hardiplank construction to the

For colour key, see page 226

North Harbour

Meadowood

Chester Park • Unsworth Heights

The Palms • Totaravale

Cuthill

Wairau Park

Bay View

Wairau Valley

Glenfield

Witheford Heights

Marlborough

Windy Ridge

Hillcrest

Pinpoint Map data supplied by Critchlow Associates Ltd and contains material subject to Crown copyright.

Population profile	Population in 2001 30,099	% Aged Under 15 years 22.34	% Aged over 65 Years 6.73
% European 69.65	% Maori 8.04	% Pacific Peoples 4.59	% Asian 18.01

newest developments including the Manuka Cove terrace houses and Treeview.

The group houses built, street by cul-de-sac street in the 1960s and 70s, have come back into favour. They may not be the height of architectural style, but they're everything else a house needs to be – and they're popular with homeowners in the middle to lower income spectrum.

The townhouses in the Manuka Cove development weren't initially popular with locals, but the weatherboard construction adds variety to the area. There are larger executive homes in Unsworth Heights and The Palms. Glendhu Rd has an almost rural feel, a striking contrast to the busy Glenfield Rd thoroughfare.

Amenities
Schools ★★★

Glenfield College is the main state high school here. It was one of the first secondary schools to attract fee-paying international students and it has a strong pastoral emphasis to its curriculum.

For single-sex education, the secondary boys' and girls' high schools at Westlake are the closest, but it's important to check the latest zones. This area is well-served with primary schools including a special school (Wairau Valley School). For a full list, see page 272.

Shops ★★★★

Glenfield shoppers are spoilt for choice, whether it's the many little suburban blocks of shops, the mall or the Link Dr retail area at Wairau Park. On Glenfield Rd, the Westfield mall is the largest on the North Shore. Its "family destination" style includes 114 shops, department stores, a food hall, cafes and Foodtown and Countdown supermarkets.

Leisure ★★★★

Glenfield has many small parks and a coastal walkway as well as the nearby East Coast Bays beaches. Rosedale Park is close to the wastewater treatment park, but you'd never know now that the odours have been eliminated by new technology. The walkway around the Manuka Reserve has had a recent upgrade. There's a boat ramp for use when the tide is right and a children's playground.

The Glenfield Leisure Centre is hugely popular for its indoor heated pools, hydroslides and diving boards, saunas and spas. Facilities include conference rooms and a gym. The North Shore Events Centre, that has seen many a Silver Ferns netball tussle, is also in Glenfield.

Wairau Park has a cinema complex and bowling alley. There are several cafes for breathing space and a chance to check the shopping list. Eateries include Asian restaurants and Valentines on Wairau Rd. The Glenfield Tavern is a quaint watering hole opposite the Glenfield mall.

Real Estate
Trends

Glenfield has come of age, and the confidence among families in the area is evident. As first home buyers drift west, local real estate agents are selling to buyers trading up from other areas, and long-established residents and self-employed people reinvesting in rental property.

Glenfield went through a negative patch when buyers turned their attention to

Albany's townhouses, but that appears to have dissipated. The influx of Asian buyers into Unsworth Heights and The Palms has eased off, as it has elsewhere in Auckland.

With scores of near-identical homes in Glenfield it's relatively easy for real estate agents to give a realistic estimate of the value of a house, depending on whether it has a carport, a garage or is on an elevated site with views.

Executive homes in the upmarket Glendhu/ Daldy's Lane are average $520,000, compared with the $305,000 average for a three-bedroom house elsewhere.

Rental and investment

Investor interest is always strong in Glenfield because the yields are better than the more highly priced areas of the North Shore. Competition for investment property is stiff because local people are reinvesting in their own patch. Larger homes are generally owner/occupied.

Best streets

High Rd and Glendhu Rd in Glenfield; Calypso Way, The Palms and Westminster Gardens, Unsworth Heights.

House prices

House	
Bedrooms	🛏 🛏
Price	$250,000 – $300,000
Bedrooms	🛏 🛏 🛏
Price	$300,000 – $320,000

New house in Glenfield

Bedrooms	🛏 🛏 🛏 🛏
Price	$400,000 – $550,000

Executive home in Unsworth Heights

Price	$600,000 plus

1.4ha lifestyle block with older house on Glenfield fringe

Price	$800,000 – $850,000
	($1.5 million if subdividable)

Rental prices

Unit	
Bedrooms	🛏 🛏
Price	$250 – $280/wk
House	
Bedrooms	🛏 🛏
Price	$280 – $300/wk
Bedrooms	🛏 🛏 🛏
Price	$320 – $350/wk
Bedrooms	🛏 🛏 🛏 🛏
Price	$360 – $420/wk

Travel times

CBD	off-peak 15 min
	peak 60 min
Airport	20 – 25 min
Westfield Glenfield	10 min

Once the widening of Glenfield Rd is completed (scheduled for 2009), a bridge link will be constructed between the two parts of Glendhu Rd. Locals have pushed for this so that children can walk to schools such as Bayview. The Glendhu link will also create alternative routes into and out of Glenfield so ease pressure on Glenfield Rd.

Once upon a holiday time, this region was Auckland's summer playland. People would head north to their baches at Orewa and the Hibiscus Coast for summer; these days they don't bother to go home afterwards. They're settling here lock, stock and city lifestyle, into the new executive family homes, the units (that are popular again among the retirees) and the apartments at Gulf Harbour. The beaches are where it's all happening, and Orewa's 2.5km stretch of white sand is one of the best. Along both sides of the Whangaparaoa Peninsula a dozen or so beaches run from Red Beach to Shakespear Bay. Gulf Harbour has the marina as its focus, with a canal development for apartment dwellers and a planned harbour village. The rural landscape is fast disappearing into suburbia.

Who lives there?

Beyond the seasonal hordes of holiday makers there's a different Orewa, a place that's popular with retired people who appreciate the flat walk to the beach and the shops, and professional families settling in for a year-round seaside lifestyle.

On the peninsula there's a mix of families and couples including retired people who've lived here long-term. Many young elderly (in their 60s rather than 80s) sell the family home and trade up to a hip version of retirement at Gulf Harbour. Gulf Harbour School's expansion, just six years after it opened, is proof of the influx of families. Migrants like the coastline and there's an increasing number of North Shore buyers relocating to an easier pace of life with a bit more green space around the houses.

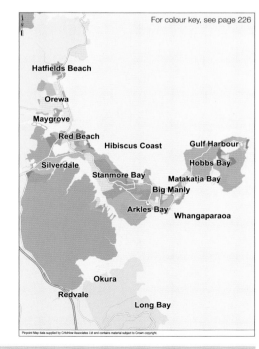

For colour key, see page 226

Hatfields Beach
Orewa
Maygrove
Red Beach
Hibiscus Coast
Gulf Harbour
Silverdale
Hobbs Bay
Stanmore Bay
Matakatia Bay
Big Manly
Arkles Bay
Whangaparaoa
Okura
Redvale
Long Bay

Pinpoint Map data supplied by Critchlow Associates Ltd and contains material subject to Crown copyright.

Population profile
% European 90.39

Population in 2001 31,488
% Maori 6.67

% Aged under 15 years 21.34
% Pacific Peoples 1.45

% Aged over 65 Years 19.83
% Asian 2.49

Typical dwellings

Near the motorway, Orewa's elevated new housing developments have views of Orewa Beach. Near the township, there's a mix of modern contemporary homes and 60-year-old holiday baches. Brick and tile units, built 30 years ago, are popular once again. Orewa got its first Gold Coast-style semi high rise a couple of years ago – some people love it, some hate it.

Throughout the peninsula the mix includes baches, older weatherboard houses and new plaster-clad homes. Many have great sea views. As well as the marina and its apartments, Gulf Harbour has subdivisions with large homes and terraced apartments.

At Waiwera a hotel/apartment complex is planned for land between the beachfront and the thermal pools complex.

Amenities
Schools ★★★

There are primary schools scattered throughout the area. Gulf Harbour Primary School is expanding to meet increased demand. Orewa has Kingsway College, which is a Christian school. Hibiscus Coast Intermediate on the peninsula has merged with the new Whangaparaoa College that opened in 2005 and will eventually take the full intermediate/secondary range. At Silverdale a new Catholic primary, Stella Maris School, opened in 2005.

For a full list, see page 272.

Shops ★★★

Orewa's town centre has a friendly small-town feel. It's also the headquarters of the Rodney District Council. Whangaparaoa township has the Pacific Plaza complex which includes some major stores such as Farmers. There are shops at Red Beach, Manly Village and Gulf Harbour. Heading inland, the popular Silverdale shopping centre offers plenty of options for bargain hunters with its mix of designer label factory outlets, boutique shops and an industrial park. The weekly Saturday markets are popular too.

Leisure ★★★

Relaxing in this part of Auckland involves extremes of climate. On one hand, there's the endless summer, with miles of beaches. And now there's endless winter too, with indoor skiing at Silverdale. The new Snowplanet with its 8000m2 "snowdrome" is a first for New Zealand.

By the beach, Orewa Reserve has a skating rink and holiday park. The numerous sandy beaches along the peninsula offer lots of choices – swimming, surfing, fishing, windsurfing, boating, or just beach walking. Red Beach has a surf club and surf life-savers, which makes it a hugely popular teen beach. The Whangaparaoa Coastal Walkway goes from Amorino Reserve in Red Beach to Matakatia Beach.

If the beach isn't your style, the Hibiscus Coast Leisure Centre at Stanmore Bay has an indoor heated swimming pool, squash courts

and fitness facilities. There are two golf courses at Gulf Harbour, and a miniature steam railway at Whangaparaoa plus activities such as rock climbing, 10-pin bowling, mini golf and horse riding.

At the tip of the peninsula, Army Bay includes a heritage trail of World War II Army defences and Shakespear Regional Park has sheltered bays, pastureland, regenerating native forest and a lookout with fabulous views.

Wenderholm Regional Park and the Waiwera Thermal Resort are a short drive north.

Eating out is improving. Local restaurants include The Rock Salt Restaurant and Cafe Kaizen Coffeehouse. Manly Village has some well patronised little restaurants.

Real Estate
Trends

Orewa's brick and tile units are enjoying a revival after a period in the doldrums, with demand among buyers and renters exceeding supply. The market includes older local people downsizing and others retiring north from Auckland city and the North Shore. Most families move into the newer areas of Orewa that are close to the motorway, including the prestigious Grand Dr and the area overlooking the Orewa River.

The beach communities along the peninsula are highly sought after. Gulf Harbour is attracting attention from returning ex-pat Kiwis and migrants from the United States, Britain and throughout Europe (particularly Germany and France). Buyers are also trading up from older homes along the peninsula.

Gulf Harbour is popular because there's plenty of land that hasn't been bought by housing companies for their own packages.

Houses are not necessarily cheaper the further you go along the peninsula. As a guideline, an executive four-bedroom home with views would cost $750,000 to $850,000 in Gulf Harbour, $850,000 to $1 million at Tindalls Bay and $2 to $3 million if it were beachfront Manly Beach. An average older home in middle-of-the-road Stanmore Bay on the peninsula costs about $100,000 less than a similar home in Orewa.

Rental and investment

Whangaparaoa rentals do get cheaper towards the end of the peninsula because it's further from the motorway. It's harder to rent property beyond Red Beach and Stanmore Bay. Renters often won't even look at a home without garaging. Garaging and sea views each add a $10 weekly premium to rentals. Orewa is popular for its proximity to the motorway, with supply barely meeting demand.

Best streets

In Orewa any of the beachside cul-de-sac streets off the Hibiscus Coast Highway; also Grand Dr and West Hoe Heights. Along the peninsula anything on the beachfront or clifftop in any of the bays. Chalverton Tce in Red Beach; Duncansby Bay Rd in Stanmore Bay; Tiri Rd in Big Manly.

House prices

Orewa

Brick and tile unit

Bedrooms 🛏 🛏
Price $340,000 – $390,000

Older house

Bedrooms 🛏 🛏 🛏
Price $430,000 – $450,000

Townhouse

Bedrooms 🛏 🛏 🛏
Price $450,000 – $680,000

Executive house

Bedrooms 🛏 🛏 🛏 🛏
Price $600,000 – $900,000

600m2 section

Price $300,000 plus

Whangaparaoa peninsula/Gulf Harbour

House

Bedrooms 🛏 🛏 🛏
Price $330,000 – $360,000

Clifftop 1960s house with northern views

Price $650,000 – $700,000

Karaka Cove sections

Price $310,000 – $379,000

Two-bedroom Santa Rosa apartment

Price $295,000 – $320,000

Three-bedroom canal apartment

Price $550,000 plus

450m2 section

Price $200,000

Old house on big section with sea views

Price $1 million

Rental prices

Unit

Bedrooms 🛏 🛏
Price $250 – $300/wk

Older house

Bedrooms 🛏 🛏 🛏
Price $320 – $340/wk

Newer house

Bedrooms 🛏 🛏 🛏
Price $380/wk

Executive house

Bedrooms 🛏 🛏 🛏 🛏
Price $500 – $600/wk
With sea views $600 plus/wk

Beachfront house

Bedrooms 🛏 🛏 🛏 🛏
Price $700/wk

Gulf Harbour apartment

Bedrooms 🛏 🛏 🛏
Price $300/wk

Travel times

From Orewa

CBD	off-peak 35 min
	peak 60 min plus
North Shore Hospital	20 min
Pacific Plaza	10 min
Airport	60 min plus
Motorway	a few seconds
From along the peninsula	
Motorway	20 - 40 mins
Silverdale to the bridge	off-peak 15 min
	peak 60 min plus

Regular bus services run from Orewa and the peninsula to Takapuna (takes about an hour) and central Auckland. The Fullers ferry service between the CBD and Gulf Harbour has been expanded to meet the rising demand.

The northern motorway extension linking Orewa to Puhoi is due to be completed in March 2009. The Weiti toll road project has funding issues that need to be resolved before construction can begin. The proposed 7km road would provide a second route out of the peninsula from Stanmore Bay, across the Weiti River and past Stillwater before joining State Highway One at Redvale. It is expected to cut travel time from the top of the East Coast Bays to Whangaparaoa from 30 minutes to 5 to 10 minutes.

Some locals reckon this is the Parnell of the North Shore. Mairangi Bay has village-style boutique shops, the people scrub up very nicely, it's by the sea and it's more demure than the showy suburbs of Milford and Takapuna down the road. Maybe it's the x-factor these picturesque little bays have ... in bucket-loads. The area's more affordable than the city-side Parnell but if you're after lifestyle you can't really go wrong. Many of the houses have sea views, there's a pretty little bay just down the road, most of the area is zoned for the desirable, albeit very large, Rangitoto College and the shopping and cafe scene is growing in sophistication. Who wouldn't love living so close to the water, whether it's taking a workday lunch break at the beach or packing an evening picnic for the family?

Who lives there?

People fall in love with this place and are reluctant to leave. It's comfortable and secure territory, and those who've settled here like to think they've put their home ownership struggles behind them. The community spirit is part of the appeal, helped by geography that creates little communities within the wider area that hugs the coastline. People here are very outdoors orientated with the focus on the beach, walking and picnics.

A large number of South Africans and Asians have settled here in recent years as much for the school zoning as for the area's quiet, restful appeal.

Typical dwellings

Throughout the bays, homes have been built to make the most of the picture-postcard

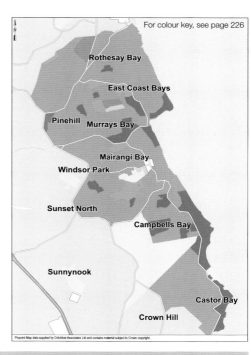

For colour key, see page 226

Rothesay Bay

East Coast Bays

Pinehill Murrays Bay

Mairangi Bay

Windsor Park

Sunset North

Campbells Bay

Sunnynook

Castor Bay

Crown Hill

Pinpoint Map data supplied by Critchlow Associates Ltd and contains material subject to Crown copyright.

eastern aspect and elevated topography with ridges and gullies leading down to the waterline. The houses are an eclectic mix with architecturally designed homes, developments and renovations. Any original 1950s houses have generally been demolished or substantially renovated.

In Mairangi Bay, apartments add to the buzz of the village.

Amenities

Schools ★★★★

The highly sought-after Rangitoto College has more than 3100 students on its roll, and many families hope to live within its extensive zone. Murrays Bay Intermediate, next to Murrays Bay Primary School, is the only intermediate. For a full list, see page 272.

Shops ★★★

Village shopping is what Mairangi Bay is all about – when you're not at the beach that is. Boutiques caters for every taste in stylish clothing, jewellery, footwear and homewares, while an About Face skincare clinic pampers the local ladies. There's a Woolworths supermarket in Hastings Rd, and a Seamart, grocery store and stationery shop in the block around the corner.

Leisure ★★★

The sacred Rahopara Reserve has a hand-crafted Maori-style viewing platform that takes in the wider Hauraki Gulf. Recreational walking is a treat, through Centennial Park and along little foreshore spots that dot the coastline.

Pupuke Golf Course is off East Coast Rd. All other sports enthusiasts have world-class facilities at the Millennium Institute of Sport and Health by Rangitoto College.

For the culturally minded, the Mairangi Arts Centre offers a range of classes.

There's a wide choice of cafes and restaurants including The Edge Restaurant in Castor Bay and Feathers Olde English Restaurant in Campbell's Bay. Mairangi Bay has the pick of the eateries and there are quality takeaways and plenty of beachfront pohutukawa trees to scoff them under.

Real Estate

Trends

A recent Bayleys Real Estate survey turned up the surprising revelation that half their sales had gone to buyers from well south of the harbour bridge, including such diverse areas as Henderson in the west and Botany Downs in the east. The common lure is the lifestyle.

A "Rangi zone" (Rangitoto College) address is the big carrot that dangles in front of parents virtually from the time of their children's birth. The 34 sections in the Rangitoto Ridge Estate off Windsor Pl (built on surplus college land) are the focus of families paying the $350,000-plus to get as close as possible to the school. Once developed, the properties with a house will be worth around $1 million.

First entry point in the area is around $400,000. There's very little on the market in the next bracket up of $400,000 to $600,000 and it's a common comment that one million dollars doesn't buy much in this area.

Rental and investment

Lower East Coast Bays rentals are on a par with Milford and Takapuna. Renters include migrants looking to buy and people renovating or building new homes. As a result,

Why we live there

Business people
Christine and Brian Davis

Christine and Brian Davis' passion for Mairangi Bay is absolute. They live here, work here and, in the evenings, they love nothing better than walking to the restaurants or collecting takeaways for a picnic at the beach. Mairangi Bay became the couple's business location of choice 23 years ago when they opened their designer stores, Jolissas Jewellers and Lejose Fashion House. More recently they redeveloped the old Post Office site with a new building that includes their apartment (plus two more) and a ground floor retail area that houses their shops side by side. Says Brian: "We feel we have helped a little way in improving the area, but then Mairangi Bay has been very good to us, too. It's a wonderful place to be."

short-term tenancies are common, but there's a dearth of quality homes to meet demand.

Best streets

Anything on the seaward side of Beach Rd. The Esplanade in Campbells Bay, Brighton Rd, Sidmouth St and Whitby Rd in Mairangi Bay, Churchhill Rd and Portal Pl in Murrays Bay.

House prices

House		
Bedrooms		🛏 🛏
Price		$400,000 – $420,000
Bedrooms		🛏 🛏 🛏
Price		$500,000 – $550,000

Executive house with no views

Bedrooms		🛏 🛏 🛏 🛏
Price		$950,000 – $1.1 million
With views		$1.1 million plus

Large cliff-top house

Price	$3 million

Rental prices

Unit		
Bedrooms		🛏 🛏
Price		$330 – $350/wk
House		
Bedrooms		🛏 🛏 🛏
Price		$380 – $450/wk

House with sea views

Bedrooms		🛏 🛏 🛏 🛏
Price		$600 – $800/wk

Travel times

From Mairangi Bay

CBD	off-peak 20 – 25 min
	peak 45 – 60 min
Northern motorway	5 – 10 min
Airport	45 – 60 min
Albany Mega Centre	10 min

Regular bus services run along East Coast Rd and Beach Rd.

This area includes a couple of Auckland's niche market real estate gems. With their harbour views across to the city and elegant villas, Birkenhead Pt and Northcote Pt tend to be described in the same breathless tones as Devonport and, of course, have the price tags and status to match. The rest of the area is well-established and has good quality homes.

The big difference is accessibility. Disregarding the often congested Onewa Rd, this is the closest the shore comes to Auckland's CBD – you can be there in a matter of minutes during non-peak times. There's lots of bush (in fact, the amount is second only to Titirangi), open space and family-friendly spots. There's a rich Asian influence in these suburbs, as you can see at the Birkenhead shops.

Who lives there?

Northcote Pt and Birkenhead Pt attract buyers who love old homes generally, and villas in particular. There's been a migration from southern shore suburbs like Ponsonby, Kingsland and Grey Lynn – people who have been priced out of those areas and are looking for similar character but better value. Northcote Pt is said to be more conservative than Birkenhead Pt.

There is a lot of trading up here. Families move three, four or five times, often only a few streets at a time, as their lifestyle and budgets change. Families like Northcote central for its good schooling for all ages. Chatswood's value for money and comparatively easy access to the city appeals to buyers. Birkenhead central's apartments are popular for all the same reasons.

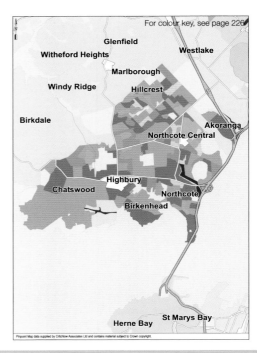

| Population profile | Population in 2001 32,346 | % Aged Under 15 years 19.23 | % Aged over 65 Years 11.78 |
| % European 73.51 | % Maori 7.94 | % Pacific Peoples 3.74 | % Asian 16.11 |

Typical dwellings

Historic cottages that were built for Chelsea Sugar Refinery workers in the late 1880s are still dotted around the suburb and they're popular renovation projects for young buyers. The original brick cottages on the refinery grounds can be leased from the refinery owners.

Character homes define Northcote Pt and Birkenhead Pt, which were established in the late 1880s. Near the centre of Birkenhead there are a number of near-new apartments.

Chatswood estate was developed as an executive subdivision in the early 1970s, offering a range of modern homes on big sections. The 34 sections on former harbour board land in Onetaunga Rd were subdivided into 1000m2 sections and have harbour or city views.

Northcote central and Hillcrest have around 6000 houses with styles ranging from renovated ex-state houses, townhouses and older quality weatherboard homes. The crème de la crème of more modern homes are in the Onepoto Basin area and along Sylvan Ave.

Amenities
Schools ★★★★

Local co-ed secondary schools Birkenhead College and Northcote College both have high profiles, with sporting, cultural and academic achievements. Northcote's jazz band regularly wins regional awards. Auckland University of Technology's Akoranga campus is in Northcote.

For a full list of local schools, see page 272.

Shops ★★★★

Shopping at Birkenhead Pt is becoming increasingly sophisticated with boutique shops, cafes and restaurants. Birkenhead central's comprehensive range of shops along Mokoia Rd and Birkenhead Ave complement the mall where there's a food hall with ethnic eateries, The Warehouse, a Countdown supermarket and plenty of undercover parking.

Northcote's town centre supports some 80 businesses while the centre facility itself includes specialty shops, Woolworths and a 50-seat Asian food hall. Northcote now boasts the largest range of Asian food stores on the North Shore. Northcote's energetic business association is working with the North Shore City Council on a town centre redevelopment.

Northcote Point's interesting mix of local shops includes a boutique wine shop, a secondhand children's toys/clothing shop and a fish and chip shop aptly named Point Taken.

Leisure ★★★★

The historic Northcote Point Walk encompasses old villas, coastline and spectacular views. To walk round the coastline, take the tunnel under the harbour bridge at the bottom of Tennyson Ave to where Sulphur Beach used to be before the harbour bridge was built in 1959.

The Harbourside Art Trail through Birkenhead and Northcote visits artists' studios and workshops. Arts have a strong profile here, with the Northart Community Arts Centre and many artists and crafts people working out of local studios.

The annual 2.36km Chelsea Swim takes place in November/December, with some 500 proven ocean swimmers stepping into the water at Herne Bay.

The Chelsea Sugar Refinery grounds are a

beautiful spot for a picnic. Birkenhead has numerous bush reserves, including Kauri Glen Reserve near Little Shoal Bay. For youngsters there's rock climbing at the Birkenhead Leisure Centre and a skate park next door. In Akoranga Rd, there's the Takapuna Athletics Club and the YMCA.

The well-known Bridgeway cinema is on Northcote Pt.

Real Estate
Trends

Locals wanting clifftop character homes are increasingly having to fight off competition from buyers from the city side of the bridge in a trend that has gathered momentum during the past six or seven years. $1.5 million buys water views – you'd pay twice as much in Herne Bay.

Hillcrest is often marketed by real estate agents as part of Birkenhead, Glenfield and Northcote, depending on the streets. Chatswood has come through a spell in the doldrums some five years ago with renewed interest in homes that respond well to renovation for family living.

Hillcrest's top homes are $500,000. First entry point into Birkenhead Pt and Northcote Pt is now close to $600,000 for a basic do-up. Birkenhead Pt streets well back from the clifftop have reached the $1 million mark.

Rental and investment

There's big demand for rental properties, including Birkenhead's wide range of investor apartments, and houses in Hillcrest. Homes in Birkenhead Pt and Northcote Pt fetch an extra $30 a week. Clifftop homes can fetch up to $800 a week. Houses in Hillcrest are at the upper end of the rental range.

Why I live there

Former All Black captain Gary Whetton

Gary has lived in both Northcote Pt and Birkenhead Pt and says he wouldn't live anywhere else. His was one of the first young families to move into a street that's now predominantly family orientated. "It's a fantastic place," he says. "It's out of the so-called big city but the city is visually right there in front of you. The ferry is right there, there are beaches, plenty of green parks and great people, lovely people." He'd rather not let slip any more secrets though. "It's an undiscovered part of Auckland and we don't really want to tell too many people about it," he quips.

Best streets

Clarence Street, Queen St and Princes St on Northcote Pt; Tizard Rd, Wanganella St and Palmerston Rd on Birkenhead Pt, Puawai St in Northcote; seaward Onetaunga St in Chatswood; Mountbatten Ave and Lynngate Pl in Hillcrest.

Travel times

CBD	off-peak 7-10 min
	peak 20 min
Northern motorway	5 min
Airport	40-45 min
Glenfield Shopping Centre	10 min

For buses and car poolers, peak-hour priority lanes cut the driving time into the city considerably. But don't try cheating. Enforcement officers along Onewa Rd regularly sting sole drivers sneaking along the green lane. Northcote Pt's big plus is the sole traffic light allowing traffic to flow into Onewa Rd for the straight run over the harbour bridge.

Birkenhead Transport runs a bus service throughout Birkenhead and Beach Haven. The new Kaipatiki Bridge now gives Beach Haven residents much quicker access to Glenfield. For city-bound ferry users, Fullers collects commuters from Fisherman's Wharf.

House prices

Unit
Bedrooms	🛏 🛏
Price	$260,000 – $280,000

Apartment or terrace house
Price	$240,000 – $400,000

House
Bedrooms	🛏 🛏 🛏
Price	$400,000 – $500,000
Bedrooms	🛏 🛏 🛏 🛏
Price	$400,000 – $500,000
With sea views	$600,000 plus

(add $100,000 or more for Chatswood)

Executive Onepoto Basin house
Price	$700,000 – $800,000

Clifftop historic house on the points
Price	$1 million – $1.8 million

Rental prices

Unit or apartment
Bedrooms	🛏 🛏
Price	$250 – $320/wk

Townhouse
Bedrooms	🛏 🛏 🛏
Price	$320 – $450/wk

House
Bedrooms	🛏 🛏 🛏
Price	$350 – $400/wk

House on the points
Bedrooms	🛏 🛏 🛏
Price	$420 – $460/wk

Clifftop house
Bedrooms	🛏 🛏 🛏 🛏
Price	$600 – $800/wk

This is Auckland's own little piece of the Gold Coast – without the brashness, the high rises or the Australians. An address in Takapuna or Milford spells prestige and affluence. Location is everything and more with the greatest kudos going to those who live in the Golden Mile – the streets that run between the main drags and the sea. Life centres around the two gorgeous beaches – whether it's being able to step right onto the sand from one of the elegant beachfront homes or about the stunning views from the medium-rise apartments. These apartments are fairly new to the area. While they offer up resort-style living, with cafes, restaurants and entertainment within walking distance, it's hard to believe that our beloved city coastline will ever look like the stuff across the Tasman.

Who lives there?

The smart, the stylish and the suitably suntanned all live here. Takapuna and Milford are the suburbs to which everyone on this side of the bridge aspires. A stroll along Takapuna beach tells you lots about the locals, whether it's the gold and the glitz that adorns the beachgoers or the fabulous homes right on the beach. Most of the wealthy residents who live in the Golden Mile between Lake and Kitchener Rds and the sea are Kiwis, not foreigners.

In Milford there are affluent families with boating in their blood, and many older people who like the flat walk to the mall and the beach. The city side of the landscape is where the upwardly mobile are settled – for the meantime – until they can edge their way street by street towards the water.

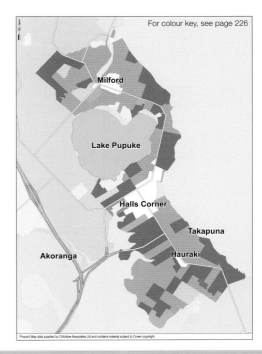

For colour key, see page 226

Milford

Lake Pupuke

Halls Corner

Takapuna

Akoranga

Hauraki

Pinpoint Map data supplied by Critchlow Associates Ltd and contains material subject to Crown copyright

Population profile	Population in 2001 12,819	% Aged under 15 years 14.84	% Aged over 65 Years 19.1
% European 83.1	% Maori 4.05	% Pacific Peoples 1.31	% Asian 10.45

Typical dwellings

For all its affluence, Takapuna has a wide choice, from basic weatherboard houses to larger family homes, palatial mansions and high-rise apartments. Many original cottages have been renovated beyond recognition or demolished to make way for a contemporary house. Takapuna's popular modern multi-storey apartments include Promenade Terraces, the Takapuna Sands, the Rocks and the Mon Desir.

At the other end of the market, brick and tile units built during the 1960s and 1970s by developers Franchi and Ion are still in demand. In between, there's a wide range of housing styles.

Amenities
Schools ★★★★★

Families throughout the area have abundant choice with state and Catholic primary schools, an intermediate school in both Takapuna and Belmont, and several secondary schools to choose from. Takapuna Grammar School at Hauraki is the only co-educational secondary school.

For a full list, see page 272.

Shops ★★★★★

Traditionally the shopping hub of the entire North Shore, Takapuna's retailers have withstood the competition from other shore retail centres. The revitalised resort-style shopping strip along Hurstmere Rd has boutiques and good cafes. On Sunday mornings there's a colourful market in the Lake Rd carpark.

Westfield Takapuna has more than 70 shops and there's a substantial mall at Milford. To the south, there's a shopping block and supermarket at Hauraki Corner.

Leisure ★★★★

The long, golden-sand beaches of Takapuna and Milford offer swimming, boating and plenty of people-watching at all times of the day. The extended dog walking hours before 10am and after 6.30pm are bringing owners and their pets from throughout Auckland.

The Takapuna Boating Club on The Strand hosts international regattas and the Milford Cruising Club and marina are much-loved fixtures of the Milford community.

There's a popular coastal walk between Takapuna and Milford with plenty to see, including stunning harbour views, sculptural rock pools – and multi-million dollar seaside mansions.

Lake Pupuke is popular for sailing, wind-surfing and rowing, with school rowing teams chopping their oars through the waters at day break. For swimmers preferring the indoors, there's the Takapuna Aquatic Centre on the lake edge.

Other local sports facilities include the 18-hole Takapuna Golf Course and driving range and a 10-pin bowling centre.

For the culturally-inclined, the North Shore

Literary Walk encompasses Takapuna (as well as Devonport and Castor Bay) and commemorates well-known North Shore authors. Indoor amenities include the Pumphouse Theatre and gallery, the Bruce Mason Centre and the Berkeley Cinema complex.

The flourishing dine-out scene includes restaurants, gourmet takeaways and cafes along Hurstmere Rd and down the side streets. Milford has fewer eateries. Nighclubbers have the Poenamo Hotel on Northcote Rd.

Real Estate
Trends

In Takapuna, Milford and Hauraki there's steady demand from buyers from throughout greater Auckland and overseas. During the recent property boom, waterfront property out-stripped the rest. A locally-based American recently bought a 2ha property in Gibbons Rd for $12.78 million – breaking the previous record of $8.4 million paid by an ex-pat Kiwi for a neighbouring property.

Agents often have waiting lists for older homes on generous sites and building sites.

The sausage-block units of yesteryear remain popular with investors and older people downsizing from large homes.

There's now little difference between clifftop prices in Milford and Takapuna. Milford may be a little cheaper but only because properties are generally smaller.

Clifftop and beachfront prices range from $4 million to $10 million.

For first, or even second home buyers, there's little under $500,000 for the most basic house in the most modest part of town.

Rental and investment

There's a wide variety of rental stock throughout the area. Properties on Takapuna's premium Golden Mile return between $800 and $1000 a week, with demand coming from corporates for staff on transfer or people between million dollar house purchases who need a temporary home.

Best streets

Any street east of Lake Rd towards Takapuna Beach, for example Minnehaha Ave, Brett Ave and O'Neills Ave. In Milford, the streets between Kitchener Rd and the beach – Tiri Rd, Cecil Rd. At Hauraki, it's Clifton Rd, overlooking the beach.

Look Out ⓘ

Big trees blocking out your sea views? As with other seaside suburbs, there are strict rules about even pruning those glorious seaside pohutukawas, so you'll need to talk to your local council for advice and formal consent. North Shore City Council will despatch an arborist for professional advice before any work can start.

Why I live there

Entertainer
Tina Cross

For a girl who grew up in South Auckland, the suburb of Milford was, Tina says, "somewhere else on the planet". She knew nothing about the North Shore as a place to live until she spotted the Milford house on the market that has now been her family's home for 13 years. Her savvy instincts told her that it was worth a drive over the harbour bridge to check out the property.

Tina and her husband Wayne, a West Auckland boy who also knew nothing about the North Shore, fell in love with the 1970s-style house and its picturesque cul-de-sac location running down to Milford beach.

It's the only home their children Sean (15) and Leah (11) have ever known, and they've made wonderful friendships among the swag of kids who were always playing in the street.

Says Tina: "It's the beach, the location, the kids and the fact that we're all like-minded people, which makes Milford really special to me."

House prices

Unit	
Bedrooms	🛏 🛏 🛏
Price	$320,000 – $350,000

Basic house	
Bedrooms	🛏 🛏 🛏
Price	$450,000 – $500,000

Modern executive house inland	
	$700,000 – $1.5 million
Near the sea	$1.5 million – $3 million +

Apartment	
	$800,000 – $1 million
Penthouse	$1.2 million – $1.5 million

Rental prices

Unit	
Bedrooms	🛏 🛏
Price	$280 –$350/wk

House	
Bedrooms	🛏 🛏 🛏
Price	$400 – $480/wk
Near the sea	$550 – $750/wk

Townhouse	
Bedrooms	🛏 🛏 🛏 🛏
Price	$500 – $650/wk

Executive house near the sea	
Price	$800 – $1000/wk

Travel times

CBD	off-peak 15 min
	peak 45 min
Harbour bridge	off-peak 5-10min
	peak 20 min
Airport off-peak	40-45 min

Regular bus services into the city via the bus lanes help peak-time traffic flows a little. By car it can be a slow trip, as Takapuna traffic merges with Devonport traffic at Esmonde Rd.

Urban Express runs a bus service from Bayswater through Hauraki and from Milford into the CBD.

This part of Auckland is a seductive mix of city living and casual beachy lifestyle. The beaches and bays are pretty, and easy to get at. The unspoiled Long Bay reserve is fairly unique for a city this size and the shops at Browns Bay have a laid-back feel that makes you slow down to an amble. The schools are excellent and the houses reasonably affordable. This area still has the wide-open feel you get at the edge of suburbia – even though the city is growing beyond it. As the neighbouring Albany infrastructure continues to grow, the upper bays appeal to an increasing number of people whose work is based there. For those who prefer greener pastures to come home to, the lifestyle blocks at Okura are a bit of a best-kept secret but probably the most accessible in Auckland.

Who lives there?

Buyers stepping up to a coastal lifestyle move here from the cheaper inland shore suburbs. Those concerned about schooling will settle for any style of house in the desired zone. South African, Asian and English migrants like putting down roots here – the African Carnival looks set to become an annual mid-March fixture. Browns Bay's apartments are giving locals the chance to downsize from family homes to holiday-style living.

Overseas buyers include one American couple who paid $665,000 for a holiday apartment that they say would be worth $6.5 million on the Californian coast.

Typical dwellings

Sea views are the big focus of all the homes built anywhere along the bays. The large

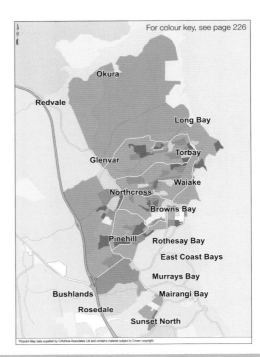

For colour key, see page 226

Okura
Redvale
Long Bay
Glenvar
Torbay
Waiake
Northcross
Browns Bay
Pinehill
Rothesay Bay
East Coast Bays
Murrays Bay
Bushlands
Mairangi Bay
Rosedale
Sunset North

Pinpoint Map data supplied by Critchlow Associates Ltd and contains material subject to Crown copyright.

Population profile	Population in 2001 28,626	% Aged under 15 years 21.21	% Aged over 65 Years 10.68
% European 86.08	% Maori 4.37	% Pacific Peoples 1.36	% Asian 8.79

numbers of 1970s architecturally designed family homes give the area a sense of individuality that is lacking in some parts of Torbay/Glenvar, where streets were defined by the housing development company of the day. Newer houses tend to have a Mediterranean style and subtropical gardens. Pinehill has big new homes popular with Asian buyers. Browns Bay's village now includes several apartment developments.

Amenities
Schools ★★★★★

The local high school, Long Bay College in Torbay, is nationally known for its creative arts and technology teaching. It's much smaller than the huge Rangitoto College, further down the bays, but that appeals to many parents keen for what they see as more personalised schooling. Some homes at the southern end of the upper bays are in zone for Rangitoto College, but it pays to check with the school.

For a full list, see page 272.

Shops ★★★

Browns Bay's village is the retail hub of the East Coast Bays. With the beach just 100m away, it may be casual but has everything – and everyone – covered whether you're a tweenager, a surfie beach bum, a lady who lunches or the pooch of such a lady who needs a diamante collar. There's the major supermarket chains, Whitcoulls, Farmers, banks and supermarkets, boutique shops, two fabulous pet stores plus multiple choices of short-order food and coffee short or long. On Sundays, there's a market.

Torbay has a small shopping centre and several restaurants and takeaway bars. For Okura and Long Bay residents, the nearest shops are Torbay, Albany and Northcross. The Albany Mega Centre is only a quick drive along Oteha Valley Rd.

Leisure ★★★

All the beaches are beauties, but Waiake Beach is the best. Its 1ha beachfront reserve has an impressive block of phoenix palms and Norfolk Island pines, as well as being home to Torbay Sailing Club.

The hugely popular Long Bay Regional Park has a 1km long golden beach, with a restaurant and playground. You can't fish or collect seafood because it's within the Long Bay-Okura Marine Reserve.

The northern East Coast Bays area has plenty of typically Kiwi sports grounds and clubs as well as the East Coast Bays Leisure Centre in Browns Bay. The Pupuke Golf Course is close by.

Art Ducko at Torbay is a popular local restaurant. Browns Bay has a great selection of eateries including Spaghetti and Speakers Corner Ale House.

Real Estate
Trends

Cyclical real estate movement is stalling the upper end of the market, from $1 million and up, on the seaward side of Beach Rd. Demand for homes in the $600,000 to $800,000 bracket is huge. Interestingly, Asian families who came to the area four or five years ago are starting to adopt the Kiwi practice of trading up towards the sea views.

Apartment dwellers have moved within Browns Bay and others, including professionals, have come from other parts of the North Shore. With the city council looking at changing some of the light industrial zones of Browns Bay to mixed use, there are more apartment developments likely.

Torbay and Glenvar were originally the cheaper areas when they were built by developers for the then first home market. They've picked up solid capital gains recently. New homes without views in the Pinehill area behind Rangitoto College range in price from $600,000 to $800,000. Basic homes on full sites still fetch much the same prices as those on subdivided half sites. It's difficult to find a home close to the water (east of Beach Rd) for under $600,000.

Rental and investment

Rental returns are standard throughout these bays. Demand for furnished executive homes comes largely from English and South African migrants looking for six to 12 months tenancies while they settle into the area, and there's generally plenty available.

Best streets

All the coastal top-spots, including Sharon Rd in Browns Bay, Churchill Rd in Rothesay Bay, and Cliff Rd and Gilberd Pl in Torbay.

House prices

Apartment	
Bedroom	🛏
Price	$300,000
Penthouse (two-bedroom)	$900,000

Basic house	
Bedrooms	🛏 🛏 🛏
Price	$350,000 – $370,000

Ten-year-old house	
Bedrooms	🛏 🛏 🛏 🛏
Price	$400,000 – $500,000

Executive house away from the water	
Bedrooms	🛏 🛏 🛏 🛏
Price	$500,000 – $600,000
Close to water	$900,000 plus

Clifftop mansion	
Price	$2 million – $5 million

Rental prices

House	
Bedrooms	🛏 🛏
Price	$280 – $320/wk
Bedrooms	🛏 🛏 🛏
Price	$350 – $380/wk

Executive house with sea views	
Bedrooms	🛏 🛏 🛏
Price	$400 – $450/wk

Travel times

CBD	off-peak 25 – 30 min
	peak 45 – 50 min
Northern motorway	10 min
Airport	50 min
Milford mall	15 min
Albany Mega Centre	10 – 15 min
Massey University in Albany	15 min

Stagecoach provides bus services through the area to Takapuna and Auckland's CBD. One goes along Beach Rd, another along East Coast Rd. Buses run every 30 minutes during the weekend.

Service towns don't come much prettier than Warkworth. It's in an idyllic spot that hugs the languid curves of the Mahurangi River. Little more than 2.5 square kilometers in area, it fizzes with community spirit and is the gateway to the busy road to Matakana, Omaha, Leigh and Kawau Island. Less than 10 years ago, Matakana was a two-shop, pub stop, Holden and Harley Davidson drive-thru town – but things are different now. It has a high-profile market and a new village plan which includes an arthouse movie theatre, wine centre and boutique foodie and health shops. Omaha is best known for the huge contemporary holiday homes that rise out of the sand dunes. Snells Beach is the hub of the Mahurangi peninsula and has a coastal/suburban flavour to match.

Who lives there?

Warkworth, Snells Beach and Leigh have a mix of young families and long-term older residents. They're very popular with elderly people retiring from Auckland and professionals commuting to work in Albany and the North Shore. There's a great community spirit. Local people stumped up $50 a plank to fund the riverside boardwalk; sausage sizzles and garage sales pay for the museum building's upkeep.

Omaha is a high profile spot for those with enough cash to fund a sophisticated holiday home (not a bach). It had some 110 permanent families at the last unofficial count, but the population swells to more than 1000 during summer as hip young holiday makers and families take to the sand and the surf to soak up the status and the sunshine.

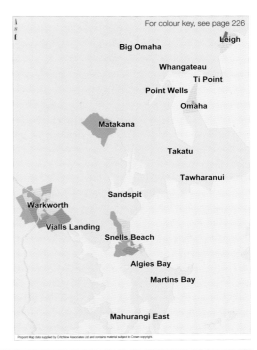

For colour key, see page 226

Leigh
Big Omaha
Whangateau
Ti Point
Point Wells
Omaha
Matakana
Takatu
Tawharanui
Sandspit
Warkworth
Vialls Landing
Snells Beach
Algies Bay
Martins Bay
Mahurangi East

Pinpoint Map data supplied by Critchlow Associates Ltd and contains material subject to Crown copyright.

Population profile	Population in 2001 7,836	% Aged Under 15 years 20.52	% Aged over 65 Years 20.75
% European 91.42	% Maori 7.27	% Pacific Peoples 1.34	% Asian 1.91

Matakana has some 250 residents and 60 houses, about half of which are long-time residents. It takes 20 years here to qualify as a "local".

Typical dwellings

There's a wide mix of housing in each community. Warkworth has villas and weatherboard houses, and stylish renovations of these. Two new subdivisions off Falls Rd and Pulham Rd will offer about 50 houses on 0.4ha-plus sections.

Matakana's mix of traditional bungalows, farm cottages and relocated villas now includes a group of new brick and tile houses in a development behind the bakery. Famous for its lifestyle, Matakana has older houses around the village and lifestyle blocks around the fringes.

Leigh has everything from caravans on 600–700m2 sites to large coastal lifestyle blocks. There's also the Wonderview subdivision of large executive homes.

Old Omaha to the north was developed in three stages from the 1960s to the 1980s, so there's everything from board-and-batten, group-style housing to two-storey houses that were the fashion of the day. To the south, houses are sprouting up in the 600-section The Dunes development where strict design criteria have to be met.

Amenities
Schools ★★★★

Preschoolers and primary school children are catered for in both Warkworth and Matakana. Snells Beach children travel to school in Matakana. A primary school is to be built in Dawsons Rd, Snells Beach, with a tentative opening date of 2007. A Ministry of Education decision is due soon on whether it will include intermediate-age children or primary-age only. Mahurangi College in Warkworth is the local secondary school. For a full list, see page 272.

Shops ★★★★

Warkworth's main shopping area runs through the centre of town, and offers everything from fishing gear to flooring, home appliances to chiropractic care.

There's a dairy on the road to Omaha, but no shops in Omaha itself. Five shops and a restaurant have been designated in the latest Omaha development but they haven't been built yet.

Snells Beach has its Mahurangi Shopping Centre, including The Warehouse. Leigh has a general store and a fish and chip shop.

Leisure ★★★★

Being outdoors is everything here, whether it's canoeing down the Puhoi River or riding horses, admiring the tuataras and water dragons at New Zealand's only reptile zoo at Leigh or peering at the fish at Goat Island Marine Reserve from the glass-bottom tourist

boat. Boat tours of the Mahurangi River are popular. The less adventurous can stroll along the river's edge.

The jewel in the crown is Tawharanui Regional Park, the first to be granted "open sanctuary" status – allowing the public access to the landscape that's a pest-free haven for native plants and animals. Scandrett Regional Park, which opened in 2004, is a short drive beyond Snells Beach. The ferry to Kawau Island leaves from Sandspit.

Omaha has bowls, a harbourside golf course and an ocean beach.

Warkworth has many historical treasures, including the Warkworth Museum, the Parry Kauri Park, the site of New Zealand's first Portland cement operation and the Kowhai Park limestone kilns dating back to the 1880s. The Warkworth show grounds hosts an annual A&P show every January and riding events throughout the year.

There are a handful of art galleries and foodies have the Matakana Village Farmers' Market for artisan foods and wine. There's also the Matakana Country Park that includes an art gallery, hands-on pottery and farmyard animals.

Warkworth cafes include the River View Plaza Cafe and the Queen St Cafe. Towards Matakana there's the Morris & James cafe, the Dragonfly Cafe, the Rusty Pelican and the Matakana pub. At Leigh there's the Sawmill Cafe. There are plenty of wineries, some with cafes/restaurants including Ascension, Heron's Flight, Ransom and Mahurangi Estate.

Real Estate
Trends

Interest by ex-pat Kiwis is as strong as ever in the area as is the interest among Asian inves-

tors for large tracts of coastal land that might be ripe for future subdivision.

Prices have jumped hugely recently and there is a big difference between first entry prices and those at the top. In Warkworth, strong interest in subdivision sites has seen many on-sold with significant capital gain even before the title has been issued. Executive houses in Warkworth sell quickly and hold their value well because they're in comparatively short supply.

Values continue to go up in Matakana. As an example, in three years, a typical 1.2ha farm in Matakana has risen in value from $350,000 to $650,000, according to one local resident. Large blocks of bare land around the coastline continue to carry rising multi-million dollar price tags.

Rental and investment

Rentals are similar throughout the area. Homes at the Wellsford end of Warkworth rent for less. Apart from the odd exception, $400 is top rental for big homes here.

Best streets

Westpark Glen and Coquette St in Warkworth (they're the winners of Warkworth's annual Best Street competition).

Travel times
From Warkworth

CBD	off-peak 60 – 90 min
	peak 2 hours
Leigh	25 min
Matakana	10 min
Omaha	15 mins
Snells Beach	off-peak 10 min
	peak 20 min

Intercity Coachlines and Northliner Express Coachlines operate daily services between Warkworth and Auckland's CBD. There is no public transport serving Leigh, Snells Beach and Matakana.

Why I live there

Unofficial mayor David Parker

David Parker grew up in Matakana, Snells Beach and Warkworth and his community work CV stretches to some 13 groups that he has either started or coordinated. He chaired the committee that organised the town's 150-year celebrations in 2004. David loves Warkworth with a passion. "It's the beauty, the natural environment and the people. It's everything that small town New Zealand really cherishes. I love the ambience of the village and the river that meanders through the historic village. It's the people who make this place such a success with their huge contribution."

House prices
Warkworth
House

Bedrooms	🛏🛏
Price	$280,000 – $300,000
Bedrooms	🛏🛏🛏
Price	$370,000 – $450,000

Executive house

Bedrooms	🛏🛏🛏🛏
Price	$450,000 – $550,000

1.2ha section

Price	$230,000 plus

Matakana / Leigh
Caravan on 600m2

Price	$280,000 – $300,000

House on 1100m2

Bedrooms	🛏🛏🛏
Price	$420,000 – $450,000
Bedrooms	🛏🛏🛏🛏
Price	$355, 000 to 500,000

Villa on 2ha

Price	$500,000 – $600,000

Large coastline property

Price	$3 million

Omaha
House

Bedrooms	🛏🛏🛏
Price	$500,000

1970s house

Bedrooms	🛏🛏🛏
Price	$600,000 – $700,000

Modern house with beach frontage

Price	$2 million

Rental prices
House

Bedrooms	🛏🛏
Price	$220 – $260/wk
Bedrooms	🛏🛏🛏
Price	$260 – $350/wk
Bedrooms	🛏🛏🛏🛏
Price	$300 – $380/wk

Westlake is the name synonymous with its two local and highly regarded secondary schools. The area is quiet, solid and, well, just nice and handy to everything that's important to the people of the North Shore – shops, beaches, the motorways and the cafes. It's right next to Takapuna and Milford but is a lot more affordable. Sunnynook used to be one of the shore's "nappy valley" suburbs but is now shrugging off its more down-market image. Forrest Hill and Crown Hill are more upmarket and popular with people who can't quite afford the seaward east coast bays. Many homes on elevated properties here have fabulous views of the city. For a group of suburbs that are often overlooked, these four have a lot going for them ... once you take a proper look.

Who lives there?

Affordable housing compared with Takapuna and Milford and good schools appeal to families looking to get established and raise their youngsters. For those for whom it's "the shore or nothing", this is a choice location close to Milford, CBD-style amenities in Takapuna and the beaches of the East Coast bays.

Forrest Hill and Crown Hill attract modest income-earners who can't afford near water prices and professionals who choose not to pay them.

Sunnynook was created as a subdivision of affordable housing and it's a natural stepping stone for young families moving up from neighbouring Glenfield. The Smales Farm Business Park by the Northcote motorway interchange, adds to the appeal of the area as a place to live close to work.

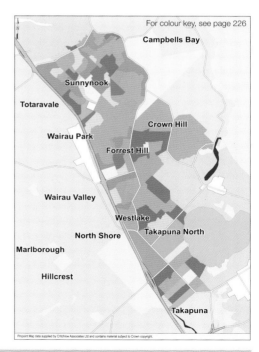

For colour key, see page 226

Campbells Bay
Sunnynook
Totaravale
Crown Hill
Wairau Park
Forrest Hill
Wairau Valley
Westlake
North Shore | Takapuna North
Marlborough
Hillcrest
Takapuna

Pinpoint Map data supplied by Critchlow Associates Ltd and contains material subject to Crown copyright.

Population profile	Population in 2001 20,631	% Aged Under 15 years 18.44	% Aged over 65 Years 14.70
% European 74.76	% Maori 4.57	% Pacific Peoples 2.02	% Asian 18.92

Typical dwellings

There is good solid Kiwi housing here. Sunnynook's group homes have lasted the distance. In Forrest Hill there's more choice of housing styles that reflects the era in which sprawling farmland was carved up into residential plots 40 years ago.

There a plenty of 1970s style homes which suit a contemporary renovation much better than the bungalows and villas of older areas. Forrest Hill has new executive housing stock off Manutara Ave, which brings welcome diversity to the area and lifts its profile.

When Sunnynook was subdivided and built by developers, buyers had several different housing plans to choose from which meant that houses of similar styles were dotted throughout the community.

Amenities
Schools ★★★★

One of the biggest drawcards here is Westlake Boys and Westlake Girls. Co-ed school options are limited. Primary and intermediate schooling is well catered for with primary schools in both Sunnynook and Forrest Hill. Wairau intermediate school is in Forrest Hill.

For a full list see page 272.

Shops ★★★

Sunnynook's shopping centre includes a Foodtown supermarket as well as the mix of bakery, video, chemist shops and the like. Forrest Hill has no local shops. Large-scale retail therapy is easily satisfied close to home with malls in Glenfield and Takapuna and Milford as well as the bulk retail centre at Wairau Park.

Leisure ★★

A couple of eateries in Sunnynook include a large Chinese restaurant. There isn't a cafe scene as such; that requires a short trip to Takapuna, Milford or Mairangi Bay. This is where everyone here heads to for the restaurants too.

Parks and facilities include Becroft Park for rugby and soccer and Greville Park which has soccer grounds. The beach is a short drive from everywhere here.

Real Estate Trends

Forrest Hill is both a favourite middle-class destination and a popular stepping stone for those who aspire to live closer to the water.

Homeowners continue to move from the neighbouring, less desirable suburbs to settle long term. Elevated homes with views back across the city in Forrest Hill fetch good prices as do the Crown Hill homes that catch a water outlook.

Some parts of Sunnynook also have views.

Developers continue to look for older properties that have potential for rebuilding or renovating.

The single-level brick-and-tile units continue to appeal to elderly people and are also popular with first homeowners. Understandably, homes near the main arterials and the motorway are much cheaper than those in streets close to the water, which makes them a more affordable first entry point.

Real estate values are continuing their steady rise. Steady movement continues to move Sunnynook's houses (not units) out of the first entry range.

Executive homes in the Manutara Ave estate sell in the high $500,000s and early $600,000s.

Rental and investment

Location is a big factor here because there are not-so-good, good and even better areas to rent in. Elevated sections and garaging cost more. Sunnynook's cheaper homes fetch $20 or $30 a week less than Westlake/Forrest Hill.

Best streets

Sycamore Dr in Sunnynook; Knightsbridge Ave, Grenada Ave and Ravenswood Ave in Forrest Hill; Gordon Ave in Crown Hill.

Look Out ⓘ

The schooling here is great but double-check the zones of your preferred school if that's the main reason you're buying in a particular street. Study the school zones at the back of this book, check the school's website and then contact your school in person.

House prices

	Bedrooms	Price
Units	🛏🛏	$300,000 – $330,000
Original house on half site	🛏🛏🛏	$340,000 – $370,000
Basic house on full site	🛏🛏🛏	$320,000 – $420,000
Large modern house		$650,000 – $750,000

Rental prices

	Bedrooms	Price
Unit in Westlake/Forrest Hill	🛏🛏	$275 – $350/wk
House	🛏🛏🛏	$360 – $450/wk
New executive house	🛏🛏🛏🛏	$430 – $500/wk
House in Sunnynook	🛏🛏🛏	$330 – $375/wk
	🛏🛏🛏🛏	$380 – $400/wk

Travel times

CBD	off-peak 10 – 15min
	peak 40 min
Airport	50 min
Shopping malls	10 –15min

An upgrade of the Taharoto Rd/Wairau Rd corridor is in the planning stages at the North Shore City Council to relieve one of the city's worst traffic bottlenecks by Westlake Girls College.

A regular bus service runs along East Coast Bays Rd to Takapuna and the CBD.

East

These are some of the scenes evocative of east Auckland: families swimming at safe beaches lined with pohutukawa and Norfolk pines; hectare after hectare of new cloned houses; millions of dollars'-worth of boats bobbing in marinas.

The suburbs of east Auckland have long been the embodiment of New Zealand suburbia. Pakuranga was known as Vim Valley in the 1970s, after the cleaning product endorsed on TV by housewives in Pakuranga – everything was shiny, new and clean.

Botany Downs has taken over the mantle of super-suburbanness now, and it's emblematic in another way. The eastern suburbs have long been part of Manukau City but, until Botany Downs

and its neighbours were developed, the eastern and southern parts of that city were physically separated by farmland. Now the farmland has become suburbs, and the division has become blurred.

A major drawcard for this part of Auckland is the proximity to the sea. The area is so built-up that you often can't see the ocean until you're right next to it, but it's still very accessible. The beaches have white sand and are, in general, safe for swimming. The convoluted coastline and nearness of the islands of the Hauraki Gulf make it a haven for boaties, as the number of boat clubs (and two large marinas) testify.

safe and secure settled suburbia a boatie's dream new, new, new

The horsey set are well established in the east, too. Whitford, Clevedon and Brookby are particularly known as being havens for horse-lovers. Clevedon is home to the busiest polo club in the country; Brookby has a top-rate equestrian centre; and some days in Whitford you can't move for horse floats.

Many eastern residents who commute to Auckland's CBD for work or study have the option of doing so by ferry, from Pine Harbour near Beachlands, or from Half Moon Bay. It makes a very pleasant alternative to a long journey by road. The service would be even better if it were more frequent and cheaper, but both of those qualities should improve as it becomes more widely used.

Suburbs such as Howick have attracted many Asian immigrants in the past decade. While inter-racial relations were strained in many quarters initially, there doesn't seem to be an issue now. Indeed the pakeha population now probably wonder how they survived without the Asian food shops and restaurants which now abound.

AUCKLAND

EAST

In the days when we travelled at a leisurely pace – not by choice, but because we had to – Beachlands and Maraetai were the preserve of farmers and holiday-makers. These settlements have managed to feel removed from the madding crowd for an impressively long time but times are changing. The area's desirable seaside location and relative ease of access to the city means farms are being sold and subdivided. Ironically, the rural landscape provided by the remaining farms helps make the place look attractive to weary city-dwellers. For those who can afford it, these two hamlets are still a great way to hang on to traditional Kiwi family values. Being at the end of the road with no through traffic, Beachlands is especially safe for riding bikes and walking to school.

Who lives there?

These two seaside hamlets are family-oriented communities, popular with lifestylers who want access to the city without having to tolerate crowded suburbs. Indeed, many people moving here are coming from other eastern suburbs – it's sort of a beachy alternative to Clevedon. Being near the sea is a huge bonus for most people.

There isn't a lot of employment here, so most people commute to work. This is still an area where you can expect to know your neighbours and be part of a strong comm-unity network – especially if you're into join-ing community groups.

Although occupants of the two hamlets identify closely with their individual com-munity, a strong spirit unites the two parties, proud as they are of the area in general.

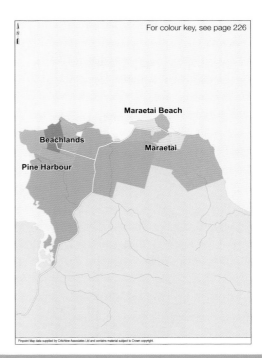

For colour key, see page 226

Maraetai Beach

Beachlands

Maraetai

Pine Harbour

Pinpoint Map data supplied by Critchlow Associates Ltd and contains material subject to Crown copyright.

Population profile	Population in 2001 4,419	% Aged Under 15 years 25.19	% Aged over 65 Years 10.39
% European 89.61	% Maori 7.6	% Pacific Peoples 1.97	% Asian 1.7

Typical dwellings

The fibrolite baches which were the norm here 20 years ago are now a rare and quaint sight. Many have been demolished and replaced with substantial modern homes. Until recently, the area had a fairly even selection of homes from every decade since the 1920s, but new subdivisions mean that large, quality contemporary homes now dominate.

Amenities
Schools ★★

Beachlands and Maraetai each have a combined primary and intermediate school. For the secondary school years, pupils generally go to Howick College: a free bus is provided for the half-hour journey. For a full list, see page 272.

Shops ★★

Most residents take advantage of the fact that they're out of the area almost daily by doing the bulk of their shopping where there's more choice and lower prices. But if you were marooned here indefinitely, it wouldn't be so bad. All the basics are covered, including grocery, hardware, baked goods, grog, pharmaceuticals and videos!

Leisure ★★★

Part of the great Kiwi dream, this area provides easy access to outdoor activities. Beachlands and Maraetai both have great swimming beaches, hence the endless line of day-trippers heading out to Maraetai every sunny summer weekend.

Omana Regional Park, between the two hamlets, has beach, bush and farm.

Neighbouring Te Puru Park has sports fields. Nearby Whitford Forest has tracks for mountain biking, walking and horseriding.

A hidden treasure is Shelly Bay, a classic little east coast beach backed by pohutukawa lined cliffs and reached via a short bush track.

The Formosa Auckland Country Club has a golf course designed by Bob Charles, as well as a small gym, tennis courts and a swimming pool and spa pool with sea views.

Experienced and novice horseriders and sailors are well catered for.

As for dining out, the focus is on takeaways rather than silver service here – which reflects the family-oriented culture rather than any down-at-heel demographic. And let's face it, if you don't feel like catching the ferry into the CBD to make your selection from hundreds of dining establishments, then a picnic on the beach is probably just the ticket.

Real Estate
Trends

Beachlands and Maraetai experienced the highest growth in the wave of Auckland-area sales activity during the recent boom but, while most of the area's sales have levelled out, Maraetai, in particular, has continued on a buoyant path.

The image of Beachlands and Maraetai as backwater locales has definitely changed to one of desirability by Aucklanders and others.

New subdivisions in Beachlands (bye bye, farmland) mean there are sections and new homes available – and lots of construction busy-ness.

There are fewer places available in Maraetai,

generally no more than six at any given time. Prices are very similar in the two areas.

Rental and investment

Rental opportunities are not abundant, especially in Maraetai. The properties are so valuable that investors are looking more for the capital gain on a sale.

Best streets

There's really no unfortunate street in Maraetai. Even Maraetai School Rd, back from the sea, isn't very far back at all.

In Beachlands, the clifftop streets are still the favourites: Hawke Cres, Ealing Cres and First View Ave.

A good address doesn't automatically guarantee top dollar – it's still very dependent on the quality, age and style of the residence.

Why we live there

Artist John Botica and Karen Botica

For John and Karen Botica, Beachlands is heaven. "It's a wonderful enthusiastic community," John says. The couple and their daughter emigrated from Germany six years ago and have lived in Beachlands for three years. "We have visitors come from Europe and they can't believe what we have here – such a beautiful place, with swimming and kayaking at the beach, and everything available that we need, and so close to the city." Since moving to Beachlands, John has discovered artisitic passion and talent, resulting in lavish decoration of their home. He's now busy with commissions for other people.

Look Out ⚠

If you're after a quiet bucolic retreat, this probably isn't it. Sure, it's prettier than most parts of Auckland, but the population is growing very rapidly and it's not the backwater (no seaside pun intended) it was until a few years ago.

Local Hero: Pine Harbour Marina

Arriving at Beachlands by ferry you have the bonus of a tour of the rather splendid Pine Harbour Marina, home to 600 beautiful boats. The marina has a full complement of on-site tradespeople, 24-hour security, a 24-hour fuel service, and a complete haul-out and hard-stand facility, with a boatlifter capable of handling boats up to 28m long and weighing 44 tonnes.

All of this doesn't come cheap: to buy a maritime parking space for your humble nine-metre yacht will cost at least $25,000 a year plus operating fees of more than $460 a quarter. For a 20-metre yacht the website says POA: if you need to ask, you probably can't afford it.

Rental prices

Unit	
Bedrooms	🛏 🛏
Price	$250 – $350/wk
House	
Bedrooms	🛏 🛏 🛏
Price	$350 – $450/wk
Executive house on the water	
Bedrooms	🛏 🛏 🛏 🛏
Price	$700 – $890/wk

House prices

Unit without a view	
Bedrooms	🛏 🛏
Price	$300,000
Bach with a sea view	
Price	$400,000
Good house with a sea view	
Price	$1 million
Modern house	
Bedrooms	🛏 🛏 🛏
Price	$400,000-plus
Executive house	
Bedrooms	🛏 🛏 🛏 🛏
Price	$750,000-plus
Sections	
(only really available in Beachlands, eg, Spinnaker Bay subdivision)	
Price	$250,000

Travel times

From Beachlands

CBD	off peak 40 min
	by ferry 25 min
Southern motorway	20 – 25 min
Airport	25 – 30 min
Manukau City shopping centre	25 min
Botany Town Centre	15 min

The ferry to Auckland's CBD is now sailing hourly and is a wonderful alternative to driving. It takes 25 minutes and services also go to Waiheke and Rakino Islands. From Beachlands, you can walk along the cliff-top or the beach to the ferry terminal at Pine Harbour.

For more information and to keep abreast of the latest schedule changes, visit www.pineharbour.co.nz or telephone 09 536 4725.

Howick & Eastern run buses to and from Maraetai and Beachlands and Auckland on weekdays.

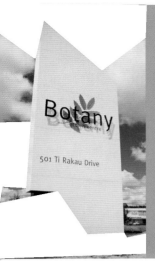

Botany
Town Centre

501 Ti Rakau Drive

It was inevitable that the easy-on-the-eye rural landscape between south and east Auckland would eventually be gobbled up by developers. On the whole, they've done a great job. The area is very popular, and it's a pleasant place to be because of good urban planning. Facilities are good, especially considering how recent this all is, and the Botany Town Centre has become renowned throughout Auckland for its innovative street-based design. If you go to Botany Downs and its surrounding suburbs and feel a bit swamped by the myriad copy-cat residences and the huge number of short curved streets, drive up to the high point of Whitford Rd for a good view of the extent of it all – it's certainly very impressive.

Who lives there?

This is a racially-mixed middle class area with many immigrants – those from Asia make up perhaps a third of the population. There are also South Africans and Middle Easterners. The variety of nationalities was obviously expected by those who dish out the street names: they include Billabong Pl, Kilimanjaro Dr and Napa Ct! Whatever the nationality, the family profile tends towards those with teenagers or kids who have grown up and left home. Judging by the number of signs outside houses advertising services such as beauty therapy and hairdressing, they're an enterprising bunch.

Residents are drawn by the newness of the houses and the amenities. Many people have relocated here from more established parts of east Auckland, seeking low-

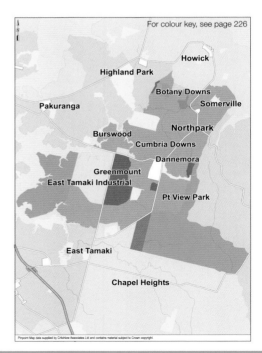

For colour key, see page 226

Howick
Highland Park
Botany Downs
Somerville
Pakuranga
Northpark
Burswood
Cumbria Downs
Dannemora
Greenmount
East Tamaki Industrial
Pt View Park
East Tamaki
Chapel Heights

Pinpoint Map data supplied by Critchlow Associates Ltd and contains material subject to Crown copyright.

Population profile	Population in 2001 26,064	% Aged Under 15 years 22.43	% Aged over 65 Years 7.38
% European 62.43	% Maori 3.36	% Pacific Peoples 1.55	% Asian 31.64

maintenance homes with desirable features such as internal-access double garaging and ensuites.

Typical dwellings

Because this area was farmland just a few years ago, the houses are virtually all new. Brick-and-tile four-bedroom one-level houses dominate, although there are also terraces. There's a definite sense here of the homogenous American suburban dream: although the reality of land prices (and people's desire for big houses) means that the sections are smaller than they'd be in a dream. The style of some of the more dramatic homes, where classical-style columns support two-storey-high porticos, seems ostentatious to some.

The Sacramento terrace housing development bordering the town centre was seen as innovative at the time but the dream soon came unstuck when many of the dwellings were affected by leaky building syndrome.

Amenities
Schools ★★★★

Botany Downs Secondary College opened for business in 2004 – and won an award from the NZ Institute of Architects, who described it as "a spectacular learning environment". That's more than could be said for most high schools! On a smaller and less dramatic scale, Catholic high school Sancta Maria College also opened in 2004. For a full list, see page 272.

Shops ★★★★★

They sure know how to do retail therapy around here! Botany Town Centre endeavours to deliver the best of both retail worlds – it's mall and mainstreet, all bundled into one mega shopping experience. It attracts curious sightseers from all over, just as the first shopping malls must have a couple of decades ago.

Like the residential development, it all feels a little unreal, like you might have stepped into a movie set. They've done good work putting lots of architectural variety into the shop fronts, which should help it to age gracefully.

In 2004 an eight-screen Berkeley cinema opened on-site, as well as the new library.

Leisure ★★★

Botany Downs will soon be rivalling Ponsonby Rd for the number of cafes per kilometre – they're fast becoming a standard part of the local social scene.

And as long as shopping is your idea of leisure, you won't put a foot wrong here. There is also 10-pin bowling and ice skating on offer just over the road from Botany Town Centre. Quiet walks in the country are a little further down the road, but they're not what most people come here for.

All manner of land sports and maritime activities are available in nearby Howick. Lloyd Elsmore Park in Pakuranga has excellent recreational facilities, including a swimming pool complex.

Real Estate
Trends

The booming real estate market of the past couple of years has now levelled off. The strongest demand is at the lower half of the market and for those in the highest bracket. A year ago everybody wanted to live near the town centre; now Botany College (which opened in 2004) is the big draw card.

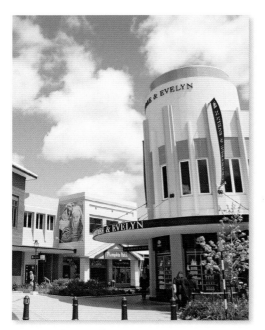

Rental and investment

The level of demand for rental properties fluctuates greatly, but this is considered a safe area to live, with good schools, so the demand will always be there.

Best streets

Fairfield Lane is sought-after because it has a good number of masonry homes which look established and respectable. Also popular are John Brooke Cres, Brook Ridge Rise, and anything near the new Botany College.

Look Out ⚠

Only time will tell how well this area will mature. The newness of everything is quite attractive, but obviously won't last – there is a certain sameness to the area which might become claustrophobic for many Kiwis.

House prices

Unit	
Bedrooms	🛏 🛏
Price	$260,000 – $310,000
House	
Bedrooms	🛏 🛏 🛏
Price	$360,000 – $410,000
Executive house	
Bedrooms	🛏 🛏 🛏 🛏
Price	up to $700,000

Rental prices

Apartment	
Bedrooms	🛏
Price	$260 – $300/wk
Bedrooms	🛏 🛏
Price	$300 – $350/wk
Bedrooms	🛏 🛏 🛏
Price	$350 – $400/wk
House	
Bedrooms	🛏 🛏
Price	$280 – $320/wk
Bedrooms	🛏 🛏 🛏
Price	$380 – $420/wk
Bedrooms	🛏 🛏 🛏 🛏
Price	$450 – $550/wk

Travel times

From Botany Downs	
CBD	off-peak 25 min
	peak 50-60 min
Southern motorway	10 min
Airport	25 min

There is a regular bus service provided by Howick & Eastern; the bus takes about an hour from Botany Town Centre to Britomart. Another option is to bus to the Half Moon Bay ferry and get into town by sea.

Bucklands Beach and Eastern Beach occupy a spectacular little peninsula that reaches as far north as St Heliers – but the area is so built up that it's perfectly possible to be unaware of the fact that you're on such a narrow piece of land. That is, until you reach Musick Pt at the tip of the peninsula, and the fabulous 180-degree panorama of the Hauraki Gulf and its islands opens up to you. Browns Island seems so close you could almost leap down on to it. (No, please don't try it.) Apart from the hidden drama of the geography, these suburbs feel like any established eastern suburb with pleasant family homes and leafy streets. It's a very settled place, with people staying put for a long time because they love the place so much.

Who lives there?

Families who appreciate being near the sea have long gravitated to this area. They also appreciate the good schooling available and, to a certain extent, the relative isolation of the peninsula.

While many properties are the preserve of the wealthy, there is also a range of more affordable properties, which means a good mix in the population. The residents here are predominantly pakeha and Asian.

Typical dwellings

Because the area has been developed over many decades, there is no such thing as a typical style of house. Many homes, though, are large and set on lovingly landscaped sections. Those with sea views make the best of them with huge expanses of window.

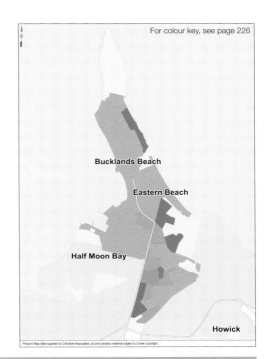

For colour key, see page 226

Bucklands Beach

Eastern Beach

Half Moon Bay

Howick

Pinpoint Map data supplied by Critchlow Associates Ltd and contains material subject to Crown copyright

Population profile	Population in 2001 10,875	% Aged Under 15 years 21.63	% Aged over 65 Years 9.57
% European 72.3	% Maori 2.57	% Pacific Peoples 1.32	% Asian 23.48

Away from the sea views, there are more modest townhouses and units.

Amenities
Schools ★★★★

There is no shortage of good educational institutions here which is a major drawcard for families. Waimokia School is a special-needs primary.

Macleans College is the big cheese among high schools, and being in zone means a lot to people (and to the house prices they pay). For a full list, see page 272.

Shops ★★★

All the basics are catered for at small centres dotted around the peninsula, but for anything major you need to venture further afield to Highland Park, Howick, Pakuranga or Botany Downs. They're also the places to head for when you want to dine out.

Leisure ★★★★

The Howick Golf Course at Musick Pt is a treat, even if you have no interest in golf. It looks like an old-fashioned park, complete with pot-holed road wending its way through the golf course. Right at the tip of the penin-

sula at Musick Pt is a wonderful Art Deco building, built in 1939 as a base for marine radio communications and now leased by a group of amateur radio enthusiasts.

Yachties are well served of course, with the Bucklands Beach Yacht Club and the Half Moon Bay Marina, as well as public boat ramps at both Bucklands and Eastern Beach. The latter has a ski lane, picnic area and children's playground.

There are tennis clubs and, not far away, the various delights of Lloyd Elsmore Park in Pakuranga.

There are several beach-themed restaurants in Eastern Beach, and a plethora of ethnic eateries in other nearby eastern suburbs.

Real Estate
Trends

Bucklands Beach is seeing a lot of redevelopment and renovations. Cliff-top homes, in particular, are soaring in value thanks to those unbeatable sea views, and a lot of money is being spent on making them into top-notch contemporary homes.

Anything with sea views (and, preferably, Macleans College zoning) is seen as a great investment.

After a period of giddy increases, prices here have levelled out somewhat.

Rental and investment

The range of rental prices is huge, affected by such factors as location, view, age and quality of construction.

Best streets

The Parade and Clovelly Rd are the places to be if you've got big money to spend on a huge view.

Local Hero: Musick Pt

Musick Pt, on the end of the peninsula, is home to a wonderful Art Deco building constructed in 1939 as a base for marine radio communic-ations. It's now leased by a group of amateur radio enthusiasts, and it's well worth the slow pot-holed drive through the course of the Howick Golf Club to get there.

The fabulous sea views north into the Hauraki Gulf include Browns Island (Motukorea), which is just off the point, surprisingly close to the mainland.

House prices

<u>Unit</u>

Bedrooms	🛏 🛏
Price	$300,000 plus

<u>House</u>

Bedrooms	🛏 🛏 🛏
Price	$350,000 – $400,000, up to $900,000 with a view

<u>Executive house</u>

Bedrooms	🛏 🛏 🛏 🛏 🛏
Price	$500,000 – $900,000 +

Rental prices

<u>House</u>

Bedroom	🛏
Price	$180 – $240/wk
Bedrooms	🛏 🛏
Price	$260 – $330/wk
Bedrooms	🛏 🛏 🛏
Price	$330 – $420/wk
Bedrooms	🛏 🛏 🛏 🛏
Price	$440 – $600/wk
Bedrooms	🛏 🛏 🛏 🛏 🛏
Price	$520 – $800/wk

Travel times

CBD	off-peak 30-45 min peak 90 min
Southern motorway	20 min
Airport	30 min
Manukau City shops	20-30 min
Botany Town Centre	15 min

There are regular buses to the CBD and to Manukau. There is also a regular ferry service from the adjacent suburb of Half Moon Bay.

Beautiful but not bland, Half Moon Bay has much to brag about - beaches, boat ramps and a marina, a large park and several great shopping centres close by. With its waterside areas and views along the Tamaki River and into the Hauraki Gulf, it typifies the modern Kiwi suburban dream in many ways. Developed in the early 1970s, Half Moon Bay was soon joined by its neighbours Sunnyhills and Farm Cove, which share in the waterside location and have become very desirable places to live. Unlike other newer eastern suburbs, the streetscapes are leafy and the houses fairly diverse and interesting, ranging from renovated original houses to some grand contemporary homes. These suburbs offer all the modern family could ever want.

Who lives there?

People who appreciate the sea and the beach feel right at home here. It's considered a great place to raise children; the schools are good and the house prices not astronomical. Hence, it's filled with many families mainly with school-age and teenage kids. Residents are very comfortable financially and own their own homes.

Once the kids have grown up, people tend to stay put, so there is a good mix of generations in the area.

Typical dwellings

Although there is a huge range of styles from the past four decades of development, those that really stand out are the palatial waterfront residences, many of them with a nod to Mediterranean style.

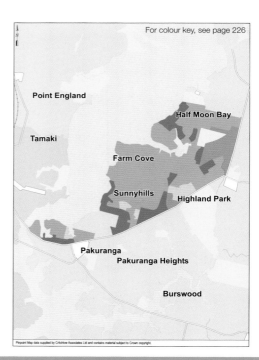

For colour key, see page 226

Point England

Half Moon Bay

Tamaki

Farm Cove

Sunnyhills

Highland Park

Pakuranga

Pakuranga Heights

Burswood

Pinpoint Map data supplied by Critchlow Associates Ltd and contains material subject to Crown copyright.

Population profile	Population in 2001 9,150	% Aged Under 15 years 20.79	% Aged over 65 Years 10.62
% European 71.64	% Maori 4.33	% Pacific Peoples 9.05	% Asian 21.74

There are certainly many 1970s and 1980s houses on generous sections, many updated and refurbished. But if you're into retro style, you would also easily find a 1970s three-bedroom home in fairly original state.

If you want new, there's the Compass Pt development (see below).

Amenities
Schools ★★★★

Locals are justifiably proud of the great schools they have here, at all levels. St Kentigern College is a private school, originally only for boys but now co-ed. The genders are kept separate within the school during Years 7-10, but they get to mix and mingle in Years 11-13.

For a full list, see page 272.

Shops ★★★

There's no huge mall here, but you're never far from a shop in these suburbs. If you need more than a video, loaf of bread, bunch of flowers or bottle of sauvignon blanc, you only need to head to nearby shopping meccas such as Westfield at Pakuranga, The

Hub or, of course, Botany Town Centre. The marina offers a surprising range of goods and services, including a pharmacy, doctor and hairdresser.

Leisure ★★★★

Residents are spoiled for choice, starting with the beautiful 500-berth marina. There are reserves and parks in every direction, and public boat ramps at Bramley Dr Reserve in Farm Cove and at the Ara Tai Reserve in Half Moon Bay.

Sunnyhills has its own well-regarded tennis club, and there's another nearby in Pakuranga.

Lloyd Elsmore Park is an absolute asset to all the eastern suburbs. Half Moon Bay residents wanting to dine out can catch the ferry to the many splendoured offerings of the CBD, or enjoy the international cuisine at neighbouring suburbs Pakuranga, Highland Park and Howick.

Real Estate
Trends

Half Moon Bay people love the fact that most sections in their area can't be subdivided, so the character of the place is guaranteed to remain similar, if not exactly the same.

One area of major change is the former 6.5ha site of the Pakuranga Children's Health Camp, which has been subdivided into 64 sections and named Compass Pt. Most of the sections sold at auction for between $400,000 and $500,000; one larger one with very good views fetched $1.5million. At the beginning of 2005, about a third of the sections had homes on them, and people were starting to move in. Most of the houses have four, five or more bedrooms. Height restrictions are in force to protect the view as much as possible.

An increase in interest in seaside property, combined with the high prices gained at Compass Pt, last year gave Half Moon Bay properties a bigger boost than other areas.

Rental and investment
Rents here tend to keep pace with those in Howick and Mellons Bay.

Best streets
Takutai Ave residences have an impressive view over Half Moon Bay and the Hauraki Gulf. In Farm Cove and Sunnyhills, desirable streets include Sanctuary Pt, Bramley Dr and Fisher Pde.

House prices

Unit	
Bedrooms	🛏 🛏
Price	$270,000 – $320,000
House	
Bedrooms	🛏 🛏 🛏
Price	$400,000 – $487,000
Executive home	
Bedrooms	🛏 🛏 🛏 🛏
Price	$400,000 – $1.4 million

Rental prices

Unit	
Bedroom	🛏
Price	$180 – 220/wk
House	
Bedrooms	🛏 🛏
Price	$220 – 320/wk
Bedrooms	🛏 🛏 🛏
Price	$300 – 400/wk
Bedrooms	🛏 🛏 🛏 🛏
Price	$400 – 570/wk

Travel times

CBD	off-peak 20 min
	peak 40 min
Southern motorway	5 – 12 min
Airport	25 – 40 min
Manukau City shops	15 min
Botany Town Centre	10 min

There are regular buses to the CBD and to Manukau as well as regular ferry services to the CBD from the marina.

Howick's a bit of a paradox. To many it's been that new area out east but today, by the sheer volume of new suburbs that have sprung up around it, it's now the older kid on the block. To those in the know, it's a place with a strong history. Old, new, take your pick. It has it all. Now a leafy, affluent seaside area, it was settled in the 1850s by Fencibles: retired soldiers and their families who were brought to New Zealand from the British Isles in the 1850s to defend Auckland in return for land. For the next 100 years the town was dominated by holiday homes and farms. The rural land was gradually developed into housing during the 1950s and 1960s – much like Botany Downs in the last few years, although in a more gradual manner.

Who lives there?

The area was particularly popular with Dutch and English immigrants in the 1950s and 1960s, and it has long had more "exotic" foods on offer than other, more staunchly Kiwi areas.

More recently, the immigrants have been South African and Asian – the arrival of the latter group ruffled some feathers for a while, but that doesn't seem to be a problem any more.

There's a strong sense of community here, borne from the fact that there are many established families with older children. Not all of the youngsters move out of the area when they first leave home – there's certainly a good percentage of young professionals and students living near the town centre. When they're ready to settle down and raise

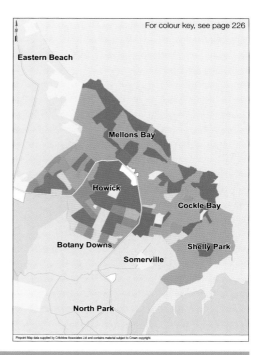

For colour key, see page 226

Eastern Beach

Mellons Bay

Howick

Cockle Bay

Botany Downs

Shelly Park

Somerville

North Park

Pinpoint Map data supplied by Critchlow Associates Ltd and contains material subject to Crown copyright.

Population profile	Population in 2001 18,888	% Aged Under 15 years 20.9	% Aged over 65 Years 12.74
% European 86.47	% Maori 3.72	% Pacific Peoples 1.41	% Asian 9.15

a family, they'll often strive to buy in the area. Boat clubs are very active here – it's a great spot for weekend sailors. And as you'd expect, around the waterfront properties, you'll find some folk with fairly deep pockets.

Typical dwellings

Howick's gradual development over many decades has resulted in a vibrant mix of architectural styles. There are century-old cottages and villas, but the majority are mid-20th-century brick-and-tile or weatherboard homes. This has long been a wealthy area, so the homes tend to be well built and have been well maintained.

The influx of Asian buyers has meant that many of the homes built in the past decade have Botany Downs-style features such as plaster exteriors, double-height porticos and classical-style pillars.

A heritage zone has been imposed on the seaward side of Bleakhouse Rd, which means the sections can't be smaller than 1400m2. In other areas, large sections have succumbed to in-fill housing, particularly in the Macleans College zone.

Amenities
Schools ★★★★

The high quality of the local schools is a matter of considerable pride around here.

Macleans College is particularly admired but only some of Howick is in its coveted zone. For a full list, see page 272.

Shops ★★★★

Howick Village has a wide range of shops, with more than 100 owner-operated stores offering everything from the basics to upmarket luxuries. The footpaths are wide, making this pleasant mainstreet shopping for pedestrians.

At the beginning of 2005, Howick's oldest building, the 99-year-old Rishworth Building, was demolished to make way for a new retail development on the corner of Picton St and Park Hill Rd.

The range of eateries reflects the ethnic diversity and the cosmopolitan nature of the locals – there are Asian restaurants of many flavours, including Japanese, Vietnamese, Malay, Korean and Indian.

Leisure ★★★★

Beautiful beaches below pohutukawa-clad cliffs are a major drawcard for relaxing locals. Although they do get crowded in summer, there are numerous small coves accessed by steep pathways which only a few know about and where you are almost guaranteed peace and quiet.

The reserves are plentiful and beautiful here, too. The Mangemangeroa Reserve walkway from Somerville Rd to the Shelly

Park Yacht Club, part board-walk over mangroves, part beach-walk and part bush-walk, is well worth the effort.

The number of moored yachts and boat ramps testify to the popularity of sailing here. Howick also has sports clubs for cricket, netball, rugby league, squash and tennis, and Cockle Bay has a petanque pitch.

There is an active cultural scene, too, with Howick Little Theatre and the Howick Operatic Society.

Howick Historic Village (physically in Pakuranga, but spiritually in Howick!) is a fascinating showcase of olde worlde every-day life. Here are gathered, and restored some 30 buildings built between 1840 and 1880. Regular live days, when the voluntary staff dress the part and perform such mysterious acts as making butter and writing on slates, are deservedly popular.

Real Estate
Trends

House-proud and spurred on by high real estate values, many Howickians are investing in renovations of older homes. In other cases,

old houses are being removed to make way for a contemporary home.

Most sections which can be subdivided, have been. This area is no longer surround-ed by farmland, so is a bustling, urban place rather than the quaint little villagey back-water which attracted many families in the past. Many people still find it more attractive than the newer eastern options such as Botany Downs.

While prices are showing no signs of flag-ging, the slower rate of Asian immigration which has been seen throughout the whole city during the past year probably means the increases are less in Howick than they might otherwise have been.

Rental and investment

Demand for rental properties is steady – and the tenants are generally of good considerate calibre.

Best streets

Pleasant Pl in Mellons Bay, Island View Tce in Howick, Pounamu Pl in Shelly Beach, Seaview Tce and Pah Rd in Cockle Bay.

Local Hero: Uxbridge Centre

Dynamic, bustling and diverse, Uxbridge Centre is the very model of a community arts and leisure centre. Every year some 40,000 people attend its programmes and events. A couple of the more unusual offerings are: a drawing and painting class mainly for Mandarin speakers (non-Mandarin speakers are also welcome); conversation groups for those whose first language is not English; and a painting workshop where the canvas is a human body!

The Uxbridge Centre was founded in 1981, when the former Howick Borough Council purchased the Uxbridge Presbyterian Church and associated buildings – extensive redevelopment is planned for the future once funding is organised.

House prices

House or unit
Bedrooms 🛏 🛏
Price $229,000 – $299,000

Family house
Bedrooms 🛏 🛏 🛏
Price $319,000 – $399,000

House with sea views
Bedrooms 🛏 🛏 🛏 🛏
Price $430,000 – $1 million

Rental prices

Apartment or house
Bedroom 🛏
Price $210 – $220/wk
Bedrooms 🛏 🛏
Price $270 – $290/wk
Bedrooms 🛏 🛏 🛏
Price $325 – $445/wk

House
Bedrooms 🛏 🛏 🛏 🛏
Price $430 – $490/wk

Travel times

CBD	off-peak 25 min
	peak 40 min
Southern motorway	20 min
Airport	40 min
Botany Town Centre	10 min

There are regular buses to the CBD and Manukau and a regular ferry service from the neighbouring suburb of Half Moon Bay.

It's probably fair to describe Pakuranga as the Botany Downs of the 1960s. That's when the farmland in this area was subdivided and turned into the great Kiwi suburban dream. It was considered a great place to raise a family and, although it's been mocked relentlessly during the years for being embarrassingly suburban, it's still got a lot going for it. It's relatively affordable for east Auckland, and has easy access to good beaches, boating and schools. And simply by merit of the era in which it was developed, sections are family-sized with mature trees – a rare commodity in newer parts of the city – and the houses are family-friendly. Recent immigrants from many countries find it particularly attractive. Expect to see a lot of demand for this area in the near future.

Who lives there?

After being THE place to bring up kids for many generations, Pakuranga's population has aged in recent years: recent generations have grown up and moved on to more desirable areas. But now the well-built and well-maintained homes on large sections with mature trees are starting to be seen by young families as a compelling alternative to a tiny townhouse on a small section.

As well as the Pakeha families who've been here since it was first developed, Pakuranga has proven attractive to immigrants from a variety of countries in the past decade, especially Asians. And it's a perfect spot for those who love to be near the sea.

Typical dwellings

If you're after a solidly built, three or four

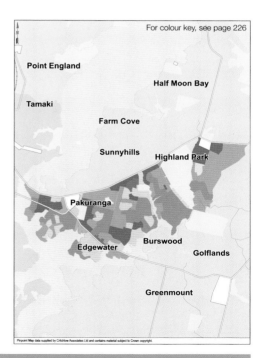

For colour key, see page 226

Point England
Half Moon Bay
Tamaki
Farm Cove
Sunnyhills
Highland Park
Pakuranga
Burswood
Edgewater
Golflands
Greenmount

Pinpoint Map data supplied by Critchlow Associates Ltd and contains material subject to Crown copyright

Population profile	Population in 2001 23,451	% Aged Under 15 years 20.21	% Aged over 65 Years 13.06
% European 66.18	% Maori 6.95	% Pacific Peoples 4.35	% Asian 24.36

bedroom weatherboard or brick home with internal-access garaging, which has hardly been altered since it was built in the mid to late 1960s, you'll have plenty of choice. Similar but more modest homes are available in Edgewater, southeast of Pakuranga. Highland Park, which developed more recently, has homes of a similar style, but the prices are generally higher.

Amenities
Schools ★★★★

Appropriately for such a family-oriented area, Pakuranga abounds with schools at all levels. Be warned however, that decile ratings vary wildly from one school to the next and this, unfortunately, can impact on the quality of the education. As always, do your research. For a full list, see page 272.

Shops ★★★★

The Pakuranga Town Centre shopping mall, which opened in 1965 to serve the new growing suburb, is now a much-improved Westfield Shopping Centre, with about 80 retailers.

The retail competition around here is intense. Just a few minutes' drive from Westfield is The Hub on Ti Rakau Dr, with its emphasis on home décor retailers. Opposite The Hub is the inimitable Botany Town Centre. Highland Park has its own shopping centre, with some 30 shops and cafes.

Leisure ★★★★

Pakuranga residents are spoiled for choice when it comes to open recreational spaces. Lloyd Elsmore Park has everything from tennis courts and golf courses to horse riding and croquet, badminton and bowls.

The new Lloyd Elsmore Pool & Leisure Complex includes a 25-metre pool for lane swimming, a 15-metre teaching and water therapy pool, and a 25-metre leisure pool, which incorporates a toddlers' splash pool, complete with fun fountains. Entry to these pools is free! There is also a crèche, cafe, gym, spa pool, sauna and steam room.

As if that weren't enough, Pakuranga also has several gyms, a big skate park, a beautiful golf course (the Pakuranga Country Club) on Cascades Rd, and a boat ramp at Tiraumea Drive reserve, which gives access to the Tamaki Estuary.

Te Tuhi – The Mark on Reeves Rd is a vibrant and diverse centre for community, cultural and arts events and exhibitions. Just opposite is the library.

Real Estate
Trends

Pakuranga seemed completely developed by the 1980s, because all the empty sections had gone. After a lull of about 10 years, however, smaller sections became acceptable and infill housing really took off. Extensive subdivision was still happening in Highland Park, Golflands and Edgewater

until very recently but in the past year there have been no new developments and no significant infill construction.

Currently the strongest demand is for lower-priced homes in this area, although people will still fork out for quality and, to some extent, a good location. Prices are considerably higher in Highland Park.

Rental and investment

There's a good range of rental property and steady demand from immigrants who have moved to the area but haven't yet bought.

Best streets

Fisher Pde is probably the stand-out address, with its waterfront location and relatively affordable substantial homes. What you get for $1 million here would cost you several times that amount in most other waterfront Auckland spots.

Other desirable streets include Kentigern Cl, Browns Ave, Udys Rd, Portadown Ave and Chatsworth Cres. Once-drab Ennis Ave is apparently an up-and-comer.

House prices

Unit	
Bedrooms	🛏 🛏
Price	$250,000 – $280,000
House	
Bedrooms	🛏 🛏 🛏
Price	$350,000 – $450,000
Executive house	
Bedrooms	🛏 🛏 🛏 🛏
Price	$450,000 plus

Rental prices

Flat	
Bedroom	🛏
Price	$210/wk
House	
Bedrooms	🛏 🛏
Price	$266 – $285/wk
Bedrooms	🛏 🛏 🛏
Price	$320 – $340/wk
Bedrooms	🛏 🛏 🛏 🛏
Price	$408 – $473/wk

Travel times

CBD	off-peak 20 min
	peak 60 min
Southern motorway	5 min
Airport	30 min
Manukau City shops	15 – 20 min

There are regular bus services to the CBD and to Manukau, but a ferry trip taking about 35 minutes from Half Moon Bay is a low-stress alternative for city commuters. There is a reduced ferry service on weekends, and no service on public holidays. See www.fullers.co.nz for more details.

Whitford, Brookby and Clevedon are to Auckland as Surrey is to London – a rural escape for the well-heeled reasonably close to the city. With the endless stretches of wooden-rail fencing, mature trees and rolling fields, it's a very English-feeling place. And although the prices put it out of reach of most Aucklanders, what you get for your money here would be astronomically expensive in most other countries. Development has been very tightly controlled, so most residents have plenty of room to swing a pony or two. The only downside to the sparseness of population is a lack of local amenities – there is no school in Whitford and there are no shops at Brookby. Still, there aren't many jobs out this way, either, so most people commute out of the area most days.

Who lives there?

Community-minded people seem to gravitate to this area. It's been noted that people actually turn up to public meetings! The vast majority of locals are white, some being recent immigrants taking advantage of the relative affordability of this lifestyle. A recent increase in the number of Asian buyers is possibly due to the advent of subdivisions, making smaller properties available to buy. And, of course, you have to love the land or love having a bit of it around you to live here. It's a lifestyler's mecca.

Typical dwellings

A typical dwelling here is one you can't see from the road, because it's set far back, behind huge mature trees and vast expanses of paddock. Lifestyle blocks and equestrian

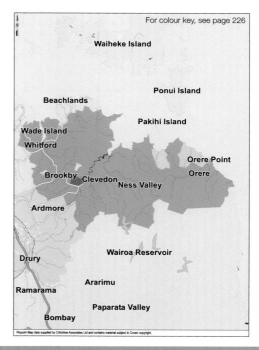

For colour key, see page 226

Waiheke Island

Ponui Island

Beachlands

Pakihi Island

Wade Island

Whitford

Orere Point

Brookby Clevedon Orere
Ness Valley

Ardmore

Wairoa Reservoir

Drury

Ararimu

Ramarama

Paparata Valley

Bombay

Pinpoint Map data supplied by Critchlow Associates Ltd and contains material subject to Crown copyright.

Population profile	Population in 2001 5,121	% Aged Under 15 years 23.73	% Aged over 65 Years 9.26
% European 89.98	% Maori 7.03	% Pacific Peoples 1.11	% Asian 1.7

properties are very popular. In Brookby, a group of 1970s houses makes it obvious when that farm was carved up for housing. Clevedon has some century-old villas and cottages. Apart from having a certain graciousness and spaciousness in common, the style of houses is very diverse.

Amenities
Schools ★★

Whitford children have to go elsewhere for their schooling: many of primary age go to Point View School in Howick. Brookby and Clevedon both have full primaries, which include the intermediate years.

Unsurprisingly, given the real estate prices around here, many opt to send their children to private high schools. In fact, there's a bus service to Pakuranga's co-ed St Kentigern College. Two new relatively local colleges, Botany Downs and Alfriston, may prove more attractive than the public schooling previously on offer.

For a full list, see page 272.

Shops ★★

Whitford retailers provide the basics for locals (videos, petrol, groceries, saddlery) and the non-essentials for tourists (gift shops,

an olde worlde restaurant and a cafe/bakery). There are no shops at Brookby.

At Clevedon, there are more horsey and touristy stores (including antiques), but also a wider range of shops, including an organic food store.

Leisure ★★★

For many people out this way, life revolves around horses. Polo at Clevedon is a major event for a certain set and their big hats. There's also a pony club at Whitford, and an equestrian centre in Brookby. And whether you're on horse, foot or mountain bike, the numerous trails through the Whitford Forest are a great place to burn off some calories. Other sports are catered for, too, with Clevedon having clubs for bowls, lawn tennis and cruising yachts.

The Whitford Park Country Club will be undergoing a major renovation soon. It has 56ha of native trees and hosts many national and international golf tournaments.

Duders Regional Park is an historic and beautiful seaside farm, with numerous tracks for walking and riding. It's popular with bird watchers and picnickers, and the adjacent beach is a haven in summer – being a little further away than the likes of Maraetai, it never gets quite as crowded. There are cafes and restaurants at Whitford, Clevedon, Pine Harbour Marina and the Formosa Country Club.

Real Estate
Trends

Subdivision is continuing, but at a much slower rate than in other areas. Locals are resisting change by contesting resource consent applications. The Auckland Regional

Council is also determined to contain the city's sprawl. Properties are selling steadily, and prices are rising steadily.

The huge desirability of properties here, plus their diverse nature and the fact that they're relatively few in number, all makes it impossible to give accurate price guides. Whether you're looking at a house on a quarter-acre or a lifestyle block, prices are all over the place in every category. It's still possible, but not easy, to buy a home for $600,000. And you can pay as much as $5 million for small and large places alike.

Many of the bigger, better-equipped properties are being marketed on the internet to those with US dollars or UK pounds in their pockets, and this is undoubtedly driving prices up. At the time of writing, an 18ha rural Clevedon property with a two-storey, four-bedroom villa and various outbuildings was being marketed for $2.2 million. If you're after a piece of Brookby, you need to be patient or lucky – there is rarely much available because it's such a small settlement and people tend to stay put.

Best streets

Here they do things differently – you're looking at best peninsulas rather than best streets! Clifton or Broomfields Peninsulas are the places to be, no contest.

Garden owner
Beverley McConnell

Beverley McConnell's magnificent 5ha country garden Ayrlies is well-known to green-thumbed Aucklanders. She and her husband moved to Whitford 40 years ago because he needed easy access to his newly established business in the city. They wanted their five children to grow up in the country, however, with the work (harvesting sweetcorn, milking cows) and the community spirit that it entails. In 2000 Beverley turned part of their farm into a wetland area, including a large lake, and she's been thrilled with the way that the project has been embraced by the local community. Ayrlies is open to visitors year-round, by appointment - ph 09 530 8706.

Local Hero:
The Auckland Polo Club

The Auckland Polo Club has its home on the Clevedon-Kawakawa Bay Rd. Founded in 1899, it's the largest (with 40-plus members) in New Zealand, and one of the longest established. Although New Zealand polo doesn't have the extreme elitism that the sport is known for internationally, it's still a rich person's sport, and makes great sightseeing for lesser mortals. There is polo at Clevedon every summer weekend from November to the end of March, but it's the New Zealand Open, held each February, which is the glamour event on the polo calendar.

Smart Buy ✓

If you can afford this area and you like the country life, go for it! Development is occurring here, but at a suitably dignified pace. And it's always going to be desirable compared with nearby suburbs.

House prices

If you're lucky	$600,000
18ha with house and outbuildings	
Price	$2 million

Rental prices

Small cottage	
Price	$270/wk
House	
Bedrooms	🛏 🛏 🛏 🛏
Price	$800/wk
6ha land for horse grazing	
Price	$150/wk

Travel times

From Whitford	
CBD	off-peak 35 min
	peak 55 min
Southern motorway	12 min
Airport	25 min
Botany Town Centre	10 min

The Pine Harbour Ferry service is a boon for those who need to get to the CBD every day but don't want the stress of driving and parking. The ferry timetable is at www.pineharbour.co.nz. Howick & Eastern buses also serve this area.

South

If you believed everything you heard in the media about South Auckland, you'd probably imagine it as an unsavoury cross between Harlem and Soweto, with all the poverty, crime and racial tension that entails.

But you have to ask yourself, would businessman Eric Watson even consider establishing a stud farm worth tens of millions of dollars in Harlem or Soweto?

South Auckland is so much more than its shallow media image, and it has to be said that the Manukau City Council has done a great job during the years of raising local pride and celebrating cultural diversity.

Each March, for example, the Auckland Secondary Schools Maori and Pacific Island Cultural Festival – colloquially

known as Polyfest – sees more than 13,000 students from some 50 Auckland secondary schools deliver their traditional and contemporary performances. There are performances on five separate stages from Cook Islands Maori, Niuean, Samoan and Tongan groups, as well as non-competitive performances from a range of other ethnic groups, mainly south-east Asian and Indian.

A different crowd is lured to Manurewa in south Auckland for the huge Ellerslie Flower Show, which takes place each November and just keeps getting bigger and bigger. In 2004, the show's 10th anniversary, there were almost 65,000

multicultural & exciting
colourful
character-filled
diverse
easy-going

visitors from throughout New Zealand. Real estate agents tell of people moving to the Manurewa area after visiting the show and "discovering" the suburb.

That show takes place at the Auckland Regional Botanic Gardens, which is an impressive place in its own right. It's one of hundreds of reserves in south Auckland, many along the foreshore of the Manukau Harbour and major streams. South Auckland is the place where you can still buy waterfront property for prices that won't make you turn pale with shock. Many newly established suburbs have impressive houses that would rival any in the more expensive parts of the North Shore, for example.

And while Waitakere might be more famous for its bush, south Auckland has the Hunua Ranges, a reserve which covers some 16,000 hectares and contains the largest block of forest on the mainland of the Auckland region, as well as the only northern mainland habitat of the kokako. It's a great place for tramping, camping, mountain biking and horse riding.

AUCKLAND

SOUTH

including Mangere Bridge and Favona

Although there are still pockets of Mangere where desolate, ramshackle homes are the norm, on the whole the area is looking brighter. Former farms and market gardens have been snapped up by developers and the new homes they are building bring a look of relative affluence and respectability to the place. Also important is the fact that the Mangere sewage purification works by Mangere Bridge no longer stink constantly, thanks to a $450 million overhaul. During the five-year project, 500ha of oxidation ponds were returned to the sea and 13km of shoreline returned to the Manukau Harbour. The wildlife has returned in droves, and the waterfront reserve is a great place for walking and bird-watching. And the area's most prominent neighbour – Auckland international airport.

Who lives there?

This is a very multicultural area, with Europeans, Maori, Pacific Islanders and Asians all having called Mangere home for a long time. Facing each other across Favona Rd are a Vietnamese Buddhist temple (a former state house, with a gold Buddha in the front yard) and a huge Tongan church (built in traditional style). More Indians are moving into the area, too. Mangere Bridge prices are higher, than Favona or Mangere, so it appeals to people with more money.

Typical dwellings

Being next to the sea, Mangere was one of the earliest parts of Auckland to be settled, so there is a smattering of villas and bungalows, often on the site of old farms or market gardens. Much of Mangere was developed

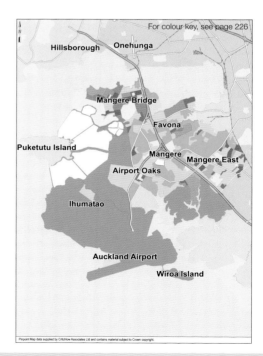

For colour key, see page 226

Hillsborough — Onehunga
Mangere Bridge
Favona
Puketutu Island
Mangere — Mangere East
Airport Oaks
Ihumatao
Auckland Airport
Wiroa Island

Pinpoint Map data supplied by Critchlow Associates Ltd and contains material subject to Crown copyright.

Population profile	Population in 2001 53,304	% Aged Under 15 years 31.61	% Aged over 65 Years 6.61
% European 24.37	% Maori 19.01	% Pacific Peoples 53.83	% Asian 9.1

by the state during the 1940s, 1950s and 1960s, with street after street of weatherboard homes. In Mangere Bridge, large brick-and-tile homes from the 1960s and 1970s dominate.

Amenities
Schools ★★★

This is a very family-oriented area, and the families are often big, so you're never far from a school. Something a bit different is the Muslim school, Al-Madinah. For a full list, see page 272.

Shops ★★

As befits its senior status in the area, Mangere Bridge has an established shopping centre. Tucked between the slopes of Mangere Mountain and the Kiwi Esplanade Reserve, it has an almost village-like atmosphere and offers most of the daily basics. Mangere Town Centre also sells the basics, but it is run-down and rather depressing. Still, the mainstreet and mall shopping of Otahuhu, Papatoetoe and Manukau are never far away.

Leisure ★★★

Mangere Mountain, once the site of one of the largest fortified pa in the region, is now a much-loved haven for recreation. It's a great place for walking (the view from the top is spectacular) and the sports fields are regularly used.

Ambury Farm Park is a large working farm where visitors are welcome; the park is on the foreshore of the Manukau Harbour, where more than 86 species of birds make their home, for at least part of the year. The park is also has a horse-riding centre for people with disabilities.

The 100ha Otuataua Stonefields Historic Reserve near the tiny settlement of Ihumatao is fascinating, offering plenty of scope for picturesque walks and discovering remnants of early Maori and European occupation, including walls, garden mounds and cooking areas.

There's a narrow strip of reserve along the pretty foreshore at Mangere Bridge, and the abandoned bridge is now a popular spot for fishing and relaxing.

Moana-Nui-a-Kiwa Leisure Centre offers a full range of gym and swimming facilities, and there are regular exhibitions at the Mangere Community Arts Outreach Service. Dining out here generally means grabbing takeaways, although there are also casual ethnic cafes.

Real Estate
Trends

Land formerly occupied by farms and market gardens is being converted into residential developments, such as Peninsula Park and Puriri Grove. Large houses are always in demand here because big families and extended families are the norm. With homeowners trying to get away with creating as much room as they can for the lowest cost, authorised and unauthorised sleep-outs are a common sight.

This is still an affordable area for buyers who will never be able to contemplate buying a home in other parts of Auckland, but it hasn't been immune to house price rises. What you might have bought for $180,000 to $190,000 in August or September of 2004 would have cost you more than $200,000 by February 2005.

Rental and investment

There's high demand for rental properties here, but some landlords have problems with tenants not caring for properties – this is not an investment for the faint-hearted.

Best streets

Kiwi Esplanade in Mangere Bridge has water views, nice houses, mature trees, and a reserve along its entire length. Nothing else in this area can compete with that!

Why I live there

Organic gardener Linda Lee

Linda Lee's grandfather was a Chinese market gardener in Mangere and her grandmother was Maori. Linda (Ngati Whatua, Te Arawa and Ngapuhi) grew up here and finds great sustenance for her soul in being back home. She established the Pukaki Worm Farm, a centre for educating the community about organic gardening and recycling, in 1999 as a way of giving back to the community that nurtured her. "This is a very historic and significant place, with an active volcano, the Manukau Harbour, fossilised kauri forests, good agricultural land, and two pa – Pukaki and Ihumatao. The people who live here are the remnants of Te Aakitai-Wai-o-Hua, the ancient tribe that was here before the great Maori migration."

House prices

Unit	
Bedrooms	
Price	$140,000 – $180,000
House	
Bedrooms	
Price	$200,000 – $400,000
Executive house	
Bedrooms	
Price	$350,000 – $500,000

Rental prices

Flat	
Bedroom	
Price	$170/wk
Bedrooms	
Price	$220/wk
House	
Bedrooms	
Price	$250/wk
Bedrooms	
Price	$295/wk
Bedrooms	
Price	$355 – $425/wk

Travel times

From Mangere	
CBD	off-peak 30 min
	peak 60 min
South-western motorway	2 min
Airport	5 min
Manukau City shops	10 min

Mangere is well-served by buses; the nearest train stations are Middlemore or Otahuhu.

including Totara Heights, Flat Bush, East Tamaki Heights, Goodwood Heights, Chapel Downs, Wiri and Puhinui

Many people living in other parts of Auckland wouldn't give these suburbs a first look, let alone a second! But they're worth considering if you like variety in geography, people and houses. You could even get a very good view at a reasonable price. Most of this area has developed quickly, which gives it a certain homogeneity. The newest subdivisions – where dairy cows crossing the road at milking time were a common sight a fews years ago – look very brash and man-made, but will soften in time. Large parts of East Tamaki, Wiri and Manukau are devoted to commercial and light industrial premises. The juncture of Manukau/Wiri/Puhinui is dominated by the Manukau City shopping centre, endless streets of bulk retailing and by Rainbow's End amusement park.

Who lives there?

Auckland in the 21st century is ethnically a very diverse place, and you can see it all in these suburbs. Newer areas like Chapel Downs are attracting young families who want a contemporary home at a good price. Totara Heights, with its views and leafy surroundings, appeals to a more affluent and generally older demographic.

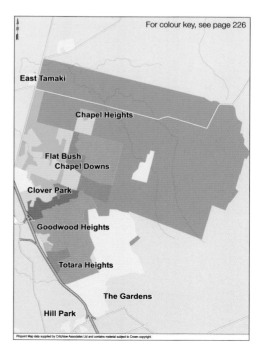

For colour key, see page 226

East Tamaki
Chapel Heights
Flat Bush
Chapel Downs
Clover Park
Goodwood Heights
Totara Heights
The Gardens
Hill Park

Pinpoint Map data supplied by Critchlow Associates Ltd and contains material subject to Crown copyright.

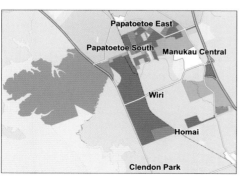

Papatoetoe East
Papatoetoe South
Manukau Central
Wiri
Homai
Clendon Park

Population profile	Population in 2001 31,632	% Aged Under 15 years 29.47	% Aged over 65 Years 5.73
% European 35.27	% Maori 17.61	% Pacific Peoples 36.47	% Asian 16.29

The area appeals to Asians, too, with many moving here as renters, and then buying once they're established.

Typical dwellings

The standard Kiwi three-bedroom brick-and-tile house is everywhere, some meticulously maintained and some woefully neglected. With smaller sections and less time spent at home, townhouses are becoming very popular with developers and buyers. The majority of homes have been built as cheaply as possible.

Up at Manukau Heights and Totara Heights, it's a different story, with many multi-storey houses, often surrounded by mature gardens or tucked into patches of native bush.

Manukau and Wiri have extensive areas of fibrolite-clad state housing which, generally, has not aged well.

Amenities

Schools ★★

There are ample primary and intermediate schools, but high school students need to travel to neighbouring suburbs. Much of the Manukau/Wiri/Puhinui area is in the highly regarded Papatoetoe High School zone, and this has an impact on property prices. Others go to high schools in Manurewa or Otara.

For a full list, see page 272.

Shops ★★★★

The Manukau City shopping centre – now rebranded as Westfield Shoppingtown Manukau – was one of the first shopping malls in Auckland, and continues to go from strength to strength. It's a vibrant place with more than 120 stores.

In the past decade the streets surrounding the centre have become an ocean of retail and wholesale outlets, with the emphasis on big, bargain-style shopping. This is far from mainstreet shopping – without a car, it would take you forever to get around.

There is a shopping centre at Chapel Downs, and you're not far from The Hub and Botany Town Centre.

When Flat Bush is further down the track, residents should be able to buy most of what they need simply by strolling down the road.

Leisure ★★★★

Hayman Park next to the Manukau City shopping centre is a bonus for local families and for workers who want to take their lunch break outside. It is full of mature trees, lawn, and has a duck pond and a creek. There's a concrete in-ground skate park, which is a hit with local youth.

If you're travelling by car, the world of leisure activities is your oyster. Totara Park is a haven of leafy tracks through native bush, with pleasant picnic spots and playgrounds, and a beautiful swimming pool. Some parts of the reserve are okay for mountain bikers.

Right next to Totara Park is the Auckland Regional Botanic Gardens.

Rainbow's End theme park entices families from all over Auckland, and is on the must-do list for many visitors to the city.

For eating out, there is ample choice in the shopping centre, as well as pubs and steak houses in the surrounding areas. Something a bit different which is getting great reviews is the Touch of Nature vegetarian restaurant on Lakewood Rd near the shopping centre.

Real Estate

Trends

The numerous new subdivisions are luring people from the east and west of Auckland – there is not a lot of rural land left in these areas now, which is a huge recent change.

Flat Bush is set to become New Zealand's most comprehensively planned new town – and in 15 years' time it will probably be home to at least 40,000 people. The model town is being built according to designs which encourage walking, cycling and use of public transport. Strict planning will make this a very pleasant place to live. For example, huge garage doors dominate the front of many new houses elsewhere. Here, the garage must be to the side of the house and set back from the road, so the front door is the public face of the house.

Prices have risen considerably in the past year, and they're still climbing. This area is very popular.

Rental and investment

With a mix of affordable properties and a large number of potential tenants, this area has long been popular with renters and landlords.

Best streets

For their elevation and views, Goodwood Dr in Goodwood Heights and Eugenia Rise in Totara Heights.

Smart Buy ⊘

When development is well under way, Flat Bush should be a great place to live – the way all our suburbs ought to be, if only we'd thought about planning them properly.

House prices

Apartment	
Bedroom	
Price	$159,000 – $220,000
Unit	
Bedrooms	
Price	$220,000 – $235,000
Family house	
Bedrooms	
Price	$279,000 – $329,000
Executive house	
Bedrooms	
Price	$360,000 – $460,000

Rental prices

Flat	
Bedroom	
Price	$180 – $290/wk
Bedrooms	
Price	$240 – $320/wk
House	
Bedrooms	
Price	$280 – $300/wk
Bedrooms	
Price	$380 – $400/wk

Travel times

CBD	off-peak 20 min
	peak 60 min
Motorway	5-10 min
Airport	15 min
Botany Town Centre	10-15 min
Train to Britomart	20 min

There is a very good bus service. The nearest train station is Puhinui (the Wiri station closed at the beginning of 2005).

including Weymouth, Clendon Park, Homai, Hill Park, Manurewa East, Randwick Park, Wattle Downs and Conifer Grove

Diversity is the key description for this area, which includes run-down state housing, luxurious contemporary homes, everything in between and some of the city's cheapest waterfront real estate. There's a lot of coastline, thanks to three peninsulas jutting into the Manukau Harbour. It also has numerous reserves, many on the waterfront, and some glorious tracts of native bush. Manurewa is home to the 65ha of gardens that make up the Auckland Regional Botanic Gardens. The entire area is becoming very popular with families, and part of it is in zone for the well-regarded Alfriston College which opened at the beginning of 2004. Choices, greenery, good schooling and sea views – if it weren't in South Auckland, you'd be paying mega-bucks.

Who lives there?

The availability of fairly cheap rental homes has made the area popular with those on low incomes, including refugees and other immigrants. Ethnicities represented include Iranians, Iraqis, Fijians, Indians (there is a Sikh temple on Great South Rd), Maori and Europeans.

Blue collar workers who live in extended families and have a good community spirit To the east of the southern motorway around the botanic gardens, the homes are new and more upmarket, so the residents are young professionals and families with a bit more money. Further east, lifestylers live on the larger blocks of semi-rural land.

Typical dwellings

Most Manurewa homes were built in the

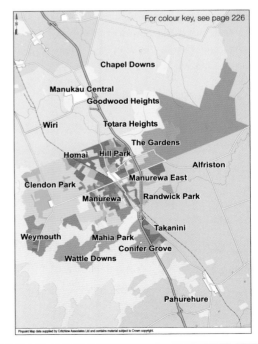

For colour key, see page 226

Chapel Downs

Manukau Central

Goodwood Heights

Wiri

Totara Heights

The Gardens

Homai Hill Park

Alfriston

Manurewa East

Clendon Park

Manurewa Randwick Park

Weymouth

Mahia Park

Takanini

Conifer Grove

Wattle Downs

Pahurehure

Pinpoint Map data supplied by Critchlow Associates Ltd and contains material subject to Crown copyright.

Population profile
% European 52.54

Population in 2001 61,434
% Maori 26.99

% Aged Under 15 years 28.84
% Pacific Peoples 19.99

% Aged over 65 Years 7.04
% Asian 8.23

212

1960s or later so the most common materials are weatherboard and brick-and-tile, and the sections are generously sized.

There are a few houses owned and rented out by the state, as well as ex-state housing. New and grander developments are typically of brick and plaster construction.

Amenities
Schools ★★★

The high number of schools reflects the high proportion of families here. The new Alfriston College, which some parts of this area are zoned for, is the most highly regarded. For a full list, see page 272.

Shops ★★

Manurewa has both mainstreet and mall shopping, but both are looking rather down at heel. It appears that those with discretionary income prefer to spend it elsewhere. There are a lot of $2-style shops, and a lot of Indian takeaways and Indian sweet shops. Most people go straight to Manukau City to do their shopping.

Leisure ★★★

Nathan Homestead, built in 1925 and still surrounded by 3.5ha of much-loved lawn and gardens, is an arts, community and function centre. The Manurewa Leisure Centre has full gymnasium facilities and a swimming pool.

For eating out, if you don't want take-aways then you'll need to head elsewhere.

Parks and reserves dotted all over the place make life more pleasant here.

Totara Park and the Auckland Regional Botanic Gardens are the key places; other parks like Weymouth Domain, which runs along more than three kilometres of coastline, are well used by locals.

The Manukau Golf Course is nestled between Wattle Downs and Conifer Grove.

Real Estate
Trends

Three-bedroom homes are very popular in this area, with demand outstripping supply at the time of writing. Hill Park, near the botanic gardens, has long been popular and its new development, The Gardens, has enhanced that popularity even further. Anything near the new Alfriston College is now considered a desirable locale, because of the school's good reputation.

The price you can expect to pay for a home here is as diverse as the area itself. However, in every one of these suburbs, prices are heading steadily up. Location and type of construction are the factors in the range of house prices.

Rental and investment

The area is popular with renters and land-lords: from the most basic humble abode through to the prestigious homes near the botanic gardens, there's plenty of demand.

Best streets

Any of the streets in Conifer Grove or next to the botanic gardens.

Smart Buy ⊘

This has got to be some of the cheapest waterfront property in the city – if you don't actually want to live here buying a renter with water views could be a very smart investment with capital gains sure to come.

Local Hero: Auckland Regional Botanic Gardens

Every year more than 800,000 visitors enjoy the 65ha of Auckland's botanic gardens, first opened in 1982. But there's no resting on laurels here. In March 2005 the new Potter Children's Garden and the much improved visitor's centre were officially opened. The children's garden includes a Coastal Garden, Sight and Sound area, Decay Garden, Vegetable Garden, Boardwalk and Creature Pool, surrounded by a grove of puriri trees. There is also a library with more than 2000 books.

Every year in November, the gardens play host to the Ellerslie Flower Show. It's been going for 10 years, attracts around 65,000 people and features exhibition gardens, floral displays, garden art and entertainment.

House prices

Unit	
Bedroom	
Price	$100,000
Bedrooms	
Price	$130,000 – $200,000
House	
Bedrooms	
Price	$180,000 – $200,000
Executive house	
Bedrooms	
Price	up to $500,000

Rental prices

Flat or unit	
Bedroom	
Price	$180/wk
House	
Bedrooms	
Price	$235/wk
Bedrooms	
Price	$275/wk
Bedrooms	
Price	$360 – $400/wk

Travel times

From Manurewa	
CBD	off-peak 20 min
	peak 1 hour
Southern motorway	2 min
Airport	10 min
Manukau City shops	5 min
Botany Town Centre	15 min
Train to Britomart	20 min

There is a very good bus service, and three nearby train stations: Homai, Manurewa and Te Mahia.

including Middlemore and Papatoetoe

The narrowest part of the Auckland isthmus (a mere 1.3km across) is home to the staunchly working-class suburb of Otahuhu. It's an established area, as evidenced by the very English-looking, red-brick façade of Otahuhu College, which opened in 1931. It's also very diverse, with a great mix of cultures living side by side. Also side by side are the park-like grounds of King's College, one of New Zealand's most expensive private schools, and Middlemore Hospital, which services some of the poorest families in the country. Papatoetoe comes in two parts: old Papatoetoe and the newer Hunter's Corner. The area's about to get a huge injection of job opportunities with big developments starting in nearby Mt Wellington and Waiouru Peninsula.

Who lives there?

Otahuhu and Middlemore are definitely blue-collar suburbs – and proud of it. The affordability of these areas, as well as their closeness to the Mangere Immigration Hostel and the airport, has made them popular with immigrant families.

Otahuhu is particularly popular with Chinese and Indians (there is a Sikh temple there), and Middlemore with Pacific Islanders. Papatoetoe High School is known in some quarters as "the grammar school of the south", attracting families who want good free education.

Typical dwellings

Some of the city's most affordable character bungalows and villas are in Otahuhu, but many are showing signs of the neglect

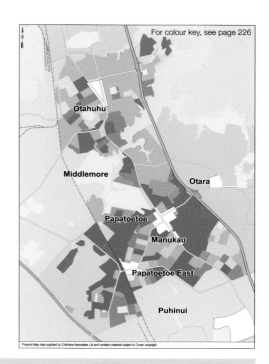

For colour key, see page 226

Pinpoint Map data supplied by Critchlow Associates Ltd and contains material subject to Crown copyright.

| Population profile | Population in 2001 39,006 | % Aged Under 15 years 25.78 | % Aged over 65 Years 10.41 |
| % European 40.66 | % Maori 17.05 | % Pacific Peoples 27.81 | % Asian 20.13 |

215

they've endured over the years.

Cheap housing has always been in demand in this area: low-rise blocks of flats here pre-date central Auckland's passion for apartments by many decades.

In Papatoetoe, there are some 1930s bungalows, but most development occurred during the 1960s and 1970s when brick-and-tile houses were the norm. They're built well and have on the whole been consistently cared for.

Amenities
Schools ★★

The fierce rivalry between the First XVs of Otahuhu College and King's College says it all – geographically, they're divided from each other only by a fence, but in every other way they couldn't be further apart. One is a public school servicing a working class community and the other is a private institution for children of the privileged classes.

For a full list of schools, see page 272.

Shops ★★★

Otahuhu's mainstreet rejuvenation must be one of the most successful in Auckland. It's a lively, pleasant place to be. Many of the big chain stores have deserted in favour of the malls, but most of what you need is here.

Middlemore has no shopping centre, but there are corner dairies and liquour stores aplenty. Old Papatoetoe also offers good mainstreet shopping; Hunter's Corner has a relatively new mall called Hunter's Plaza, and its mainstreet has also been successfully spruced up.

When the vast new Sylvia Park development opens in several years' time, it will probably pose quite a challenge to retailers in all of these areas. There are also to be support services and shops in the planned Highbrook Business Park.

Leisure ★★★

The adjacent Auckland Golf Club and Grange Golf Club attract mostly those from other wealthier suburbs: locals are more likely to play rugby, league, netball or kilikiti.

There are plenty of public reserves throughout the neighbourhood, many alongside the picturesque Tamaki River.

Papatoetoe and Otahuhu have recreation and fitness centres and ample choice for rugby and bowls players. Papatoetoe has the Centennial Pools and a roller skating rink. Otahuhu has rowing and badminton clubs, as well as a fantastic range of good, cheap, authentic Asian restaurants.

Real Estate
Trends

In the past few decades, much of the Otahuhu and Middlemore real estate has been owned by landlords rather than owner occupied, but with high prices elsewhere, first home buyers are reassessing these

suburbs. You can snap up an old railway cottage or a 1930s bungalow for a reasonable price. Call it the new Onehunga.

Unemployment rates have made the area somewhat unsettled in recent years, but that's changing. With the massive Sylvia Park development just down the road in Mt Wellington eventually providing thousands of jobs (between 5000 and 10,000, depending on who's telling the story), a continuing upward trend seems likely. There's also the huge 193ha Highbrook Business Park planned for the Waiouru Peninsula, with 15,000 jobs predicted.

While prices are extremely reasonable here compared with other parts of the city, a steady upward trend is expected to continue.

Rental and investment

A preponderance of low-income families make this area popular with investors – and considering you can buy a block of four two-bedroom units for less than $600,000 and rent them out for around $200 a week each, that makes sense.

Best streets

Princes St East, Church St, Hutton St and Ave Rd in Otahuhu. Omana Rd, Fitzroy St and St George St in Papatoetoe.

Smart Buy ⊘

They're calling Otahuhu the next Onehunga, with predictions of gentrification, of a sort. It might be a good idea to get in quick before word gets around that you can buy a spacious three-bedroom bungalow on 1000m2 for $269,000. While you're at it, take a look at the houses along the estuary for affordable waterfront property.

House prices

Flat	
Bedroom	
Price	$100,000 – $110,000
Unit	
Bedrooms	
Price	$120,000 – $160,000
House	
Bedrooms	
Price	$235,000 – $280,000
Bedrooms	
Price	$280,000 – $300,000

Rental prices

Flat	
Bedroom	
Price	$160 – $195/wk
Flat or house	
Bedroom	
Price	$210 – $235/wk
Bedrooms	
Price	$225 – $290/wk
House	
Bedrooms	
Price	$375 – $405/wk

Travel times

CBD	off-peak 20 min
	peak 45 min
	by train 20 min
Southern motorway	5 min
Airport	10 min
Manukau City shops	10 min

The area has a very good bus service, and Otahuhu has a train station (although it's a bit of a hike from the centre of town). For drivers, the Otahuhu motorway interchange is to be upgraded and there's a whole new interchange being built just south of there to service the Waiouru Peninsula and the new business park.

including East Tamaki

> The name Otara is well-known outside of Auckland – and not for good reasons. This place has come to symbolise poverty, and it's true that there are areas where unkempt barefoot children mill around with malnourished dogs, and the gardens aren't as tidy as they might be (abandoned rusty cars can really ruin the look of a place). But Otara is also home to the industrious Manukau Institute of Technology, the unbeatable Saturday market, vibrant churches of myriad denominations and some of the country's best young musicians. East Tamaki, to the north of Otara, was primarily industrial until a few years ago. Now subdivisions resembling those in the eastern suburbs are springing up; some are terraced apartments with retail or office space on the ground floor and living areas above.

Who lives there?

Otara is predominantly populated by Pacific Islanders and, to a lesser extent, Maori. The new subdivisions in East Tamaki have meant an influx of Indians into the area. There's a high percentage of blue-collar workers and unemployed. Huge numbers of Asians buy and sell at the Saturday morning market, but they're not locals.

Typical dwellings

The classic mid-20th-century state house (three bedrooms, weatherboard-clad) is everywhere in Otara. There are stand-alones, duplexes and multi-unit townhouses. Over in East Tamaki, the homes (brick and tile with internal garaging) are slightly larger (with three or four bedrooms) and the sections slightly smaller.

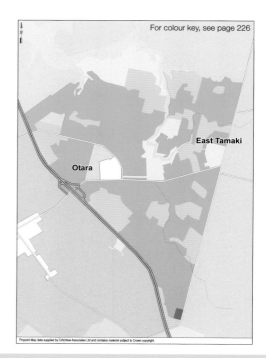

For colour key, see page 226

East Tamaki

Otara

Pinpoint Map data supplied by Critchlow Associates Ltd and contains material subject to Crown copyright.

Population profile			
	Population in 2001 16,371	% Aged Under 15 years 35.55	% Aged over 65 Years 5.24
% European 10.61	% Maori 21.26	% Pacific Peoples 71.49	% Asian 2.18

Amenities

Schools ★★★

The area is well served by schools at all levels. The Manukau Institute of Technology offers 1500 study programmes. For a full list, see page 272.

Shops ★★

You can get the basics at the Otara Town Centre… plus lavalava fabric by the truck-load, tapa cloth by the kilometre and corned beef by the tonne. But, given the choice, most people would probably travel to either Manukau or Botany Downs.

Leisure ★★

Otara is blessed with plentiful reserves, including an extensive one along the Otara Creek foreshore. The basketball courts at O Tamariki Reserve are in constant use. The council-run Otara Music Arts Centre has a recording studio which is used by local amateur and professional musicians. Next to the town centre is a free swimming pool.

The dining experience in Otara is largely fast food, with some exotic options at the Saturday flea market. East Tamaki has several steak-and-chips style restaurants.

Real Estate

Trends

Real estate agents note that this area is showing a general improvement in maintenance of homes, and a resurgence of local pride. While the centre of East Tamaki is still primarily commercial, the edges are developing quickly into residential. East Tamaki is more of an owner-occupier area than Otara.

House prices have grown steadily. A house that might have fetched $140,000 two years ago would now cost $180,000.

House prices			
House			
Bedrooms	🛏 🛏 🛏		
Price	$130,000 – $300,000		
Better house			
Bedrooms	🛏 🛏 🛏 🛏		
Price	$280,000 – $400,000		

Rental prices	
Flat	
Bedroom	🛏
Price	$190/wk
Bedrooms	🛏 🛏
Price	$265 – $320/wk
House	
Bedrooms	🛏 🛏 🛏
Price	$300 – $340/wk
Bedrooms	🛏 🛏 🛏 🛏
Price	$395 – $530/wk

Travel times		
From Otara		
CBD	off-peak	20 min
	peak	80 min
Southern motorway		3 min
Airport		15 min
Manukau City shops		10-15 min
The area is well served by buses.		

Rental and investment

There's plenty of demand for rental properties in Otara but, while weekly rents would indicate a respectable return, many tenants don't come from a culture of home ownership and properties are not always cared for.

Best streets

Anything near the shops or the MIT campus.

including Takanini, Red Hill, Ardmore, Rosehill, Drury, and Pahurehure

Papakura is where the city meets the country. Although it's less rural with every passing year and every new subdivision, it still feels like a country town and has its own council. As well as catering for its own population, townies and country folk, Papakura provides retail and other essential services to the lifestyle block crowd from Whitford, Clevedon and Brookby, which have few shops of their own. Although Papakura itself is considered a suburb of Auckland, it's big enough to have its own suburbs – Pahurehure and Red Hill. Pahurehure is the most desirable area, with demand outstripping supply, especially for newer homes. A lot of development is expected west of Pahurehure, into the Hingaia Peninsula and at Takanini during the next decade.

Who lives there?

Papakura is still a fairly conservative town. The community is close-knit and largely working class. Papakura is considered a good place to raise a family – although teenagers who no longer see Calf Club Day as a social highlight might not agree!

When townie residents retire, they often buy a little block of land just outside town; when farmers retire, they do the opposite.

Typical dwellings

Good solid standard Kiwi homes are the norm in central Papakura, which was mostly developed from the 1950s to the 1970s. Red Hill and Pahurehure are newer developments, and the plaster homes which have sprung up around the substantial older farmhouses reflect that.

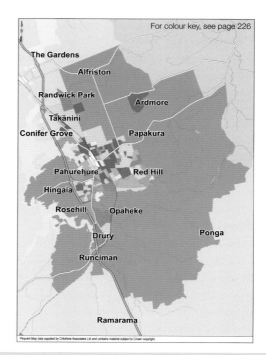

For colour key, see page 226

The Gardens
Alfriston
Randwick Park
Ardmore
Takanini
Conifer Grove
Papakura
Pahurehure
Red Hill
Hingaia
Rosehill
Opaheke
Ponga
Drury
Runciman
Ramarama

Pinpoint Map data supplied by Critchlow Associates Ltd and contains material subject to Crown copyright.

Population profile	Population in 2001 36,135	% Aged Under 15 years 25.58	% Aged over 65 Years 9.95
% European 69.95	% Maori 24.43	% Pacific Peoples 7.83	% Asian 5.23

Amenities

Schools ★★★

The area is well-served with town and rural schools. Alfriston College opened at the beginning of 2004 and is drawing some Papakura students. For a full list, see page 272.

Shops ★★★

Until recently, many necessities and luxuries had to be purchased elsewhere – but this is all changing, with bigger retailers moving in. The Southgate retail development opened in Takanini in late 2004, and mainstreet Papakura is poised for a substantial makeover.

Leisure ★★★★

There are ample parks and reserves in and around Papakura. There's also a golf course, and a pleasant drive in the countryside can take you to some lovely east coast beaches Papakura has a museum and art gallery, and many casual ethnic eateries.

Real Estate

Trends

During 2003 and 2004 Papakura house prices rose more than 27%, evidence of a resurgence of popularity – possibly thanks to the fact that it's physically somewhat removed from Auckland, but with big-city amenities within reasonably easy reach.

Sections in the new Red Hill subdivisions are selling for $150,000 to almost $200,000. Sections at Hingaia look set to fetch even more, because of the proximity to the harbour and desirable Karaka. Currently, the allowable section size is a matter of debate between the ARC (which wants smaller sections to fit more dwellings in) and the local council (which is trying to appease locals who are resisting urbanisation).

Best streets

In Pahurehure, Rushgreen Ave; in Papakura, Opaheke Rd. Red Hill Rd (in Red Hill, of course) is elevated and has beautiful views.

Rental and investment

There is steady demand for rental properties.

House prices

Unit	
Bedrooms	🛏 🛏
Price	$130,000 – $260,000
House	
Bedrooms	🛏 🛏 🛏
Price	$170,000 – $350,000
Executive house	
Bedrooms	🛏 🛏 🛏 🛏
Price	$190,000 – $500,000
Lifestyle block with modest house	
Price	$450,000 plus

Rental prices

Flat or unit	
Bedroom	🛏
Price	$150 – $220/wk
Flat or house	
Bedrooms	🛏 🛏
Price	$225 – $250/wk
Bedrooms	🛏 🛏 🛏
Price	$260 – $290/wk

Travel times

CBD	off-peak 25 min
	peak 75 min
By train	50 min
Southern motorway	5 min
Airport	25 min
Manukau City shops	15 min

There are regular bus and train services.

including Karaka

Gone are the days when Pukekohe was best known for its ability to grow great onions and potatoes – the word "onion" doesn't even appear on www.pukekohe.org.nz! Today most of the residents are more interested in motor sport or hanging out at the town's award-wining cafes. The traditional rural businesses are still there, but they're no longer the essence of the place. Pukekohe, 52km south of the Auckland CBD, was settled by Pakeha in the 1860s. Long a service town to the surrounding farmers and market gardeners, it is now the lively heart of Franklin District. From Pukekohe Hill there are panoramic views to the north and south. A stroll down the main shopping street reveals Pukekohe as a pleasant, affluent, unpretentious and substantial country town.

Who lives there?

The population is predominately European, but there are also Maori, Indian and Chinese. Pukekohe is attractive to those who need to be near Auckland but want a country lifestyle with all the amenities of an established country town. People here are mostly middle-class, and there are a few seriously wealthy people, too.

It's been noted that quite a few former All Blacks and Rugby Sevens players have moved to Pukekohe, because they don't get the unwanted attention they would in a more metropolitan area.

Typical dwellings

Typical dwellings run the full spectrum from old farmhouses, villas and bungalows, through to more modern brick-and-tile and weather-

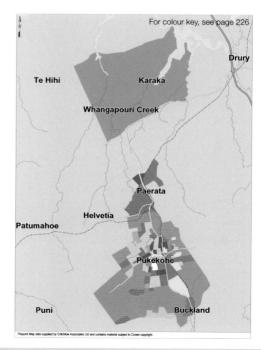

For colour key, see page 226

Pinpoint Map data supplied by Critchlow Associates Ltd and contains material subject to Crown copyright.

Population profile	Population in 2001 13,623	% Aged Under 15 years 25.32	% Aged over 65 Years 13.06
% European 69.68	% Maori 19.58	% Pacific Peoples 4.98	% Asian 7.66

board homes. The new developments tend to be brick-and-tile or have plaster finishes.

Amenities

Schools ★★★

All of the local schools are very good, which is obviously attractive for families considering moving to the area. Many locals love the fact that they can send their children to country schools which still have calf-club days and, because the population is in no danger of declining, their future seems more secure than that of most country schools. For a full list, see page 272.

Shops ★★★★

Pukekohe has excellent mainstreet shopping. And it's a very pleasant place to be. The street was revamped in a pretty country-style a few years ago. The busy town centre has more than 200 businesses offering everything from tractors to fine wines.

There is also a booming retail area in Manukau Rd, with large car parks. Big retailers like Bunnings and Harvey Norman have arrived in town, but there's no room for them in the main street – and that will ensure that it keeps its much-loved character.

Leisure ★★★★

Locals are spoiled for choice, especially if they're keen on outdoor activities.

Pukekohe Park is the home of motorsport, and horse racing is getting bigger and bigger here.

There is a stadium, tennis and squash courts, gyms, an all-weather hockey ground, playing fields for all sports, bowling greens, golf courses, swimming pools and a recreation centre with heated pool, basketball,

badminton, martial arts and aerobics facilities. The fairly new Cosmopolitan Club sports complex has indoor and outdoor all-weather bowling greens, 10-pin bowling and many other recreational facilities.

There's a clay target-shooting club not far out of town, and the traditional A & P show still pulls the crowds, as does a more contemporary Garden and Craft Show.

Drive 40 minutes east or west and you're at the sea: many locals have baches on the Coromandel Peninsula and find it easy to get away for the weekend.

And if you like the sophistication of city-style restaurants and cafes but hate the crowds, this is place for you – a relaxed weekend brunch can be just that, because you're not fighting 50 other people for a table. Imagine!

Real Estate

Trends

There's been so much development in Pukekohe in the past couple of years that it's becoming more suburban, and less like a country town. Despite the number of new homes which some may see as detracting from the area, demand is still very high, and that's driving prices ever upwards.

Hampton Park and Buckland Estate are two fairly new subdivisions where the sections are quite large and values are high. One home on a 1500m2 section at Buckland Estate recently sold for $640,000.

A few years ago you could buy something small and very modest in the worst part of town for around $100,000; now you'll be lucky if it's $170,000.

Rental and investment

There has always been good demand for

rental properties in Pukekohe, and that has increased with the population. At the time of writing, landlords were happy to buy at 5% returns because they're so confident of the town's future growth.

Best streets

Sunset Dr and its off-shoot Cloverlea Pl are sought after because they back on to a big reserve and are very close to Pukekohe Hill School.

Karaka

To the north of Pukekohe, Karaka is a lifestyle area of mainly 10-acre blocks, popular with the same sort of people who flock to Whitford to live. Numbers are a good way to get a handle on the sort of place this is. Westbury, the 253ha Karaka stud farm of London-based Kiwi businessman Eric Watson, for example, is estimated to be worth about $60 million. Bare land in the neighbourhood sells for close to $123,000 a hectare. Fees for senior students at local private school Strathallan are almost $12,000 a year. Get the picture?

The Karaka Sales Centre is well-known as the home of the National Premier Yearling Sale figure, where each year tens of millions of dollars passes from one well-shod horse-lover to another.

Strathallan is one of the largest independent school complexes in New Zealand, and goes right through from pre-school to Year 13. It's set on 14.5ha of gently rolling country with a tranquil tidal inlet winding round the property.

Yes, this is a land of privileged beings, a world away from their neighbours across the Pahurehure Inlet: Weymouth, Wattle

Local Hero: Pukekohe Park

Whether you like your racing on legs or wheels, Pukekohe Park is the place to be. More than 50,000 people gather here for some events, from premier horse racing to international motor racing, as well as rock concerts and agricultural shows.

Pukekohe Park is the home of both the Counties Racing Club (horses, that is) and the New Zealand round of the Australian V8 Supercar Series in April each year, although Wellington is bidding to host the event. From the end of 2005, after a $2.5 million re-development programme, it'll be replacing Takanini as the Auckland Racing Club's training facility for the northern region. This will lift the profile of Counties Racing Club, and lift the number of horses trained there from about 100 to 400.

Downs and Conifer Grove. But when you're just passing through, you don't see dollar signs. Karaka could be any pretty part of rural New Zealand. Except, of course, that it's so close to urban amenities. Pukekohe is less than 10 minutes' drive south; Papakura about the same to the east.

Why I live there

Racing driver Dean Perkins

Racing driver Dean Perkins and his wife moved to Pukekohe 15 years ago because they wanted to raise their family in the country. For Dean, who says he's always been a petrol-head, the fact that New Zealand's top motor racing track was nearby was definitely a bonus. They bought an 3ha block and shifted an old house on to it. The 200-pupil Buckland School was "brilliant" for their children.

Dean says Pukekohe's a very friendly place, and as a self-employed engineer it was easy for him to make good contacts and get to know everybody.

The big "muscle car" his team built and ran about five years ago was always a crowd-pleaser at the track. One die-hard fan has just bought the car with the aim of restoring it. Now Dean's involved in the New Zealand V8 Touring Car Championship, considered the pinnacle of local motor racing. In 2003 and 2004 his team finished third out of the 36 teams competing.

House prices

House		
Bedrooms		🛏 🛏
Price	$350,000 – $380,000	
Bedrooms		🛏 🛏 🛏
Price	$400,000 – $530,000	

House on a big section

Bedrooms	🛏 🛏 🛏 🛏
Price	$600,000 – $680,000

Large lifestyle block

Price	$800,000

Small lifestyle block

Price	$300,000 – $400,000 plus

Residential sections, 500m2

Price	$170,000

Rental prices

Flat

Bedroom	🛏
Price	$145 – $150/wk

House

Bedrooms	🛏 🛏
Price	$210 – $215/wk
Bedrooms	🛏 🛏 🛏
Price	$230 – $260/wk
Bedrooms	🛏 🛏 🛏 🛏
Price	$335/wk

Travel times

CBD	off-peak 35min
	peak 75 min
Manukau City shops	20 min
Southern motorway	10 min
Airport	30 min

The area is served by buses and trains; the trains are not very frequent, as most only go to Papakura further up the line.

Each neighbourhood in this book features a map colour-coded according to eleven population groups. This neighbourhood classification system, known as MOSAIC® is created by Pinpoint Target Marketing, a division of PMP Limited.

MOSAIC® combines information on consumer demographics, households, lifestyles and attitudes so you can see who might live next door if you choose to buy in an area. The detailed descriptions on the following pages highlight characteristics such as what sports and activities people enjoy, typical occupations and even what they eat for dinner.

Information is gathered from the following sources:
- Property attribute data provided by Quotable Value NZ
- New Zealand Census data from Statistics NZ
- Motor vehicle data from Cadmus
- Market research data sourced from Roy Morgan Research

For more information on MOSAIC® and other segmentation and mapping solutions, contact Pinpoint Target Marketing on 0800 938 555.

Elite Professionals

Elite Professionals are upper class mature families, located in affluent urban areas, though also increasingly on rural lifestyle blocks. They are typically between 45 and 54 years of age. Elite Professionals are successful, degree-qualified and work long hours in occupations that provide them with the highest median household incomes of all MOSAIC Groups, at over $78,000 per annum. The majority are employed as white-collar professionals and managers. Their houses are of the highest value, and consist mainly of large separate houses and apartments, with many of these being owned outright. These neighbourhoods revel in social interaction and their residents can often be seen sailing around the harbour, enjoying a game of tennis or golf, or at the beach. Keeping up with the cutting edge of fashion and technology at exclusive stores is considered a must. Fine dining at exclusive restaurants and cafes or hosting dinner parties is enjoyed regularly, especially over a premium bottle of wine. Elite Professionals like attending cultural activities such as ballet, opera and live theatre. Their occupations demand that they keep abreast of current affairs and the latest trends, so they are avid readers of newspapers and business, motoring and home lifestyle magazines.

Comfortable & Secure

Comfortable & Secure are typically middle-aged families with teenage children, or empty nesters. They are reasonably well qualified, and work as mid-level managers, professionals and technicians. Their household incomes are high, at over $60,000 the second highest of all MOSAIC Groups. They predominantly live in separate houses that they own outright. Busy with work and family commitments, these people generally don't have much time to spend cooking. When they do have a chance to relax, they like to spend it keeping up-to-date with ways to improve their homes. Given that home ownership is high this is not surprising, and many even admit to being more interested in their house than their career. Popular pastimes include jogging and going to the gym, as well as water sports such as sailing and power boating. Surfing the internet, shopping, frequenting cafes and weekends at the beach are other common ways to relax. Motor vehicle ownership is high across the group, with cars often purchased on looks - particularly by the teenaged members of the household. They keep up to date with current affairs through newspapers, television and the internet, and read major women's, home and lifestyle and business magazines.

Stylish Singles

Stylish Singles represent a mix of young professionals and students, and are typically aged between 20 and 34. The majority live in inner-suburban flats or close to tertiary campuses. Success-driven and with high qualification levels, most work in professional and technical occupations where they earn well above average household incomes - over $48,000 per annum. Stylish Singles live for the moment and will try anything once. They are extroverted and sociable, often letting their hair down at bars and clubs. Cars, clothes and accessories are seen as an extension of themselves. They wear stylish clothing with the right labels, and express  themselves through conspicuous purchases. They were born to shop, and aren't afraid to use credit to buy the things they want. These people are technologically savvy - "early adopters" - and are into computers, DVD players and associated technical gadgets. They are heavy internet users and also cultured, generally appreciating art and fine food, but are just as comfortable with takeaways and a movie. Keeping fit is important, and exercise is often slotted into their busy schedules. Stylish Singles enjoy sporting activities such as aerobics, rugby, surfing and jet-skiing. On winter weekends, they can often be seen on the slopes of the nation's skifields.

Family Balance

Family Balance are usually middle-aged families with young school-aged children, located in the outer suburbs. A high proportion have two or more children. They predominantly live in separate houses in average condition, with slightly below average property values due to their location. Home ownership rates are high, and Family Balance take pride in their homes. Balancing family and career, they work hard to support their families in a variety of occupations, from trades to professional and technical occupations. Household incomes average just under $46,000. Shopping is completed after work or on weekends. Value for money is a key factor in the purchase decision process and Family Balance make a conscious effort to buy New Zealand-made products. Family Balance are not technically minded or particularly concerned with fashion. They prefer  the familiar and simple things in life, such as motor sport, hunting and fishing. While not overly concerned with image, some are increasingly concerned with health issues, such as cholesterol. Increasing numbers are taking up physical activities such as walking, jogging, and working out at the gym.

Kiwiana

This group of classic Kiwis contains a mixture of ages and family groups - from young families to older retirees. Kiwiana live in a mixture of localities, including big city suburbs. Their houses are valued close to the national median, if not slightly below, and are in average condition. These tend to be rented privately, or owned with a mortgage. Occupations are more manual in nature or in trades, which bring home slightly below average household incomes of $38,000. Having to make their earnings stretch, Kiwiana look for bargains and are the most attracted to discounts, promotions and special offers. Although influenced by price, Kiwiana still only  buy products they know and trust, including brands they have grown up with. This reluctance to try new things is highlighted by the fact they are likely to buy the same food from week to week. When it comes to fashion these people prefer function over style, and are somewhat hesitant when it comes to technology and the internet. Traditional Kiwi sports such as rugby, rugby league and cricket are popular with younger people, with pursuits such as darts popular with older people. Magazine readership is high within the Kiwiana types.

Local Pride

Local Pride contains a mixture of young families, and older 50-somethings, with a relatively high incidence of households containing more than one family. These people are proud of their close-knit local communities. Houses are generally separate dwellings, of average quality and below average capital value. However, their homes are built on above average sized sections, typically the classic quarter acre section. Homes are generally mortgaged. Education levels are among the lowest, and consequently some struggle to find employment. The most common jobs include trades, manual occupations and work in the primary sector, such as in agriculture and fishing. Household income levels of $37,000 are below average, but this doesn't necessarily mean they struggle, as the cost of living is significantly lower in their neighbourhoods. Local Pride live conservatively and are more likely to watch television at home than hold dinner parties or attend cultural events. They do not spend extravagantly and rarely eat at expensive restaurants. They can occasionally be found buying takeaways such as fish and chips. Local Prides don't welcome change, and are not particularly interested in technology.

Blue Collar Owners

Blue Collar Owners consist of families, generally aged between 20 and 34. These households contain a mixture of married and defacto couples, along with the occasional solo parent family. Home values are low and there is a mixture of government owned, privately rented and mortgaged houses. Tertiary qualifications are not common, and the average household income, at $35,000, is below average. Common occupations include agriculture and fisheries, trades and manual jobs. Unemployment is high. Blue Collar Owners are not interested in fashion, nor exercise such as aerobics and running. However, tough team sports such as rugby and rugby league are popular. Blue Collar Owners enjoy entering competitions and using coupons. One luxury is beer, particularly New Zealand beers, which are often consumed with mates. Wine is less popular than with other consumers. These people also enjoy fast food. Blue Collar Owners are sceptical about issues such as globalisation, believing they have yet to see any benefits from the so-called "global community". They are particularly wary of genetically modified food. New technology is not found particularly interesting or important, and internet usage is below average.

Grey Power

Grey Power are the oldest MOSAIC Group, with most aged over 55. Housing types consist of separate houses, flats and retirement homes. These properties have a capital value slightly below average and conditions vary from good to poor. Average household incomes are approximately $29,000. These people are proud of their country and try to buy the New Zealand-made products that they have grown up with, wherever possible. Set in their ways, they are not interested in trying new products often, even when discounted or on special. Grey Power rarely eat out. Instead they enjoy cooking and traditional meals at home. They don't often eat new, or foreign foods. Grey Power are indifferent to new technology, particularly the internet, and usage rates are some of the lowest of all New Zealanders. They enjoy reading magazines, however, and are particularly fond of women's lifestyle and home lifestyle magazines. When it comes to activities, slower games such as lawn bowls and darts are preferred, though they do enjoy watching active sports such as rugby and cricket on TV. They also watch horse racing which they occasionally flutter on. They spend more time watching TV than other consumer groups, though pay television subscriptions are low.

Cultural Diversity

These neighbourhoods are the most culturally diverse, with strong representations of Maori, Pacific Islanders and Asians. Households range from large young families to one-person retirees. Single parents are more commonly found in these neighbourhoods, making use of lower cost services and accommodation. Housing is low cost and below average quality, with the average home value being $139,000. A significant proportion of these people live in government-owned rental accommodation. Education levels are lower, and unemployment is higher, than all other MOSAIC Groups. Workers are usually employed in manual or service occupations, earning an average household income of just under $30,000 per annum. Bargain basement emporiums, factory outlets and traditional stores are favoured, with more expensive items frequently bought on credit. Takeaways and pre-prepared meals are regularly purchased to eat at home. They believe environmentally friendly products are overpriced. Betting on sport and racing is a popular pastime, albeit with minimal disposable income. Cultural Diversity also enjoy watching TV, recording the heaviest television viewing levels of all MOSAIC Groups. Tough sporting activities such as rugby and league appeal to this group.

Rural Lifestyle

Rural Lifestyle are located in country farming areas and rural service towns. This group includes school children with middle-aged parents, with grandparents, ranging in age from 25 to 64. Employment is generally on the farm, however there are lifestyle types within this group, such as Suits & Gumboots, who work in the city while living on lifestyle blocks or "toy farms". Rural Lifestyle types spend a disproportionate amount of time tending the land, and as most live at work, they find it difficult to switch off from their jobs. Average household income is approximately $48,000. Rural Lifestyle like to have traditional meals at home, often eating meat, and rarely buy frozen or ready prepared meals. New Zealand beer is popular, and preferred over wine. Self sufficient, they consider themselves as do-it-yourself kind of people, and are surprisingly adept at using computers and other technology. They are light internet users, however, as the technology is often not practical in remote areas. Rural Lifestyle don't trust the government, feeling the agricultural sector is increasingly neglected in favour of more "fashionable" industries. They enjoy a beer after a hard day and rarely eat at restaurants.

Brand New Houses

Brand New Houses are predominantly found in new subdivisions on the outskirts of the city. Many of these new subdivisions are being built on what was farmland. Some new houses are also found within established areas, where in-fill and higher density housing is occurring as vacant land runs out. These are typically homes built by executive families, but also include some lower cost first homes and retirement homes. Brand New Houses contain a cross section of age groups, and are mainly family households occupying larger than average sized homes. Although these homes are larger than average, mean prices are lower due to lower land prices further away from the central city. There are more Asian and fewer Maori and Pacific Islander new homeowners than elsewhere, and quite a few new homeowners are recent immigrants. Occupations are often managerial, technical or trades oriented. Brand New Houses are slightly more educated than the rest of the population, which results in an above average median household income of approximately $45,500. Internet access is high in these neighbourhoods. Motor vehicle ownership is high, with many households having three or more vehicles, and very few have only one car.

WHO LIVES WHERE?

Suburb		2001 Population	% Change since 1996	% Aged Under 15 Years	% Aged Over 65 Years	% European	% Maori	% Pacific Peoples	% Asian
CENTRAL	Auckland City	11193	89.01	4.02	4.10	51.38	5.49	3.46	31.20
	Avondale	25206	11.61	22.80	10.08	45.11	10.93	24.57	20.02
	Blockhouse Bay	26283	6.12	22.44	12.24	50.43	5.95	14.67	29.06
	Eastern Bays	24801	3.35	17.54	14.47	83.41	4.68	2.03	9.19
	Epsom	9849	2.88	20.32	9.53	61.29	2.56	1.83	32.32
	Glen Innes/Pt England	16125	4.15	26.98	11.81	46.79	15.50	31.83	8.89
	Grey Lynn	23781	2.87	18.09	9.84	73.05	8.58	14.82	8.14
	Hauraki Gulf Islands	7242	12.33	20.05	13.84	86.12	11.10	3.15	2.03
	Kingsland	5421	10.59	13.61	3.98	65.52	8.36	15.05	9.96
	Meadowbank	24351	3.98	17.51	10.95	71.75	4.92	4.36	18.60
	Mt Albert	18591	5.12	19.40	9.29	62.27	6.99	11.46	18.28
	Mt Eden	36075	2.82	19.53	7.97	66.15	6.61	8.79	18.99
	Mt Roskill	21936	7.03	20.90	13.09	50.56	5.44	13.65	30.06
	One Tree Hill	11271	5.5	19.11	12.86	70.91	4.07	3.09	23.02
	Onehunga	25890	6.85	20.03	10.76	61.45	8.90	17.46	14.77
	Pamure	26049	5.57	23.62	8.81	45.02	16.01	24.42	18.93
	Parnell/New Market	7593	7.79	10.27	8.06	81.59	4.27	1.82	8.85
	Ponsonby	14415	0.38	14.19	7.62	82.39	6.66	8.14	4.79
	Remuera	18660	2.76	19.98	12.28	81.74	2.17	1.53	12.68
WEST	Helensville	6819	13.54	25.34	8.84	83.99	15.35	3.52	1.54
	Henderson	50013	12.04	23.72	10.95	64.54	14.97	14.46	11.61
	Kumeu/Huapai	14748	13.61	24.13	8.18	90.01	6.81	1.75	2.58
	New Lynn	42216	8.72	23.94	9.77	58.91	12.49	18.80	14.83
	Swanson	31485	8.53	27.59	6.03	64.70	15.46	18.11	7.37
	Titirangi	24120	2.81	24.07	8.67	87.82	7.25	3.96	4.17
	West Coast Beaches	6894	6.54	24.76	5.87	88.99	8.96	2.61	1.65
	West Harbour	16062	7.49	25.35	5.96	73.91	9.76	7.99	12.61

Area								
NORTH								
Albany	11634	60.58	24.29	5.65	84.01	7.14	1.88	8.38
Beachhaven/Birkdale	18603	0.89	24.35	7.76	74.07	14.06	9.19	8.40
Belmont/Bayswater	9015	-4.12	21.76	13.91	87.05	9.35	2.56	4.99
Devonport	7374	-5.13	21.20	10.78	92.76	5.53	1.91	2.03
Glenfield	30099	10.52	22.34	6.73	69.65	8.04	4.59	18.01
Hibiscus Coast	31488	16.99	21.34	19.83	90.39	6.67	1.45	2.49
Lower East Coast Bays	18456	0.92	19.64	11.64	87.29	2.57	0.75	9.56
Northcote	32346	2.94	19.23	11.78	73.51	7.94	3.74	16.11
Takapuna	12819	2.89	14.84	19.10	83.10	4.05	1.31	10.45
Upper East Coast Bays	28626	14.84	21.21	10.68	86.08	4.37	1.36	8.79
Warkworth	7836	14.01	20.52	20.75	91.42	7.27	1.34	1.91
Westlake	20631	3.88	18.44	14.70	74.76	4.57	2.02	18.92
EAST								
Beachlands-Maraetai	4419	8.39	25.19	10.39	89.61	7.60	1.97	1.70
Botany	26064	65.96	22.43	7.38	62.43	3.36	1.55	31.64
Bucklands Beach	10875	4.59	21.63	9.57	72.30	2.57	1.32	23.48
Half Moon Bay	9150	-0.81	20.79	10.62	71.64	4.33	9.05	21.74
Howick	18888	5.06	20.90	12.74	86.47	3.72	1.41	9.15
Pakuranga	23451	2.9	20.21	13.06	66.18	6.95	4.35	24.36
Whitford	5121	6.36	23.73	9.26	89.98	7.03	1.11	1.70
SOUTH								
Mangere	53304	5.76	31.61	6.61	24.37	19.01	53.83	9.10
Manukau/Clover Park	31632	16.71	29.47	5.73	35.27	17.61	36.47	16.29
Manurewa	61434	12.37	28.84	7.04	52.54	26.99	19.99	8.23
Otahuhu	39006	4.8	25.78	10.41	40.66	17.05	27.81	20.13
Otara	16371	-1.36	35.55	5.24	10.61	21.26	71.49	2.18
Papakura	36135	3.29	25.58	9.95	69.95	24.43	7.83	5.23
Pukekohe	13623	13.55	25.32	13.06	69.68	19.58	4.98	7.66

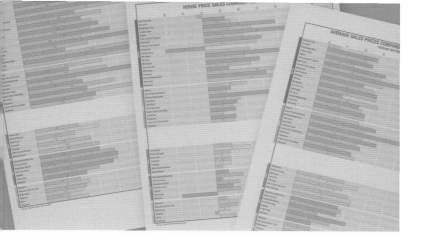

What are house prices doing?

A history of house sales is always a good yardstick on which to base your house-buying decisions. None of us wants to pay over the odds for a house but knowing what is reasonable, especially in a buoyant market, can be difficult to assess. While the information on the following pages is based on averages and is therefore broadbrush, it gives some useful guidelines, using three key measurements:

1. Average house prices 2004.

Check out the most expensive suburbs, and the cheapest. As with any figures based on averages, these can be skewed by particularly high or low sales prices in the area. If, for example, a large terraced housing development was launched and sold at very affordable rates during the year but located in an expensive suburb, it will bring the averages down.

2. House price changes from 2003 to 2004.

This shows the percentage increase in each suburb for the year ending July 2004 compared with July 2003. Again, certain sectors of the market, may appear to buck the trend in each area.

3. Average 2004 house prices compared to capital values.

Depending on when capital valuations for an area were last made, this can be a particularly good guide to market values. You can determine what premium property is attracting, say, 10% above capital valuation. This may then influence any offer you might make for a property in that area.

N.B. Average Sale Price: The average net sale price of the properties sold (excludes chattels).

Average Capital Value: The average capital value of the properties sold at the date of latest Rating Valuation.

Source: Quotable Value New Zealand
www.qv.co.nz

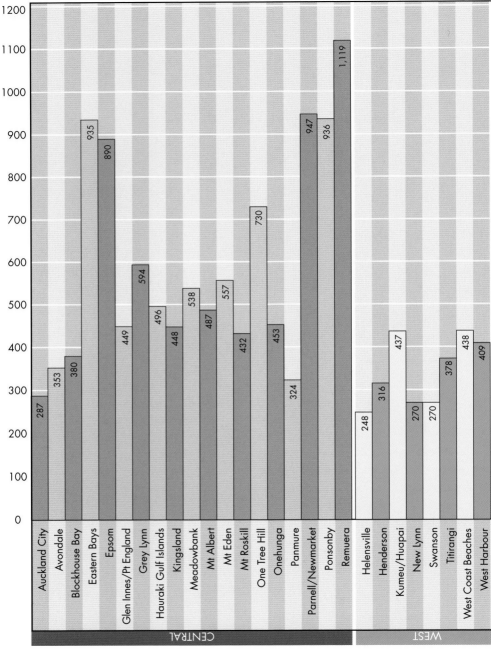

AVERAGE HOUSE PRICES 2004
HOUSE PRICES IN $'000

Suburb	Price ($'000)
Auckland City	287
Avondale	353
Blockhouse Bay	380
Eastern Bays	935
Epsom	890
Glen Innes/Pt England	449
Grey Lynn	594
Hauraki Gulf Islands	496
Kingsland	448
Meadowbank	538
Mt Albert	487
Mt Eden	557
Mt Roskill	432
One Tree Hill	730
Onehunga	453
Panmure	324
Parnell/Newmarket	947
Ponsonby	936
Remuera	1,119
Helensville	248
Henderson	316
Kumeu/Huapai	437
New Lynn	270
Swanson	270
Titirangi	378
West Coast Beaches	438
West Harbour	409

CENTRAL • WEST

Region	Area	Value
NORTH	Albany	548
	Beach Haven/Birkdale	322
	Belmont/Bayswater	628
	Devonport	910
	Glenfield	340
	Hibiscus Coast	412
	Lower East Coast Bays	660
	Northcote	425
	Takapuna	816
	Upper East Coast Bays	465
	Warkworth	363
	Westlake	444
EAST	Beachlands/Maeratai	496
	Botany Downs	478
	Bucklands Beach	600
	Half Moon Bay	497
	Howick	521
	Pakuranga	383
	Whitford	437
SOUTH	Mangere	271
	Manukau/Clover Park	287
	Manurewa	259
	Otahuhu	273
	Otara	166
	Papakura	270
	Pukekohe	266

Source: Quotable Value Limited

(QV) www.qv.co.nz

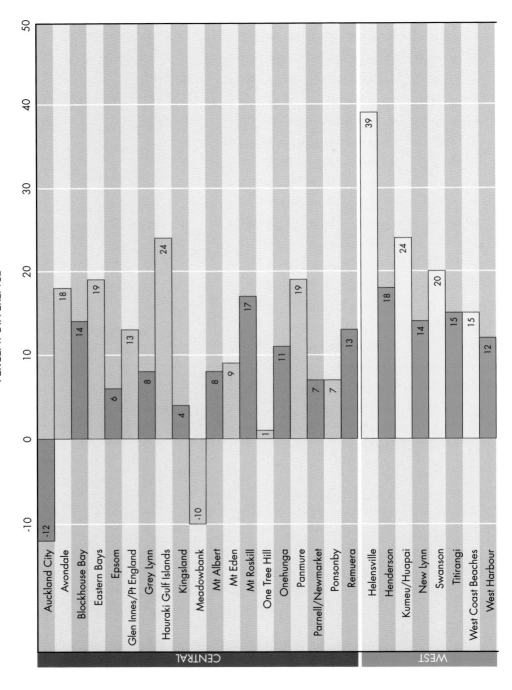

AVERAGE HOUSE PRICE CHANGES 2003 - 2004
PERCENT DIFFERENCE

CENTRAL

Auckland City	-12
Avondale	18
Blockhouse Bay	14
Eastern Bays	19
Epsom	6
Glen Innes/Pt England	13
Grey Lynn	8
Hauraki Gulf Islands	24
Kingsland	4
Meadowbank	-10
Mt Albert	8
Mt Eden	9
Mt Roskill	17
One Tree Hill	1
Onehunga	11
Panmure	19
Parnell/Newmarket	7
Ponsonby	7
Remuera	13

WEST

Helensville	39
Henderson	18
Kumeu/Huapai	24
New Lynn	14
Swanson	20
Titirangi	15
West Coast Beaches	15
West Harbour	12

NORTH

Area	Value
Albany	25
Beach Haven/Birkdale	22
Belmont/Bayswater	30
Devonport	20
Glenfield	16
Hibiscus Coast	25
Lower East Coast Bays	19
Northcote	14
Takapuna	12
Upper East Coast Bays	18
Warkworth	27
Westlake	14

EAST

Area	Value
Beachlands/Maeratai	37
Botany Downs	20
Bucklands Beach	12
Half Moon Bay	3
Howick	21
Pakuranga	11
Whitford	46

SOUTH

Area	Value
Mangere	22
Manukau/Clover Park	12
Manurewa	5
Otahuhu	14
Otara	21
Papakura	18
Pukekohe	40

Source: Quotable Value Limited

AVERAGE 2004 HOUSE PRICES COMPARED TO CAPITAL VALUES
PERCENT DIFFERENCE

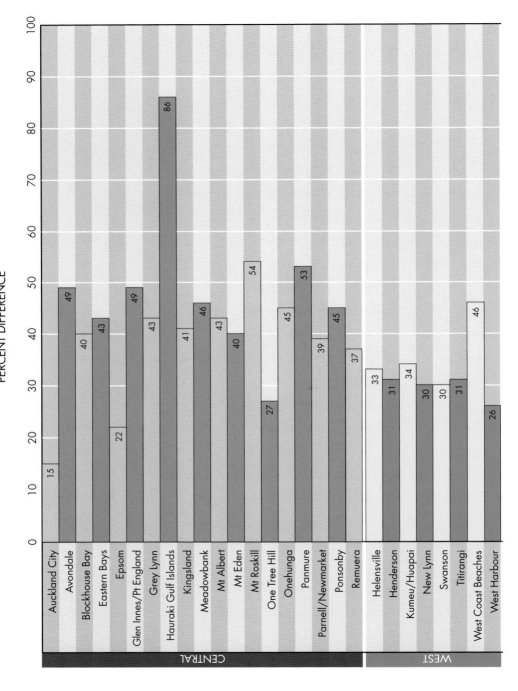

Region	Location	Value
NORTH	Albany	43
	Beach Haven/Birkdale	61
	Belmont/Bayswater	57
	Devonport	55
	Glenfield	48
	Hibiscus Coast	35
	Lower East Coast Bays	50
	Northcote	48
	Takapuna	50
	Upper East Coast Bays	46
	Warkworth	40
	Westlake	50
EAST	Beachlands/Maeratai	67
	Botany Downs	30
	Bucklands Beach	39
	Half Moon Bay	30
	Howick	44
	Pakuranga	36
	Whitford	62
SOUTH	Mangere	43
	Manukau/Clover Park	36
	Manurewa	31
	Otahuhu	42
	Otara	34
	Papakura	27
	Pukekohe	43

Source: Quotable Value Limited

www.qv.co.nz

The school zone maps on the following pages let you see which public secondary schools your children may be eligible to attend. We strongly recommend, however, that you contact the school to confirm the zone status of any particular street – or check the school's website. The star on each map shows the location of the school; roll numbers are as at 2004. If a public high school is not on these pages, it doesn't have a defined zone, so its roll is open to all-comers. Please contact your local school for more details. There is also a list of Auckland schools – primary, intermediate and secondary – grouped by region and neighbourhood. If you're considering a private school, we've compiled a list of Auckland's better-known private schools, including fees and other details.

If you have school-age children, good schools are high on the list of factors to take into account when choosing where to buy a home. Auckland has many excellent schools, but as the city's school-age population has mushroomed, access to the school of your choice can't be taken for granted.

In the past decade, student numbers at many of the city's most popular schools have rocketed, reflecting both a school's good reputation and the increased numbers of families living locally. To limit school size and prevent overcrowding, the Ministry of Education has a system of enrolment schemes, giving oversubscribed schools a home zone with clearly defined boundaries. If you live within the home zone, the school legally has to accept your child. Most schools have a few out-of-zone places available by ballot – applications close in September for the following year.

Currently around 25% of Auckland schools across all levels have enrolment schemes, including the four new secondary schools that opened in the past two years.

As a result, parents keen to send their children to prestigious state schools clamour to buy a family home in the right zone. They may not be paying private school fees, but they will certainly pay a premium for living in-zone. Real estate agents estimate, for example, that you can pay up to $100,000 more for a property in the Auckland Grammar School zone. The consolation is that these houses are seen as an investment. Once the kids are past school age, the house can be on-sold, with a heftier price tag – as long as the zone doesn't change! Some families opt out of the zoning problem by sending their children to private schools.

Don't presume a school is no good because it doesn't have a zone. There are a number of factors to take into account when assessing local schools. One source is the Education Review Office, which regularly reports on individual schools, and publishes its findings at www.ero.govt.nz. The ministry also publishes schools' academic results.

Each public school has a decile rating, which reflects the socio-economic level of the population from which the school draws its students – not academic results. Factors determining decile ratings are household income, occupation, crowding levels and tertiary educational qualifications.

Schools are rated from 1 to 10. A low decile rating reflects a low socio-economic group and a lower decile school gets more government funding than higher decile schools to help level the inequity among communities. Higher decile schools tend to have more successful parent-driven fundraising and will also charge higher school fees or "donations" – which aren't legally compulsory, but are important to a school's budget.

What is the NCEA?

The NCEA is New Zealand's rather controversial new senior high school assessment regime. It was phased into schools from 2002 and high school graduates of 2004 were the first to enter tertiary study with NCEA Level 3 (Year 13) university entrance grades.

NCEA stands for National Certificate of Educational Achievement, and it replaces the old system of School Certificate and Bursary exams and Sixth Form Certificate internal assessment. NCEA is a standards-based assessment – students are evaluated against a standard, not each other. Instead of marks or percentage ratings, students are given grades of Excellence, Merit, Credit or Incomplete gained through a combination of end-of-year exams run by the NZ Qualifications Authority and internal tests and assignments. Each NCEA subject breaks down into units so results comprehensively outline a student's strengths and weaknesses, eg units in English will include individual grades, such as Excellence for oral speech, Merit for formal writing and Achievement for comprehension.

There has been some disquiet about teething problems with the NCEA, particularly about huge discrepancies in the levels of difficulty among Level 4 Scholarship subject exams in 2004. As a result, ranking of students has been reintroduced at scholarship level and scholarships will now be awarded to a set percentage of students.

So far, though, most practitioners at the coal face are keen to see NCEA continue. They feel the new system meets the needs of a wider range of students and recognises a wider range of achievement.

However, teachers and principals have identified a number of administrative aspects that need rectifying, including external moderation consistency and reliability. Some teachers are also concerned that the increased workload of assessment and moderation cuts into teaching time too much.

Those who oppose NCEA argue it is lowering standards and weakening our students' competitive edge. Some schools (including Auckland Grammar, King's College and Macleans College in Howick) offer the English-based Cambridge International Examinations alongside NCEA. The Cambridge exams are geared to the British school system, so there are concerns that while internationally recognised, they don't have any New Zealand content.

Despite talk from traditionalists about NCEA being easier, university entrance appears more stringent under NCEA. To enter degree level study with NCEA requires not only Level 3 (Year 13) passes but compulsory literacy levels at Level 2 (Year 12). Many students, especially international and new immigrants, have struggled to meet these requirements.

Alfriston College

550 Porchester Rd, Manurewa,
ph 09 269 0080
www.alfristoncollege.school.nz

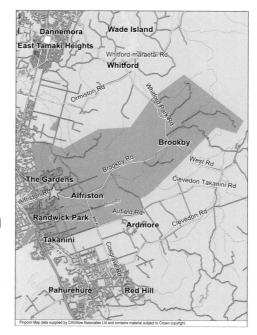

Pinpoint Map data supplied by Critchlow Associates Ltd and contains material subject to Crown copyright.

Roll 277 growing to 1500; co-educational; year 9-13

When brand new Alfriston College opened its doors in 2004 it showcased outstanding 21st century architecture and an innovative approach. The first new school to be built in South Auckland for many years, it has an ethnically diverse roll. The school will grow its roll to Year 13 during the next three years and eventually cap at 1500 students.

Located on an enviable 11ha of land, Alfriston is now in its second construction phase with a gym being built this year. Rooms feature double glazed windows, controlled air temperature and full use of natural light. While there is currently no pool, there are playing fields, tennis courts, a sit-down cafeteria and state-of-the-art performing arts theatre. The school's architectural design strongly emphasises ICT with the whole school cabled so ICT can be accessed "anytime, anyplace". Alfriston has also taken an innovative approach to education up to Year 12. Students learn through blended courses such as Nature and Balance or Crime Scene and Investigation (combining social studies and science) that tie learning into real life. Three days each term are dedicated to specific challenges, such as an enterprise or community challenge or local event. Year 12 and 13 students learn traditional specialist subjects such as Physics, English etc.

Zone boundary: Starting at Gt South Rd / Hill Rd intersection the zone travels northeast up the centre of Hill Rd to the motorway bridge. Then north, following the boundaries of the botanic gardens and Totara Park (it does not include the suburbs of Totara Heights or Goodwood Heights). The northern boundary is the intersection of Totara Park, Redoubt Rd and Hilltop Rd. From here the zone moves east, including both sides of Redoubt Rd (and its side streets) and travels northeast (excluding Bownhill Rd) and intersects Whitford Park Rd at the bridge. It continues northeast until the end of Ara Kotinga is reached and then travels southeast until it reaches the Clevedon Scenic Reserve. From the Clevedon Scenic Reserve the zone travels southwest, intersecting Twilight Rd at the Quarry, and West Rd at their highest point, then continues southwest along the Watershed until the intersection of Alfriston-Ardmore Rd with Clevedon-Takanini Rd. From here, it travels south down the centre of Alfriston-Ardmore Rd until Airfield Rd. Then down the centre of Airfield Rd until Takanini School Rd and then down the centre of Taka St. From the Gt South Rd/Taka St intersection the zone moves northwards through the centre of Gt South Rd until Hill Rd is reached.

Auckland Grammar School

Mountain Rd, Epsom, ph 09 623 5400
www.ags.school.nz

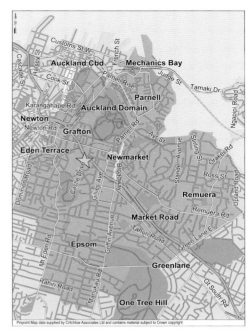

Roll 2554; boys; year 9-13

Auckland Grammar is Auckland's highest-profile school in more ways than one. It's a state school with lots of status, carrying all the born-to-win authority of the best private school (and then some). The "grammar zone" takes in some of Auckland's top suburbs and the school's reputation is responsible for adding a substantial price premium to properties in those already desirable areas. Plenty of parents keen to make sure their sons get top education and sporting opportunities in a traditional all-male school think the investment is worth it. Auckland Grammar occupies a prominent chunk of real estate on the slopes of Mt Eden, with a historic Mission-style main building overlooking the motorway. (The school also has an outdoor education centre in Ohakune.) The school's students top the exam tables year after year and it offers the Cambridge International examinations as an adjunct.

Former students are a veritable Auckland old-boys' network of business leaders, doctors, lawyers, judges, rugby and cricket stars, including famed All Black captain Wilson Whineray, actor and Auckland Festival director Simon Prast, Maori leader Professor Sir Hugh Kawharu of Ngati Whatua, and Mt Everest conqueror, Sir Edmund Hillary.

Zone boundary: Northern boundary is the south side of Victoria St East from the Queen St intersection; Bowen St (south side), Waterloo Quadrant (south side) and Alten Rd (south side). Left into Stanley St (east side) and the Strand (south side), and north to Mechanics Bay. Western boundary is the east side of Queen St, Upper Queen St, Exmouth St, New North Rd to Dominion Rd. The east side of Dominion Rd to Grange Rd. Both sides of Grange Rd. South into Henley Rd (both sides) to Balmoral Rd. The north side of Balmoral Rd to Mt Eden Rd. The east side of Mt Eden Rd to Landscape Rd. Southern boundary is Landscape Rd, Selwyn Rd, Glenferrie Pl and Rostrevor Ave (both sides of all streets) to Pah Rd. Both sides of Pah Rd and Manukau Rd to Golf Rd (both sides) and Fern Rd (both sides). The western boundary of Cornwall Park to Claude Rd, and then in a direct line from the Cornwall Park end of Claude Rd to the intersection of Greenlane West and Pohutakawa Dr. The north side of Greenlane West to the intersection of Wheturangi Rd. Greenlane West (north side) from Wheturangi Rd to Great South Rd, and then Greenlane East (north side) to the intersection with Remuera Rd. Remuera Rd (north side) to Upland Rd. Eastern boundary is Upland Rd (west side) to the northern intersection with Orakei Rd to Hobson Bay, and the western foreshore of Hobson Bay to Judges Bay and Mechanics Bay.

Auckland Girls' Grammar School

Howe St, Newton, ph 09 307 4180
www.aggs.school.nz

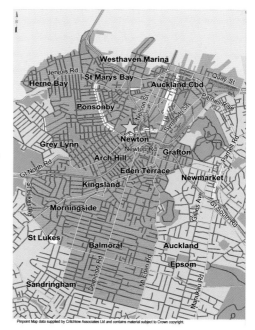

Pinpoint Map data supplied by Critchlow Associates Ltd and contains material subject to Crown copyright.

<u>Roll 1522; girls; year 9-13</u>
Auckland Girls' Grammar School (AGGS) is a diverse multicultural inner city public girl's school. There are more than 50 ethnic groups, including 53 international students.

Academic standards are high with the school winning the Goodman Fielder School of the Year Award for 2000. This award acknowledges achievement in academic, sporting, cultural, social and environmental aspects of the school.

Established on its current site in 1906, the historic and beautiful brick buildings now sit alongside modern science laboratories, classrooms and the Dorothy Winstone Centre, a theatre and auditorium. A new gym, art block and art design block are nearly completed.

Auckland Girls' has a strong sporting reputation with more than 25 sporting codes on offer, including rock climbing and lacrosse. Sporting facilities include a gymnasium, swimming and diving pools. Many students represent their sport at a regional or national level. Netball is very strong with the Open A team making regional and national finals most years.

The arts curriculum includes an annual school production, debating teams and participation in the Sheila Winn Regional Shakespeare Festival, which has been hosted at AGGS for the past three years. The school also has a childcare centre.

Influential former students include ex National Party President Michelle Boag, community leader Dorothy Winstone, politician Laila Harre, Middlemore Hospital senior manager Dr Wendy Walker and Maori politician Georgina Te Heuheu.

Zone boundary: From Waitemata Harbour via the Strand, Stanley St, Grafton Rd, Nugent St to Mt Eden Rd taking in Park Rd and Boston Rd and the streets between. Also Water, Kohutu, Enfield, Harold, Edwin, Mary and Kohekohe Sts. It runs along Mt Eden Rd to Landscape Rd, along Landscape Rd to Lambeth Rd to Sandringham Rd. Along Sandringham Rd to St Lukes Rd. Along St Lukes Rd to Great North Rd. Up China Man's Hill to Surrey Cres. Surrey Cres to Richmond Rd. Around Richmond Rd to Ponsonby Rd. Along Richmond Rd to Coxs Creek (Bayfield Park Side) to Marine Pde, along Marine Pde to the harbour. Both sides of all streets are included.

Avondale College

Victor St, Avondale, ph 09 828 7024
www.avcol.school.nz

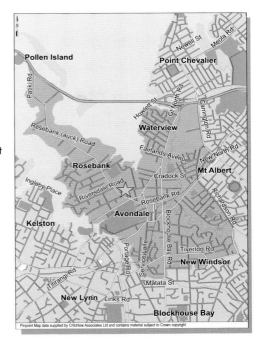

Roll 2730; co-educational; year 9-13
Avondale College is the largest secondary school in West Auckland and second largest in Auckland. The roll reflects the multicultural mix of the surrounding suburbs with the largest groupings being Asian (23.5%), Pacific (21.5%) and Pakeha (39%). It is a popular choice of school in the area and is handily situated alongside Avondale Intermediate.

In recent years the college has developed strong business relationships with the local community and is known for its innovative approach to education.

As the school roll expands, so do the facilities with a modern two-storey 14-classroom Technology Centre currently under construction.

The school has a strong reputation in contemporary, orchestral and jazz music. The Big Band, Premier Band and Concert Band regularly win national awards.

Sports are well catered for with a two-gym stadium, a water-based astro hockey turf and extensive sport fields for rugby, soccer, cricket, netball etc. In 2004 both Avondale's boys and girls' basketball teams were 2004 national champions with five of the students representing New Zealand at secondary school level. Another New Zealand representative is a Para Olympic swimmer.

The college owns and operates an Outdoor Education Camp at National Park in the central North Island where students do activities such as rafting, climbing and tramping.

Avondale boasts an eclectic number of famous exes including entertainer Rob Guest, ex Auckland mayor John Banks, broadcaster Merv Smith, novelist Maurice Shadbolt and national sports administrator Murray Halberg.

Zone boundary: From Oakley Creek to the junction of Great North Rd and Carrington Rd; the western side of Carrington Rd to the railway, along the railway to Woodward Rd. Both sides of Richardson Rd to the corner of Maioro St, across New Windsor Rd and Whitney St to both sides of Holbrook St. Across Blockhouse Bay Rd to both sides of Miranda St; across to the Whau Creek and Great North Rd; the rest of Rosebank Peninsula.

Botany Downs
Secondary College

575 Chapel Rd, Botany Downs,
ph 09 273 2310; www.bdsc.school.nz

Pinpoint Map data supplied by Critchlow Associates Ltd and contains material subject to Crown copyright.

Roll 311 growing to 1500; co-educational;
year 9-13

Opened in 2004, the groundbreaking design of east Auckland's newest school won it the New Zealand Institute of Architecture Resene Award for Architecture in Education 2004. The judges described it as "a spectacular learning environment". Environmentally sustainable features reduce the school's energy use. Classrooms have double-glazed windows, air conditioning and are designed to use plenty of natural light. Use of whanau and common space gives a 21st century twist to the old school house system. There are three two-storey Whanau House buildings with the ground floor teaching classrooms opening out onto a common space. Botany Downs has predominantly Pakeha and Asian students.

Technology plays a major part and there are support programmes for high ability/gifted students and special needs students. The school is situated on pleasant grounds with plenty of room to expand. There are currently tennis courts, a gym and performing arts centre.

Zone boundary: From Mangemangeroa Bridge, west along Whitford Rd (both sides) until Chapel Rd; south down the centre of Chapel Rd to the right-hand intersection with Kilimanjaro Dr; west down the centre of Kilimanjaro Dr to the left-hand intersection with Tarnica Rd; south-west down the centre of Tarnica Rd (including Bampton, Ravensdale, Thirlmere and Caldbeck Rises, Ambleside Dr, Keswick Cl, Embleton Cl, Bowscale Pl and Fencote Pl) to the intersection with Botany Rd; south along Botany Rd (both sides) and all no-exit roads off it, to the intersection with Ti Rakau Dr; west down the centre of Ti Rakau Dr to the intersection with Huntington Dr; south across country until the intersection of Smales Rd and Sir Wlliam Ave (including Huntington Dr, Kelvin Hart Dr, Guys Rd and all streets directly off them). Following but excluding Sir William Ave, Lady Ruby Dr and all roads off them, along Accent Dr (excluded), excluding Reg Savoury Pl, until Chapel Rd (all roads north of Accent Dr included); north until the intersection of Chapel Rd (west side only) and Baverstock Rd; east along Baverstock Rd (both sides but no roads off southern side) and across country to Inchinamm Rd (both sides) to the intersection with Gracechurch Dr; east across country until the intersection of Sandstone Rd and Whitford Park Rd; south-east along Whitford Park Rd (both sides, including Brownhill Rd until Polo Lane, included); following the Whitford-Maraetai Rd (both sides) east including Trig Rd, until the northeast intersection with Henson Rd; east to the coast and west until the Mangemangeroa Bridge.

Edgewater College

Edgewater Dr, Pakuranga, ph 09 576 9039
www.edgewater.school.nz

Roll: 1262; co-educational; years 9-13
Ethnic mix: 30% of Pakeha, Asian and
Pacific groups. There's a comprehensive
range of subjects on offer. Sport, cultural
and academic successes are encouraged.
An English Language Foundation Programme
is available for ESOL learners. The school
has extensive landscaped grounds and well
equipped classrooms, including upgraded
science laboratories and computer facilities.
The modern music rooms include recording
studios. Golf, softball, touch rugby, volleyball
and Waka Ama outrigger are just some of the
sports on offer, along with cultural activities.

Zone boundary: Left-hand side of the Pakuranga Highway.
Gossamer Dr to Pakuranga Creek then Harris Rd. Crook Rd
to Highbrook Dr. Tamaki River to the Panmure Bridge.

Epsom Girls' Grammar School

Silver Rd, Epsom, ph 09 630 5963
www.eggs.school.nz

Roll 1948; girls; year 9-13
Epsom Girls' Grammar is the girls' equivalent
to Auckland Grammar – one of New
Zealand's premier girls' schools, and also
one of the largest. Like Auckland Grammar,
the EGGS home zone takes in some of the
city's most desirable suburbs. Epsom Girls' is
on a pleasant 7.2ha campus between Gillies
Ave and the Newmarket end of Manukau Rd.
EGGS has long been respected for the high
quality state education it delivers to young
women, aiming for an ideal mix of traditional
and modern. Its success is reflected in its exam
results, and in the performance of its students

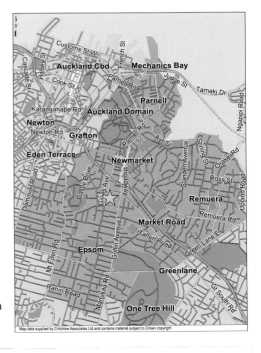

in tertiary education. The school reports that 98% of its Year 13 students go on to university or other tertiary study. It has a great reputation for teaching languages – all Year 9 students study a second language. Arts and music are also strong, with an award-winning school orchestra, instrumental groups, choirs and jazz band. Epsom Girls' students regularly work with Auckland Grammar boys to present stage shows and drama productions. A new arts centre has just been completed.

Famous ex pupils include Prime Minister Helen Clark (a boarder at the school's on-site hostel, Epsom House) and Green Party co-leader Jeanette Fitzsimons.

Zone boundary: The area bounded by Upland Rd (from the harbour), Remuera Rd, Greenlane East, Greenlane West, around One Tree Hill as far south as Golf Rd, to Manukau Rd, to Pah Rd to Selwyn Rd via St Andrews Rd to Landscape Rd, to Mt Eden Rd to Balmoral Rd. Balmoral Rd to Dominion Rd, to Valley Rd to Horoeka Ave, to View Rd to Mt Eden Rd to Normanby Rd, Boston Rd to Khyber Pass to Park Rd to Carlton Gore Rd, George St and along the eastern side of the Auckland Domain, to Parnell Rd, The Strand to the harbour at Mechanics Bay. (Note: houses on both sides of the road on the boundaries plus any cul-de-sacs off an included road are in the zone.)

Glendowie College

Crossfield Rd, Glendowie, ph 09 575 9128 www.glendowie-college.school.nz

<u>Roll 976; co educational; years 9-13</u>
Ethnic mix: 66% Pakeha, 24% Asian, 6% Pacific, 3% Maori.

The college's main emphasis is on traditional academic subjects and NCEA assessment. It offers multi-level study options, accelerant learner programmes and comprehensive ESOL programmes. Students often perform above the national mean in external examinations. A variety of vocational qualifications are also offered, including business studies, retailing and hospitality. Involvement in sport and culture is encouraged. There is a large music department, with stage, concert and jazz bands and string orchestra.

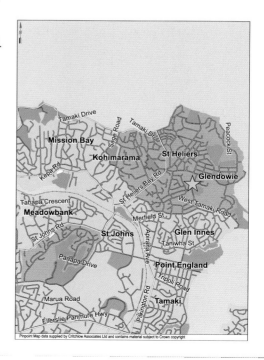

Zone boundary: In Glendowie and St Heliers, the area bounded by West Tamaki Rd, Grampian Rd, Allum St from Grampian Rd, Melanesia Rd from Allum St to Sage Rd, Sage Rd and the coastline from Sage Rd to West Tamaki Rd. Both sides of the boundary road are included. In St Johns Park, the area bounded by St Johns Rd, Remuera Rd, Koraha St, Abbotts Way and College Rd (boundary roads are excluded).

Howick College

Sandspit Rd, Howick, ph 09 534 4492
www.howickcollege.school.nz

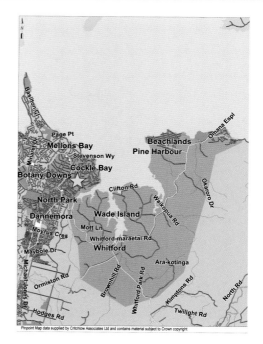

Roll 2371; co educational; years 9-13
Ethnic mix: Pakeha 55%, Asian 29%,
Maori 5%.
Howick College is well established in the
neighbourhood and has a solid academic
reputation. It provides a broad curriculum with
more than 40 subjects for senior students.
The college is recognised for cultural and
sporting opportunities, with music groups
including barbershop, chamber and rock. The
Performing Arts Department is well known for
technical and dramatic expertise.

The school has a high reputation for its
library system, ICT and learning technologies.
A new performing arts block, including
recording studios, is being built.

Note: A new zone is in place for year 9 and 10 students in 2005, and will progressively replace the old zone for other
levels from 2006 to 2008. For details of the old zone, contact the school direct.
New zone boundary: From Howick Beach via Uxbridge Rd (included), Picton St and Ridge Rd (both excluded). From
Howick Intermediate School along Botany Rd (excluded) to Millhouse Dr; both sides of Botany Rd from Millhouse Dr to
Ti Rakau Dr; Golflands Dr and all side streets (included). From the end of Botany Rd, east along Ti Rakau Dr until Chapel
Rd; north along Chapel Rd until Whitford Rd (Kingsgate included); east along Whitford Rd to Whitford including all side
roads (excluding Pt View Dr); Whitford Park Rd and all side roads (including Ara-Kotinga Rd, and Sandstone Rd and
side roads and its extension into Ormiston Rd as far as the ridgeline of the Whitford watershed) and beyond Ara-Kotinga
within walking distance of the school bus stop at Ara-Kotinga. From Whitford Rd, along Whitford-Maraetai Rd and
Maraetai Beach Dr (including all roads leading off it) to the eastern end of Maraetai Beach.

Lynfield College

White Swan Rd, Mt Roskill, ph 09 627 0600 www.lynfield.school.nz

Roll 2151; co-educational; years 9-13 Ethnic mix: Pakeha 36.8%, Asian 38%, Pacific 6.6%,
Other 6.6%, Maori 4.8%. The college offers excellent broad-based education at junior level
and flexible subject choices and multi level approaches at senior level. This includes many
vocational options. Sport, cultural and academic successes are encouraged.
State of the art technology and computer systems are used in all learning areas. It has one of
largest English as a Second Language Departments in Auckland schools and provides strong
community education, refugee support and international student exchanges.

Zone boundary: Along Dominion Rd Extension, through Richardson Rd, May Rd (not included), Stoddard Rd (not included), Mairoro St (not included) through Trevola St, across Holbrook St (not included), Miranda St (not included), Wolverton St (not included) and down Taylor St (not included). For a full list of street names within the zone boundary please visit the Lynfield College website.

Macleans College

Macleans Rd, Bucklands Beach,
ph 09 535 2620 www.macleans.school.nz

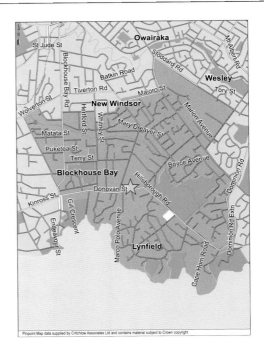

Roll 2400; co-educational; years 9-13
Opening its doors in 1980 to the affluent eastern suburbs, Macleans College is known for innovation and academic success and is now the largest co-educational Year 9-13 school in east Auckland. The school's ethnic mix reflects the suburbs: 35% Pakeha, 21% Chinese, 17% Japanese and Korean, and 15.7% other European.

Macleans offers Cambridge International Examinations (CIE) as well as NCEA. Last year a Macleans College student was first in the world to gain a first year A level in French in CIE. Sporting and musical opportunities also abound. The college was the first to introduce a physical whanau approach to classroom design for secondary schools. Facilities include a huge gym, a specialist auditorium and music blocks.

Macleans' best known former student would have to be Barbara Kendall, Olympic boardsailer gold medallist.

Zone boundary: A line from Howick Beach via Uxbridge Rd (both sides excluded), Picton St, Ridge Rd (1-47, 6-60 included) and Bleakhouse Rd (both sides included) to Gills Rd, then via Gills Rd (both sides excluded and with Udall Pl and other no exit streets off Gills Rd similarly excluded) to the junction of Pigeon Mountain Rd. Via Pigeon Mountain Rd (1-69, 2-60 included) and to the end of Ara Tai Pl (both sides included).

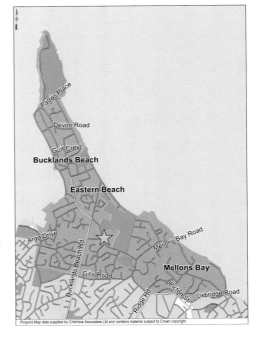

Manurewa High School

67 Browns Rd, Manurewa, ph 09 268 3888
www.manurewa.school.nz

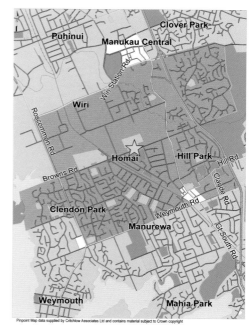
Pinpoint Map data supplied by Critchlow Associates Ltd and contains material subject to Crown copyright

Roll 2078; co-educational; years 9-13
The largest secondary school in south Auckland, Manurewa High School has a multi cultural population – 33% are European, 26% Polynesian, 22% Maori and 15% Asian. The school opened in 1960 to accommodate growth in the area and has continued to be a favoured south Auckland school.

The Year 9-13 classes are streamed to allow students to work to their full potential and an advanced placement programme provides for gifted students. External examination results are consistently above the national average so the approach is working. As well, Manurewa High School ranks among the top in academic competitions such as the Crest Science Projects, Mathematics Competitions, Ilford Shield Photographic Competition and RD Monetary Policy Challenge.

Music is strong in the school with the concert band awarded a Gold Award at the 2004 National Band Festival in Manukau City.

The school's modern amenities and advanced technological equipment have been further enhanced by a new Technology Faculty consisting of 10 classrooms (two Food Technology, two Textiles Technology, four hard materials centres and two machine bays). These state of the art facilities surround a central design space which contains 28 computers.

Famous ex pupils include gold medal winner John Walker, Silver Fern Ana Noovao, All Blacks Mark Cooksley, and Black Cap cricketer Darryl Tuffey.

This new home zone applies at the following year levels: 2005 – years 9-10; 2006 – years 9-11; 2007 – years 9-12; 2008 – all year levels.

Northern boundary is Redoubt Rd (west from the intersection with Hilltop Rd), Wiri Station Rd to Roscommon Rd. Western boundary is Cnr Wiri Station Rd along Roscommon Rd to Browns Rd. Manukau Harbour coastline from Browns Rd to Burundi Ave. Southern boundary is Burundi Ave to Weymouth Rd and east along Weymouth Rd. Alfriston Rd to motorway. Eastern boundary is Along motorway and across northern boundary of botanic gardens. Across Totara Park to the intersection of Redoubt Rd and Hilltop Rd. NB: On all boundary roads, the zone includes only those houses on the side of the road nearest the school.

Massey High School

274 Don Buck Rd, Massey, ph 09 831 0500
www.masseyhigh.school.nz

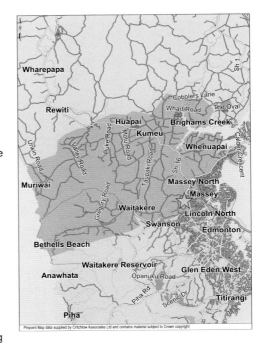

Roll 2423; co-educational; years 9-13
Situated on the northern boundary of West
Auckland, Massey High School draws on a
diverse mix of urban and rural families. The
school's roll has grown significantly during the
past few years, making it the second biggest
in West Auckland.

The school has a strong Maori population
at 20% alongside 43% Pakeha, 23% Asian
and 14% Pacific. Students are placed in one
of five "schools" on the Massey campus, and
there are two dean's working with
each school.

First established in 1969, the Year 9 – 13
school moved to its current Don Buck Rd site
in 1970. Due to the significant roll growth,
the physical school campus is now expanding
with a number of major building projects in progress, including a second gym and a new
technology block.

As well as having a strong academic record, Massey High School delivers outstanding
sports people, musicians, artists, actors and Maori, Pacific and Asian cultural groups.

It provides sporting experiences across 30 different codes with more than 150 teams
participating in inter-school competitions. Road cycling, equestrian and kilikiti are just a few of
the non traditional sports offered, alongside netball, rugby, hockey, soccer etc.

Famous former students include Olympic 2000 yachting representative Peter Nicholas,
Silver Fern Linda Vagana, All Blacks Ron Cribb and Troy Flavell and actors Karl Burnett and
Angela Blomfield (Shortland Streeters Nick and Rachel).

Zone boundary: Northern boundary is Muriwai Beach, Muriwai Rd and side roads to Waimauku. Matua Rd, Deacon
Rd, Cobblers Lane to Wake Rd. Eastern boundary is Waitemata Harbour. Southern boundary is the bottom of Don Buck
Rd, Chamberlain Rd, Crows Rd, Kay Rd, Waitakere Rd, ANZAC Valley Rd and side roads, Te Henga Rd and side
roads, Bethells Rd to Bethells Beach.

Mt Roskill Grammar

Frost Rd, Mt Roskill, ph 09 621 0050
www.mrgs.school.nz

Roll 2432 co-educational; years 9-13

In the past decade or so, Mt Roskill Grammar has grown from a relatively low-profile suburban co-ed to a school with a city-wide and even national reputation. In 2002 Mt Roskill Grammar was named Goodman Fielder Secondary School of the Year, reflecting the school's successes across the curriculum. It's now one of the most sought-after high schools on the Auckland isthmus – family homes in the Mt Roskill zone are in huge demand.

Mt Roskill is one of Auckland's bigger co-ed schools, and sits alongside separate primary and intermediate schools. The school offers a top-quality array of facilities, cultural and sporting activities to match its size, including 16 new science labs, six new computer rooms, a fully equipped music suite, floodlit artificial turf, fitness centre and two gyms.

Students reflect the rainbow cultural mix of the surrounding suburbs – 30% Pakeha, 19% Chinese, 18% Indian, 4% Maori, 8% Samoan, and 5% Tongan, among others. Academic standards are high, with the school producing the nation's top scholar in 2002. Mt Roskill Grammar aims to meet the needs of students with a wide range of abilities and interests.

Mt Roskill Grammar's most famous former student is Academy Award-winning actor Russell Crowe; other notables are Auckland City Councillor and yachtswoman Penny Whiting and former All Black coach John Hart.

Zone boundary: From the Manukau Harbour via Waikowhai Rd and Hillsborough Rd (both excluded) to Dominion Rd Extension; via Dominion Rd Extension (excluded) to Richardson Rd; then via Richardson Rd (excluded), May Rd and Stoddard Rd (both included) to Sandringham Rd; via Sandringham Rd (excluded) to Mt Albert Rd; via Mt Albert Rd (included), Renfrew Ave (excluded), Invermay Ave (included), Landscape Rd (excluded); via St Andrews Rd (excluded) to Mt Albert Rd (included); then via Hillsborough Rd (excluded) to Hillsborough Cemetery/Richardson Rd corner and the Manukau Harbour.

Mt Albert Grammar School

32 Alberton Ave, Mt Albert, ph 09 846 2044
www.mags.school.nz

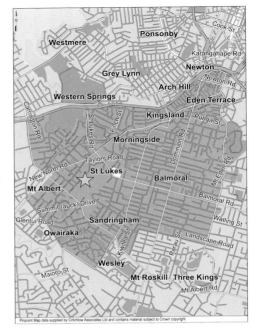

Pinpoint Map data supplied by Critchlow Associates Ltd and contains material subject to Crown copyright

<u>Roll 2474; co-educational but single-sex classes; years 9-13</u>

It's hard not to think sport when you hear the name Mt Albert Grammar School. The school has seven sporting academies, headed by noted sports people such as Kevin Fallon, Te Aroha Keenan and Bryan Williams. It is home to Philips Aquatic Centre's heated indoor swimming pool and wave pool, and has extensive sports grounds as well as a school farm and agricultural unit.

In 2004 Mt Albert Grammar's rugby sevens team were national secondary school champs and the 1st XI Soccer won both the Auckland Championship and Knockout Cup. The 2004 Premier Netball Team also performed extremely well. Traditional sports aside, students can also participate in underwater hockey, roller hockey, snow boarding and aerobics. Students also do well academically and musically.

Originally a boy's grammar school, Mt Albert Grammar opened its doors to girls in 2000. Girls and boys study separately, however, in the junior levels and only combine at senior level for option subjects. In 2005 the first cohort of girls reached Year 13 level with the overall girl's roll approximately 800. The school is also unique in that it offers boarding facilities for 100 boys, a rare service for a public school in the 21st century.

MAGS is one of the 12 biggest schools in Auckland and a school with a strong Polynesian presence. Nearly a third of the population is of Pacific or Maori descent.

Unsurprisingly, many notable ex students are national sport reps, such as Bryan Williams and Dr Peter Snell. Those from other walks of life include former Prime Minister Sir Robert Muldoon, Judge Mick Brown, Professor Sir Keith Sinclair and Sir Woolf Fisher.

Zone boundary: The northern boundary is the north-western motorway. Then all areas north of the junction of the north-western motorway and Carrington Rd, via Carrington Rd, to New North Rd, to Richardson Rd, to Stoddard Rd, to Sandringham Rd extension, to Mount Albert Rd, to Renfrew Rd, to Invermay Ave, to Landscape Rd, to Mount Eden Rd, to Symonds St, to the motorway. All no exit roads off the boundaries are included in the zone.

Northcote College

Kauri Glen Rd, Northcote, ph 09 481 0141
www.northcote.school.nz

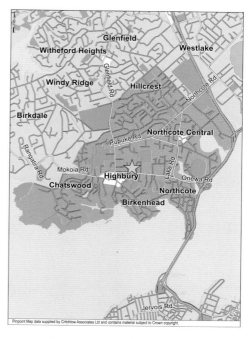

Roll 1533; co-educational; years 9-13
Northcote College on the North Shore grew increasingly popular during the past decade with students travelling across the harbour bridge from inner city Auckland suburbs. The resulting high roll growth has led to a recent zone enrolment scheme for the school – which excludes inner city Auckland! The school is predominantly Pakeha (58%) in make up, followed by 16% Asian and 9% Maori.

Established in 1877, Northcote College has expansive fields, established grounds and good facilities all within five minutes of Auckland City, North Shore City and the beaches of the North Shore.

The school is well known for its music, particularly its jazz band. The band has won the esteemed national secondary schools Tauranga Jazz Competition eight times in recent history and received many other awards.

Drama and English students are regular winners of the Auckland Shakespeare Competition and two groups of students have travelled to London to compete with other countries' secondary school Shakespearian scholars.

There is a Sports Elite programme for students in representative sport to help them pursue academic and sporting success. Along with the traditional school sports, Northcote offers watersports that take advantage of the closeness to Pupuke Lake and the beach with dragonboating, waterpolo and rowing.

Famous former students include North Shore mayor George Wood, TVNZ boss Bill Ralston and actress Stephanie Tauavahi. A current newsworthy student is Sharon Ahn, a 14-year-old golfer in the New Zealand Women's Golf Team.

Zone boundary: From Balmain Rd, Mokoia Rd, Roseberry Ave, Parkhill Rd, Glenfield Rd. Coronation Rd, Archers Rd, Sunnybrae Rd, Northcote Rd, the motorway to the harbour bridge and the harbour to Kauri Pt Domain and Balmain Rd.

Onehunga High School

Pleasant St, Onehunga, ph 09 636 6006
www.ohs.school.nz

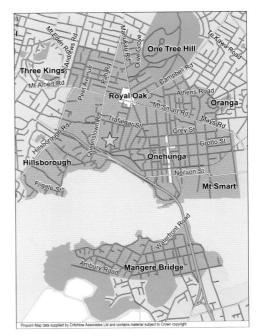

Roll 1509; co-educational; years 9-13
Business makes Onehunga High School
unique! The school has established a first
in New Zealand schools – a business
school on site for secondary students where
senior students study subjects such as
entrepreneurship, starting and running a
business, the global economy and strategic
financial management. They undertake a
cadetship/mentoring programme with a
CEO and sit the internationally recognised
Cambridge (CIE) AS Business Studies
examination. Aside from the business school,
there are a number of innovative learning
programmes running in the school.

Onehunga High School has nearly 40%
Pacific students, 30% Pakeha and 15% Maori.

Currently the school is undergoing a major facility modernisation programme. New
sports facilities are being developed to support the range of successful sports codes in the
school. These will include a premier rugby ground, an all-weather training area and an
arena for senior grade cricket. Planning is also underway for a sports and gymnasium
complex overlooking the new fields. A new administration and staffroom block is also under
construction.

Undoubtedly one of the most popular past students is Tony Falkenstein, successful Just Water
director who suggested the business school idea and has continued to support it financially.
Other famous exs include Ports of Auckland chief executive Geoff Vazey, ex National Party
President Susan Wood, performer Madeleine Sami, restaurateur Judith Tabron and Samoan
rugby national Samiu Vaha'folau.

Zone boundary: On the northern side of the Manukau Harbour the boundary runs from Hillsborough Cemetery via
Hillsborough Rd (including both sides), St Andrews Rd to Selwyn Rd, Pah Rd and Ngaroma Rd (included in each case)
to One Tree Hill Domain. From the domain across Campbell Rd at its intersection with Moana Ave then via Moana Rd,
Namata Rd, Curzon St, Mays Rd and Captain Springs Rd (included in each case) to the Manukau Harbour. South of the
Manukau Harbour the boundary follows a line south of Ambury Rd, Taylor Rd, Domain Rd and Hastie Ave so that both
sides of these streets, and the no exit streets leading off them, are included.

Orewa College

Riverside Rd, Orewa
Ph 09 426 4075
www.oc.school.nz

<u>Roll 1673; co educational; years 7-13</u>
Ethnic mix: 78% Pakeha, 8.7% Maori with
more than 100 international students from
South America, Asia, Europe and North
America. Orewa College has an emphasis
on languages from Year 8, including Spanish,
Japanese and Maori. It has top-level social
science and technology facilities, including a
new automotive workshop. There are extensive
grounds and sporting facilities.

Performing arts are important; prefects are
appointed to this area of the curriculum.
Co curricular activities range from drama and
musical theatre to community projects, charity
work and clubs such as the Astronomy Club
and Model United Nations Assembly. Gifted
and talented students are catered for with Club 100.

Pupils from rural areas are serviced by a free school bus.

Pinpoint Map data supplied by Critchlow Associates Ltd and contains material subject to Crown copyright.

Zone boundary: On the Whangaparaoa Peninsula, it crosses Vipond Rd between Shadon Pl and Dobell Pl. Excludes house numbers greater than or equal to 400 Whangaparaoa Rd and 139 Vipond Rd. Includes Rivervale Grove, Blue Heron Rise, Brian Cres and John Rd but excludes Carento Way, Dobell Rd and Gledstanes Rd. North along the coast to include Wenderholm Regional Park. From the northern tip of the park, west in a line to the Puhoi/Ahuroa Rd turnoff from SH1 (excluding Hungry Creek Rd). From the Puhoi/Ahuroa Rd turnoff, it includes the roads south of, but not including, Moirs Hill Rd, then south to include J Tolhoph Rd. Then south-west to the intersection of Krippner Rd and Tahekeroa Rd, including Rauner Rd. Then west along Tahekeroa Rd to the intersection of Tahekeroa and Haruru Rds where it follows down Haruru Rd to its intersection with Monowai Rd, including Lee Anne Rd. Then west to include Pebble Brook Rd and then south to include Drinnan Rd where it turns south-east and cuts through the junction of Forestry Rd and Ireland Rd. It includes only the beginning of Forestry Rd, north of Ireland Rd, but does not include Ireland Rd. It then follows, but does not include, Ireland Rd to the intersection at the west end of Blackbridge Rd. Along the edge of Riverhead Forest, following Blackbridge Rd to SH17. It includes only Escott Rd, Three Oaks Rd and Jean Mackay Rd, off Blackbridge Rd. Then south down SH17 to the start of Bawden Rd, to include Jeffs Rd and Postmans Rd but not including Green Rd, Sunnyside or Robinson Rd. Then following Bawden Rd to its intersection with SH1 and Coast Rd, including all of Bawden Rd and the roads off it. Then in a straight line, north east, to Stillwater Heads where it includes Stillwater Rd and all the roads off it. Then up the coastline to the eastern boundary.

Otahuhu College

74-78 Mangere Rd, Otahuhu,
ph 09 270 1170
www.otahuhucollege.school.nz

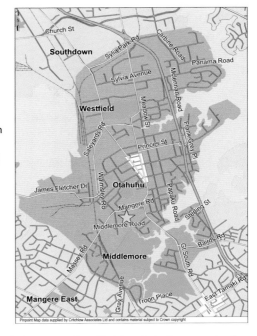

Roll 1399; co-educational; year 9-13
Otahuhu College celebrates its 75th birthday in 2006, making it one of the oldest schools in Auckland. It has always been a working-class school in a working-class area – as evidenced by its Decile 1 ranking, but that doesn't stop it offering plenty of academic, sporting and cultural opportunities. Students are from the diverse ethnic community. Pacific students make up 71.3% (Samoan 34.5%, Tongan 16.2%, Cook Island 8.4%, Niuean 5.5%) with Maori 12.3% and Pakeha 3.6%. There are also a number of Indian, Vietnamese and Chinese students.

The school has active Maori, Samoan, Tongan, Cook Island, Niuean and Indian groups which participate in the annual Auckland Maori and Pacific Islands Cultural Festival. Other major activities at the school include chess club, Christian fellowship, concert band, debating, large school and junior choirs, and the college orchestra. Drama is a growth area. In 2001, the Otahuhu College Drama Group represented Auckland in Guangzhou, China, performing a home-grown drama called Tamatane. The school has a strong sporting reputation. It offers all of the usual codes, as well as dragon boat racing and kilikiti.

Facilities include extensive playing fields, a large gymnasium and a swimming pool. The school has a new and well-equipped library with a computer ICT suite. There are specialist rooms for art, science and technology, an English-language reception centre, special education units, a guidance and transition education centre, a marae and modern music suite.

Former Prime Minister David Lange, Mayor of Manukau Sir Barry Curtis, boxer David Tua, entertainer Max Cryer and Silver Fern Temepara George are just some of Otahuhu's successful former students.

Zone boundary: The northern boundary line goes from Anns Creek at Westfield, along the railway line through Sylvia Park on a direct line to the Tamaki River. The other boundary line begins at the Favona Bridge over Harania Creek to the junction of Massey Rd (up to and including 240 and 249) and Gray Ave, along Gray Ave (both sides included in the Otahuhu College zone up to and including 102 and 115A) to the railway line, along the railway line and across Swaffield Rd (62 and 41 and over) and the Grange Gold Course (so that Middlemore Cres is included), then to the motorway (Motatau Rd is excluded and Bairds Rd east until the motorway is included) and along the motorway to the Tamaki River.

Pakuranga College

Pigeon Mountain Rd, Bucklands Beach,
ph 09 534 7159 www.pakuranga.school.nz

Roll: 2247; co-educational; years 9-13
Ethnic mix: While 50% of the roll is Pakeha
and 34% Asian, students hail from over 48
countries. The collect has a strong academic
reputation and well resourced facilities,
including the school's own television station!
It has a new state-of-the-art library and
information centre, science and English
facilities, and new gymnasium. Extensive
co-curricular activities are offered – the school
newspaper was highly commended in the
2004 national competition.

Zone boundary: Western boundary is from the Tamaki
River around the eastern boundary of St Kentigern College
to the Pakuranga Main Highway so that Grammar School
Rd is included, then along Pakuranga Rd to the Pakuranga
Creek, with the northern side of the main highway included;
along the line of the creek using Pakuranga Creek and its
tributaries as the southern boundary as far as it can be
taken, then taking a straight line to the intersection of Ti
Rakau Dr with Botany Rd, including those streets coming
west from Botany Rd and excluding Ti Rakau Dr and any
streets coming from it. Northern boundary commences at
Half Moon Bay then via Ara Tai and Pigeon Mountain Rds
(both excluded) to the junction of Gills Rd, then via Gills Rd
to Bleakhouse Rd, along Bleakhouse Rd (excluded) to Ridge
Rd and along Ridge and Botany Rds (both included).

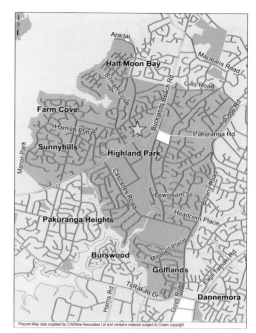

Papatoetoe High School

Nicholson Ave, Papatoetoe, ph 09 278 4086
www.papatoetoehigh.school.nz

Roll: 1831; co-educational; years 9-13
Students represent more than 50 different
nationalities (42% Asian, 21% Pakeha, 16.8%
Pacific, 15% Maori). The school has a solid
reputation in academic and sporting activities.
Senior students have over 40 subjects to
choose from and a gifted and talented

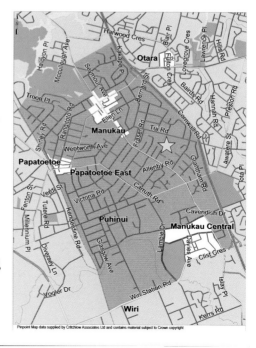

programme runs for students requiring academic extension. Ongoing roll growth has resulted in an extensive building and modernization programme. New facilities include grass hockey fields, new larger gym, sciences, technology and library blocks.

The school hosts the Richards Centre for students with physical disabilities. The zone was amended last year.

Zone boundary: To the east by the southern motorway. To the south, by Wiri Station Rd. To the west, by the railway line. To the north, following the southern edge of the Grange Golf Course from number 27 Swaffield Rd, up the eastern edge of the golf course to the intersection of Great South Rd and Motatau Rd. Then from Motatau Rd to the Southern Motorway.

Pukekohe High School

142 Harris St, Pukekohe, ph 09 238 6084 www.pukekohehigh.school.nz
<u>Roll 1493; co-educational; year 9 - 13.</u> Ethnic mix: Predominantly Pakeha (70%).
This school has a broad curriculum across all levels with a strong emphasis on information technology. It has a tradition of academic, sporting and cultural endeavours. Alternative sporting codes include weightlifting, wrestling, orienteering and equestrian. Performing Arts activities include kapa haka, lip synch, Shakespeare competition and a range of music groups. New classrooms and other facilities are under development due to roll increases.

Zone boundary: SH22 north of Pukekohe to the edge of Rosehill College's zone; Sim Rd and Burtt Rd to Needham Rd; 2km north of Runcimann Rd and Tuhimata Rd intersection; Kern Rd and including Patrick Rd; Coulston Rd, Ambush Rd, Flay Rd, Great South Rd, north of Flay Rd; north of dogleg on Hillview Rd; Chamberlain Rd, Totara Rd, Dunn Rd; Ararimu Rd from Totara Rd intersection to Steels Rd; Paparimu Rd, south of intersection with Matheson Rd; Matheson Rd; Lyons Rd, Caie Rd, Jeff Rd, McKenzie Rd; SH 2 to Mangatangi Rd intersection; Bell Rd, Homestead Rd, Chester Rd; Koheroa Rd east of no 341; SH2 to SH1(and including) Baird Rd, Dobson Rd, Serpell Rd, Irish Rd, Rimu Rd, McMillan Rd, O'Leary Rd; Nikau Rd, Razorback Rd, Beaver Rd; Jericho Rd, Ruebe Rd; Harrisville Rd, Buckville Rd, Jamieson Rd; Buckland Rd to intersection of Tuakau Rd; Ray Wright Rd, Pukekohe; Upper Queen St, Camerontown Rd, Clifford Rd, Knight Lane; Tramway Rd, Settlement Rd, Fulton Rd, Puni; Aka Aka Rd (including Riverview Rd, Shipherd Rd and Massey Rd) until intersection with Eastern Drain Rd; Eastern Drain Rd and Wiley Rd; Waiuku Rd and including Waller Rd, up to 970; Baldhill Rd to top of hill (up to and including no 160); Farm Park Rd, Glenbrook Station Rd to Gearon Rd; Gearon Rd to Quinn Rd, Martyn Wright Rd; Glenbrook Rd east of Klipsch Rd (not included), to SH 22; Glenbrook Rd (both sides) and all roads south of it (Cuff Rd, Ostrich Rd, Pearson Rd, Kingseat Rd).

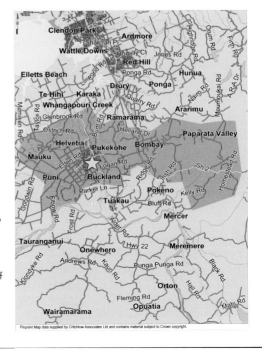

Pinpoint Map data supplied by Critchlow Associates Ltd and contains material subject to Crown copyright.

Rangitoto College

564 East Coast Rd, Browns Bay,
ph 09 477 0150
www.rangitoto.school.nz

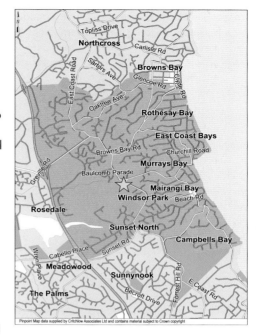

Pinpoint Map data supplied by Critchlow Associates Ltd and contains material subject to Crown copyright

Roll 3284; co-educational; years 9-13.
On a ridge overlooking the prosperous suburb of Mairangi Bay on Auckland's North Shore, Rangitoto College is not just the biggest school in Auckland, it's the biggest secondary school in the country. It's the most popular state school on the shore – a high-performing co-ed that's in big demand among shore families, longstanding residents and new migrants alike.

High-profile principal Allan Peachey leads a hugely successful staff team with a good reputation for meeting the needs of students with a wide range of learning abilities. Rangitoto has a strong tradition of academic excellence, with outstanding results in national examinations. The school's size means it has superb international-class facilities (including a new auditorium and an Olympic-standard hockey turf) and can offer a wide range of study options, both traditional and modern. A new 19-classroom maths block will be completed towards the end of 2005. Despite the large number of students, the school aims to be warm, personal and friendly, and manages to make sure each student is catered for as an individual.

Rangitoto's student body provides a snapshot of the local community demographics – 70% Pakeha, 8% South African, 8% Korean, 8% Chinese and Taiwanese.

Sports activities are high-profile here with students often winnnig national sporting titles. The school offers a Sports Talent Development Programme, which aims to support talented and committed students to achieve success in sports without sacrificing academic achievement.

Zone boundary: From Browns Bay via Anzac Rd (excluded) and Glencoe Rd (included) to the bridge over the Taiatoa Creek and then via John Downs Dr to East Coast Rd so that John Downs Dr and all no-exit streets off it are excluded. Then via Andersons Rd (excluded), the southern boundary of the sports fields to the junction of Masons Rd and Oteha Valley Rd, then via Oteha Valley Rd (excluded) to the motorway and south via the motorway to Sunset Rd (excluded to the junction of Juniper Rd), to East Coast Rd and then via East Coast Rd (included) to the southern boundary of Pupuke Golf Course, along the southern boundary of the golf course, excluding Aberdeen Rd and Rae Rd, to Beach Rd at the intersection of Red Bluff Rise (included) to the sea.

Rosehill College

Edinburgh Ave, Papakura, ph 09 295 0661
www.rosehill-college.co.nz

Roll: 1893; co-educational; years 9-13.
Ethnic Mix. Predominantly Pakeha (63.5%),
then Maori (16%) and Asian (10%).
On the rural edge of greater urban Auckland,
sport, cultural and academic successes
are encouraged. It is strong in languages,
including German and Spanish. Co curricular
activities include kapa haka, wearable arts,
debating and talent quests. Traditional codes
aside, Rosehill offers an eclectic sporting
mix including canoe polo, cheerleading,
equestrian, karate and lawn bowls.

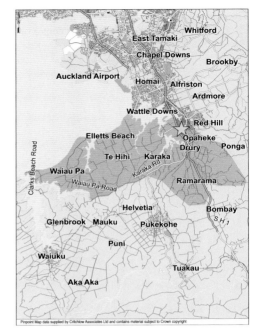

Zone boundary: Western rural boundary Waiau Beach,
Manukau Harbour, Pahurehure Inlet. Southern rural
boundary (west of motorway): North bank of Taihiki
River to Glenbrook Rd. Both sides of Glenbrook Rd. All
areas between Glenbrook and Karaka Rds and Manukau
Harbour, Gellert Rd, Sim Rd, Bycroft Rd, Woodlyn Rd, Snelgars Rd, Burtt Rd to intersection with Needham Rd (from 155
Burtt Rd onwards), Needham Rd, Solataire Rd, Cheriton Lane, Runciman Rd to the intersection with Coulston (from 377
Runciman Rd onwards, not 368 Runciman Rd). Tuhimata Rd to the first stream from the Runciman/Tuhimata intersection
(includes 479 Tuhimata Rd), Ingram Rd. Southern rural boundary (east of motorway): Ararimu Rd to intersection with
Dunn Rd includes Dale, Maxted, Fausett, Turner Rd, Steel Rd, Ponga Rd to intersection with McEntee Rd (includes all
roads off Ponga Rd up to and including McEntee Rd, from the Opaheke Rd end). Urban boundary Manurewa/ Takanini
motorway inter-change, Manukau Harbour, Pahurehure Inlet, east of motorway, main trunk railway line.

Rutherford College

Kotuku St, Te Atatu Peninsula, ph 09 834 9790 www.rutherford.school.nz

Roll: 1451; co-educational; years 9-13
Ethnic Mix: 47% Pakeha, 18% Maori, 13.5% Asian, 9.8% Pacific.
Multi-level programmes are backed by a gifted and talented programme for those students
requiring further extension, along with ESOL and special needs support. Performing arts such
as music, drama and dance are offered as academic subjects right through to a senior level.
   Rutherford's list of water based sports - water polo, underwater hockey, sailing, kayaking
– reflect its peninsula location.

Zone boundary: The Rutherford College home zone starts at Lincoln Bridge (Triangle Rd), following
a line down the centre of Lincoln Rd South until the railway line. Along the railway line south until

View Rd. Along the centre of View Rd turning south into Great North Rd. Along the centre of Great North Rd turning east into Hepburn Rd. Along the centre of Hepburn Rd until the Whau River. Along the coast of the peninsula until reaching the Lincoln Bridge.

Sancta Maria College

Te Irirangi Dr, Manukau, ph 09 274 4081
www.sanctamaria.school.nz

<u>Roll: 308, growing to 1000; co educational; years 7-13</u> Ethnic mix: 44% Pakeha, 25% Asian, 13% Pacific. Opening in 2004, the buildings of this new school are state of the art and include specialist science labs, art rooms, gym, auditorium and technology workshops. It's a state integrated school so 95% of the roll must be students with clear links to the Catholic Church. A chapel is an integral part of the attractively landscaped setting, including sports fields and walkways. Buses come from Howick, Pakuranga, Botany Downs, Maraetai, Beachlands and Whitford.

Zone boundary: From Otara Creek, following the Tamaki River north, around Musick Pt, around Whitford, Beachlands and Maraetai until the Wairoa River. Along the river and across to the intersection of North Rd, Twilight Rd and Papkura-Clevedon Rd. West until the intersection of Whitford Park Rd and Sandstone Rd, excluding Ara-Kotinga, Kimptons Rd and Polo Lane. Following Sandstone Rd until Ormiston Rd, including Regis and Shepherds Lanes. Following Ormiston Rd to the west, turning south into Murphy's Rd. Following Murphy's Rd until, and including, Hodges Rd. West down Thomas Rd and Dawson Rd (south sides excluded) until Te Irirangi Dr. North along Te Irirangi Dr (west side excluded) until Belinda Ave. Following Belinda Ave and Rongomai Rd (both excluded) until the intersection of Rongomai Rd and Dawson Rd. Along Dawson Rd (south side excluded) until Preston Rd. North along Preston Rd, East Tamaki Rd and Springs Rd (all west sides excluded) until Kerwyn Ave. West along Kerwyn Ave and south down Andromeda Cres until the Otara Creek. Note: Both sides of boundary roads included, unless otherwise noted.

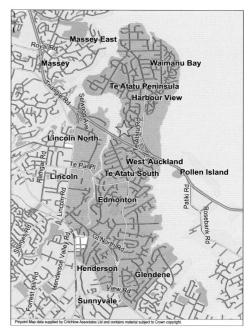

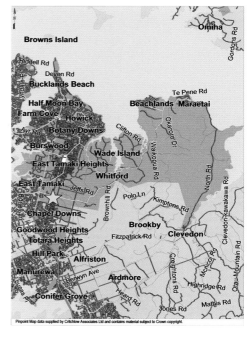

Tangaroa College

Haumia Way, East Tamaki, Manukau
ph 09 274 5764
www.tangaroa.school.nz

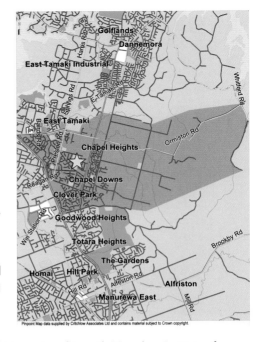

<u>Roll 1100; co-educational; years 9-13</u>
Tangaroa College has a very community-focussed, team-oriented approach to education. Tutor teachers monitor attendance and behaviour and encourage learning; the health centre includes Home and Family Liaison; and Learning Support Teachers are available for students with learning difficulties. Students can study at multi-levels according to their abilities.

A unique mentoring programme provides staff from Fletcher Challenge and law firm Bell Gully as student mentors to help keep students committed to their education.

Tangaroa was one of the first New Zealand schools to offer National Certificates within the school curriculum. Some subjects are taught in partnership with Manukau Institute of Technology and can be continued at tertiary education level.

Nearly 95% of the school's are of Pacific and Maori descent yet Tangaroa College was the surprise winner of an Auckland Indian high school dance competition in 2004, with a multicultural team of Maori, Samoan, Tongan and Nigerian students... but no Indians. The largely Indian crowd of 3000 loved the team's classical Indian dance and demanded an encore. Sport and cultural activities are strong,

A state-of-the-art technology block was completed in 2004, complementing existing facilities such as the drama theatre, music studio, science laboratories and fitness centre.

Famous former students include rugby sevens player Eric Rush, Silver Fern Temepara George, and league players Tawera Nikau and Jerry Seuseu.

Zone boundary: Western side of the Southern Motorway from East Tamaki Rd in the north to Redoubt Rd in the south. The northern side of Redoubt Rd. East Tamaki Rd from the Southern Motorway to East Tamaki War Memorial Park. Following a stream across to the corner of Te Irriangi Dr and Accent Rd. The southern side of Baverstock then across country to the intersection of Sandstone and Whitford Park Rd. The eastern side of Whitford Park Rd until Brownhill Rd and then the eastern side of Brownhill Rd and across country to Redoubt Rd.

Takapuna Grammar School

210 Lake Rd, Takapuna, ph 09 489 4167
www.takapuna.school.nz

Pinpoint Map data supplied by Critchlow Associates Ltd and contains material subject to Crown copyright

Roll 1590; co-educational; years 9-13

Takapuna Grammar School consists of an imposing set of buildings set grandly back from the entrance gates off Lake Rd with views out to sea across the school ground boundaries.

The roll's ethnic make up reflects the surrounding neighbourhood. It is predominantly Pakeha (70%) with only a small representation of Maori and Pacific Islanders. The next highest ethnic group is Asian at 14.3% and there are also 100 international students.

Takapuna claims its facilities are some of New Zealand's best. They include the Memorial Library, a weight-training room, a music suite (built in 1998) with a recording room and acoustically designed performance space, three computer classrooms, photographic facilities and pottery kilns.

The Special Education Unit provides for disabled students and their helpers; the swimming pool is also equipped for disabled users.

High goals are encouraged in the mainstream band of classes at Takapuna Grammar. Special Assistance and Accelerated and Enriched bands run on each side of the mainstream bands and close attention is paid to the student's individual ability to learn and progress. Options available in senior school include rock-climbing, canoeing, tramping, diving, surf survival, and ecology.

The school was founded with 218 students in 1929, the first co-ed school under the auspices of the Auckland Grammar School Board. The school grew quickly, and established its own Board of Governors in 1955.

Sailor Sir Peter Blake, cricketer Bert Sutcliffe, cricketer and media personality Danny Morrison and numerous others appear on the wall of fame.

Zone boundary: The Devonport peninsula from King Edward Pde and Jubilee Ave north to a boundary defined by and including Northcote Rd and its intersection with the northern motorway, Shea Tce and the southern shores of Lake Pupuke including Hurstmere Rd, Kitchener Rd and all side roads up to and including Fenwick Ave, Otakau Rd, Omana Rd and Craig Rd.

Waitakere College

42 Rathgar Rd, Henderson, ph 09 836 7890
www.waitakere.college.net.nz

<u>Roll 1435; co-educational; years 9-13</u>
Ethnic mix: Pakeha 43%, Maori 22% , Pacific
20%, Asian 10%, other 5%.

 The college offers a wide range of subjects
including an enrichment programme and
practical qualifications such as business
administration and automotive engineering.

 It runs special projects including the Maori
Mainstream Pilot (to raise the achievement of
Maori students) and the Gateway programme
(a joint venture with Skill New Zealand to
fund special work experience programmes for
students). Wrestling, rock climbing, sailing,
skiing, equestrian and kayaking are some of
the non traditional sporting codes on offer.
Kapa haka, Cook Island and Samoan groups
perform regularly, along with harmony groups
and barbershop quartets.

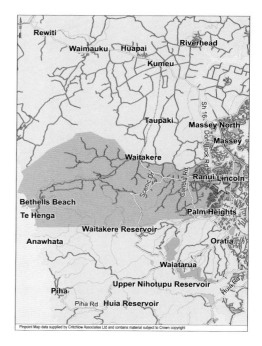

Zone boundary: Starts to the north of Bethells Beach at Te Waharoa Pt, then in a north-eastern line until it meets the Makoroa Stream, then east to the Wairere Stream. From the Wairere Stream the boundary joins Gregory Rd then to Wairere Rd (including Arrowsmith Rd). From Wairere Rd along Bethells Rd into Waitakere Township. The boundary crosses Waitakere Rd and the railway, including Township Rd and McEntee Rd. Then Sunnyvale Rd to Crows Rd. Where Crows Rd meets Birdwood Rd the boundary crosses directly to the Momutu Stream that runs through Te Rangi Hiroa Park. Momutu Stream joins the Swanson Stream and crosses Don Buck Rd at the point where Don Buck Rd meets the Huruhuru Creek. The Huruhuru Creek and Henderson Creek are the northeastern and eastern boundaries. Henderson Creek into the Opanuku Stream. The Opanuku Stream forms the southern boundary until a line from the headwaters of the Opanuku Stream crosses Scenic Dr and travels west to the coast at Wigmore Bay to the south of Bethells Beach.

Westlake Boys High School

30 Forrest Hill Rd, Forrest Hill,
ph 09 410 8667 www.westlakebhs.school.nz

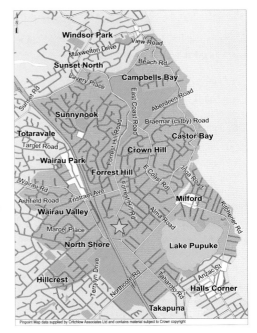

Pinpoint Map data supplied by Critchlow Associates Ltd and contains material subject to Crown copyright

Roll 2170; boys; year 9-13

Westlake Boys High School prides itself in being both traditional and progressive in its outlook, with a proud record for academic, sporting and cultural achievement. The school is very popular with North Shore parents wanting single sex boys' education. Westlake Boys reflects the surrounding neighbourhood in its ethnic make up of predominantly Pakeha (57%) and Asian (22%) students.

Cambridge International Exams are offered alongside NCEA. The college has a wide range of modern facilities including art rooms, specialist graphics rooms, technology workshops, 12 new science laboratories, an ESOL centre for English language development, an expanded computer-networked library with internet access, and extensive sports fields. Sport is important. Last year Westlake Boys' won the national secondary schools' soccer championships. Boys are expected to participate in at least one team sport a year. Music is also encouraged through the curriculum and choir Voicemale, as well as concert, stage, rock and orchestral bands.

The school was co-ed when it opened in 1958; it became boys only in 1962, when Westlake Girls' High School opened next door. The two schools enjoy a close relationship, with combined social events such as the school ball, leadership training, peer support and prefects, drama productions, music tuition and productions.

Famous former students include John Hood (Oxford University vice chancellor), TV journalist Rob Harley, artists Jeff Thomson and Dean Buchanan, and musician Don McGlashan.

Zone boundary: From the sea along Earnock (included), across Hurstmere Rd and along the edge of Lake Pupuke, excluding Killarney St and Manurere Ave to Taharoto Rd, but including Kowhai St and Pupuke Rd. It crosses Taharoto Rd at Killarney St and continues south of Dominion Rd (included) to Onewa Domain. Through the domain it crosses Northcote Rd and goes up by the golf course, excluding all streets to the west, to Benders Ave (included). Along Coronation Rd (included, also including Nicholson Pl) until Beatrice Ave (excluded). South of Archers Rd to Chivalry Rd, then north along Chivalry Rd (included, and including Edgeworth Rd) to Diana Dr. Along Diana Dr to Weldene Ave (excluded). North to Hogans Rd (excluded, Ngatoa Pl and Normanton Rd are also excluded). South of Hogans Rd and across Wairau Rd at Kathleen Pl, which is included. North of Ellice Rd (excluded), across Target Rd and south of Sunnynook Rd to the northern motorway. The northern boundary leaves the motorway at Sunset Rd and runs east along Sunset Rd (included) to East Coast Rd, along East Coast Rd (included) to Kowhai Rd (included). Along Kowhai Rd and across Beach Rd to the sea. Whitby Cres is included.

Westlake Girls High School

2 Wairau Rd, Takapuna, ph 09 489 4169
www.westlakegirls.school.nz

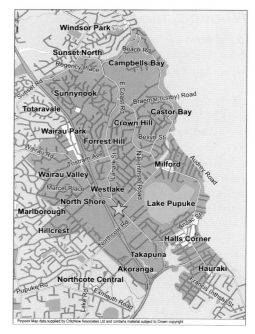

Pinpoint Map data supplied by Critchlow Associates Ltd and contains material subject to Crown copyright

Roll 2244; girls; years 9-13

As the only public secondary single-sex girls school on the North Shore, Westlake Girls' High School is very popular. The roll reflects North Shore City's ethnicity, being 60% Pakeha and 25% Asian.

Westlake Girls' High School opened in 1962; until then Westlake High School had been co-ed, operating on a neighbouring site from 1958. The girls' school has continued a close relationship with Westlake Boys, with combined social events such as the school ball, leadership training, peer support and prefects, drama productions, music tuition and productions.

The music suite includes a keyboard laboratory, classrooms and instrument practice rooms. The gymnasium, which opened in 2002, has a dance studio and fitness centre. There is also a swimming pool. The art rooms include a senior art area, design studio, photography and sculpture facilities. Students are exposed to a wide range of learning encounters, and leadership qualities are encouraged.

Sporting and cultural successes abound. Westlake Girls High School's Premier Cricket Team are the 2005 champs for the greater Auckland area; they go to the nationals in December.

Several Westlake Girls' musical groups, including their symphony orchestra and chamber orchestras, have won gold medals at regional and national music festivals. The school also recently won the North Island Inter-Secondary Schools Teams Dressage Championships for the fourth year in a row.

Zone boundary: Southern boundary is from Hauraki Rd, across Lake Rd and Jutland Rd, including all streets to the north, around Shoal Bay and to the western boundary of the Esmonde Rd interchange, along Akoranga Dr, crossing Northcote Rd, along Sunnybrae Rd to Coronation Rd, which is included, as is Nicholson Pl, until it reaches Beatrice Ave, which is excluded. It runs south of Archers Rd to the junction with Chartwell Ave, then up Chartwell Ave (included) to the junction with Diana Dr (included) and along Diana Dr until Weldene Ave (excluded). Ngatoa Pl and Normanton St are also excluded. The zone runs south of Hogans Rd and crosses Wairua Rd at Kathleen Pl, which is included. North to Ellice Rd (excluded), across Target Rd and south of Sunnynook Rd to the northern motorway. From the northern motorway down Constellation Dr to the junction at East Coast Rd, along East Coast Rd to Maxwelton Dr and done Maxwelton Dr to Ramsgate Tce and Sidmouth St to the sea.

Whangaparaoa College

15 Delshaw Ave, Whangaparaoa
ph 09 428 4724
www.wgpcollege.school.nz

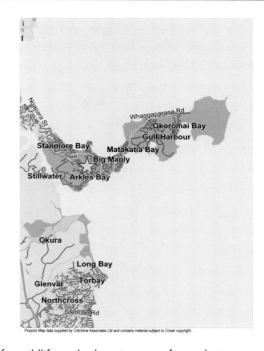

Roll 865 growing to 2000; co-educational; years 9-13

The newest secondary school in Auckland, Whangaparaoa College opened its doors in 2005 with 865 Year 7 to 9 students. This makes it one of only a handful of New Zealand state schools that incorporate intermediate level students into the school.

Another unusual and admirable aspect of the school is the focus on best environmental practice. For example, large expanses of glass mean ample natural light and savings on electricity; the lights can't be switched on if natural light levels are sufficient. A plan is being developed for water recycling and the creek that runs along one edge of the site will be turned into a wetland area – a haven for wildlife and a learning area for students. Cycleways and pedestrian ways to the school grounds will encourage people to walk or cycle rather than drive and will continue through the school so the community has easy access from the shopping centre on one side to the sports fields and beach on the other. Again the aim is to discourage vehicle use.

By the beginning of 2006, three major new buildings will open: a performing arts centre (which includes a 450-seat auditorium, music studios, dance/drama studios, practice rooms, dressing rooms and a recording studio), gymnasium and visual arts block.

Students in the junior level will be mainly taught by one teacher, but will move into different areas for specialist subjects. Approximately 85% of the roll is Pakeha, the rest is mainly Maori and Asian. The school is to cap its roll at 2000.

Zone boundary: crosses Vipond Rd between Brian Cres and Ellenbury Pl, and includes house numbers greater than or equal to 139 Vipond Rd; and Whangaparaoa Rd between Shadon Place and Dobell, and include house numbers greater than or equal to 400 Whangaparaoa Rd.

Auckland International College

Auckland City; years 11-13; co-ed; roll 100; established 2003. A three-year senior secondary school for international and New Zealand students who wish to gain entry to universities in New Zealand as well as in other countries. Fees: $11,450.

Carey College

Panmure; years 1-13; co-ed; roll 50; established 1988. "A friendly and nurturing family-based school, uncompromising in its commitment to biblical schooling, to the building of Christ-like character, and to teaching of the highest standards." Fees: years 9-10 $5600; years 11-13 $6800.

Corran School

Remuera; years 1-13; girls only; roll 500; established 1954; Christian. "A small school which allows individual attention, where the uniqueness of every student is fully acknowledged, and where pastoral care really works." Fees: $11,935

Diocesan School *

Epsom; girls only; years 1-13
1560 students including 35 boarders; Anglican; founded 1903. Fees: years 1-6 $11,056; years 7-13 $12,716.

Junior College

Parnell (alongside the domain); co-ed; 362 students; years 7-10. Established 1998. Special features: junior high school; high-interest academic programme. Fees: $10,575.

Kadimah College

Auckland City; preschool to year 8; co-ed; roll 170; established 1971. Jewish – although children from all backgrounds are welcome. "Small classes and children learning in ability rather than age groups for subjects such as maths and reading ensure individual attention and promote the joy of learning."
Fees: preschool $7011; years 1-6 $9009; years 7-8 $9423.

King's College

Otahuhu; 982 students; years 9-13; boys only up to year 11; accepts girls in year 12 and 13. Boarders and day students. Established 1896; Christian (Anglican) ethos. Offers Cambridge International examinations.
Fees: middle school $14,960; senior school $15,568.
The closest thing Auckland has to the traditional public schools of Great Britain.

King's School (primary)

Remuera; boys only; 640 students; years 1-8
Established 1922; Christian (Anglican).

Fees: years 1-3 $9164; years 4-6 $9852; years 7-8 $10,584.

Kristin*

Albany, North Shore; co-ed; 1400 students from kindergarten to year 13. Established 1972; non-denominational Christian ethos; second language teaching; International Baccalaureat syllabus and exams. Fees: years 0-6 $9100; years 7-8 $10,920; years 9-10 $11,200; years 11-13 $11,520. Established 30 years ago by a group of parents who wanted a high-quality independent school for the North Shore. It has a strong international focus, aiming to prepare students to be "responsible world citizens". Kristin provides all-round education that's "vibrant, innovative, yet rigorous".

Senior College

Central Auckland; co-ed; 451 students; years 11-13. Established 1995. Special features: Senior students only; "challenging schooling for students to reach their potential" in a pre-university environment; specialist teaching; Cambridge International Examinations. Fees $12,450.

A school for year 11, 12 and 13 students aiming to be a "specialist pre-university centre", meeting the special needs of senior secondary students.

The school's stated intention is "educating young men and women who will make a difference", and there's a focus on giving students the freedom to make choices and take responsibility for their learning.

St Cuthbert's College *

Epsom; years 1-13; girls only;1394 students; including 130 boarders. Established 1915; Presbyterian; very strong academically – in 2002 top school in country for scholarships, second for A bursary, top for School

Certificate. Fees: years 1-6 $10,664; years 7-8 $12,284; years 9-10 $12,396; years 11-13 $12,565.

St Kentigern College

Pakuranga; years 7-13; fully co-ed (since 2003); 1504 students; established 1953. Presbyterian; "broad, sound, innovative education"; strong in academics, IT and extra-curricular activities; sports academy. Fees: $11,862.

St Kentigern School (primary)

Remuera; years 1-8; boys only; 501 students.

Established 1959; Presbyterian. Fees: years 1-3 $9588; years 4-6 $10,464; years 7-8 $11,862.

Strathallan College

Hingaia Peninsula, South Auckland; years 1-13, plus kindergarten; co-ed 897 students; established 2001. Part of AGC private education group (which also includes Junior and Senior Colleges), the school offers Cambridge International exams. It's one of largest independent school complexes in New Zealand and offers a complete pathway from kindergarten to year 13. Fees: years 0-6 $9630; years 7-10 $11,160; years 11-13 $11,790.

Wentworth College

Whangaparaoa; years 7-13; co-ed; roll 152; established 2003; secular. "Wentworth College provides a high quality, comprehensive and challenging education in a positive, caring school environment. Traditional values of respect, courtesy and consideration are clearly articulated and students respond positively to the expectations of their teachers." Fees: $10,400.

Auckland Schools are listed only under the suburb in which they are physically located. Many will have wider catchment areas or zones.

A decile rating is given to each state or state integrated school, of between one and 10. The decile rating is based on census information and reflects the socio-economic level of the population from which the school draws its students – not academic results. A lower socio-economic area will have schools with lower ratings. Decile ratings are not applicable to private schools. A state integrated school is a school with a special (religious or philosophical) character, which has been integrated into the state system. It has state funding but the school owns the land and buildings.

Name	Address	Phone	Level	Funding	Gender	Decile	Roll
AUCKLAND CITY							
MindAlive	68a Nelson St	849 4780	all levels	private	co-ed	n/a	30
Kadimah College	108 Greys Ave	373 3072	primary	private	co-ed	10	176
ACG New Zealand International College	Cnr Rutland & Lorne St	307 5399	secondary	private	co-ed	8	2016
ACG Senior College	Cnr Rutland & Lorne Sts	307 4477	secondary	state	co-ed	n/a	451
Auckland Girls' Grammar School	Howe St	307 4180	secondary	state	girls	4	1522
Auckland International College	85 Airedale St	309 4480	secondary	private	co-ed	n/a	62
AVONDALE							
Immanuel Christian School	63 St Georges Rd	828 4545	all levels	private	co-ed	n/a	172
Avondale Primary School	Crayford St West	828 8929	primary	state	co-ed	3	343
New Windsor School	New Windsor Rd,	626 6356	primary	state	co-ed	5	553
Waterview School	Oakley Ave	828 7227	primary	state	co-ed	1	158
Rosebank School	217 Rosebank Rd	828 6319	primary	state	co-ed	2	650
St Mary's School	2140 Great North Rd	828 5599	prim+interm	state integrated	co-ed	2	284
Avondale Intermediate	Holly St	828 7883	Intermediate	state	co-ed	3	540
Avondale College	Victor St	828 7024	secondary	state	co-ed	5	2730
Odyssey House School	56 Bollard Ave	374 4556	secondary	private	co-ed	n/a	20
BLOCKHOUSE BAY							
Hill Top School	37 Heaphy St	627 9295	all levels	private	co-ed	8	166
Blockhouse Bay School	584 Blockhouse Bay Rd	627 9940	primary	state	co-ed	8	625
Chaucer School	Chaucer Place	626 6699	primary	state	co-ed	4	218
Halsey Drive School	106 Halsey Drive	627 9106	primary	state	co-ed	9	490
Glenavon School	340 Blockhouse Bay Rd	828 7029	prim+interm	state	co-ed	2	283
St Dominic's School	32 Bolton St	626 5391	prim+interm	state	co-ed	6	303
Blockhouse Bay Intermediate	Bolton St	626 6414	Intermediate	state	co-ed	6	583
EASTERN BAYS							
St Ignatius School	72 Speight Rd	575 7081	primary	state integrated	co-ed	10	199
St Joseph's School	16 Brenton Place	521 0866	primary	state integrated	co-ed	5	103
Churchill Park School	Riddell Rd	575 8156	prim+interm	state	co-ed	10	460
Glen Taylor School	172 West Tamaki Rd	528 6325	prim+interm	state	co-ed	1	264
Glendowie School	217 Riddell Rd	575 7374	prim+interm	state	co-ed	7	543
Kohimarama School	112 Kohimarama Rd	528 5306	prim+interm	state	co-ed	10	453
Orakei School	Grace St	521 0657	prim+interm	state	co-ed	3	167
St Heliers School	126-160 St Heliers Bay Rd	575 8311	prim+interm	state	co-ed	6	432
St Thomas School	Allum St	528 3938	prim+interm	state	co-ed	9	605
Glendowie College	Crossfield Rd	575 9128	secondary	state	co-ed	9	976
Selwyn College	Kohimarama Rd	521 9610	secondary	state	co-ed	5	1420

CENTRAL

CENTRAL

Name	Addresss	Phone	Level	Funding	Gender	Decile	Roll
EPSOM							
Diocesan School For Girls	Margot St	520 0221	all levels	private	girls	n/a	1577
St Cuthbert's College	Market Rd	520 4159	all levels	state	girls	n/a	1394
Epsom Normal School	41 The Drive	630 5144	primary	state	co-ed	10	621
Kohia Terrace School	3 Kohia Terrace	630 4525	prim+interm	state	co-ed	10	345
Our Lady Sacred Heart School	19 Banff Ave	638 6200	prim+interm	state integrated	co-ed	10	224
Auckland Grammar	Mountain Rd	623 5400	secondary	state	boys	10	2554
Epsom Girls' Grammar School	Silver Rd	630 5963	secondary	state	girls	10	1948
Marcellin College	617 Mt Albert Rd	625 6509	secondary	state integrated	co-ed	3	834
St Peter's College	Mountain Rd	524 8108	secondary	state integrated	boys	7	1260
GLEN INNES/PT ENGLAND							
Glen Innes School	Eastview Rd	528 3507	primary	state	co-ed	1	203
Glenbrae Public School	Leybourne Circle	528 5025	primary	state	co-ed	1	180
St Pius X School	103 Castledine Crescent	528 7257	prim+interm	state integrated	co-ed	1	143
Te Kura Kaupapa Puau Te Moana-Nui-A-Kiwa	26a Farringdon St	528 0210	prim+interm	state	co-ed	1	31
Sacred Heart College	West Tamaki Rd	529 3660	secondary	state integrated	boys	8	1031
Tamaki College	Elstree Ave	521 1104	secondary	state	co-ed	1	622
GREY LYNN							
Grey Lynn School	Surrey Crescent	376 3255	primary	state	co-ed	4	217
Newton Central School	Monmouth St	378 6883	primary	state	co-ed	5	222
Pt Chevalier School	Te Ra Rd	846 1359	primary	state	co-ed	7	612
St Francis School	Montrose St	846 4696	primary	state integrated	co-ed	6	192
Westmere School	Larchwood Ave	361 0014	primary	state	co-ed	8	405
St Joseph's School	456 Great North Rd	376 5456	prim+interm	state integrated	co-ed	3	163
Pasadena Intermediate	Moray Place	846 2169	Intermediate	state	co-ed	5	269
Western Springs College	Motions Rd	846 8197	secondary	state	co-ed	7	790
HAURAKI GULF ISLANDS							
Te Huruhi School	7 Donald Bruce Rd	372 0200	primary	state	co-ed	5	70
Kaitoke School	Kaitoke Lane	429 0273	prim+interm	state	co-ed	2	64
Mulberry Grove School	Shoal Bay Rd	429 0475	prim+interm	state	co-ed	3	24
Okiwi School	Great Barrier Island	429 0138	prim+interm	state	co-ed	3	14
Waiheke Primary School	26 Sea View Rd	372 2372	prim+interm	state	co-ed	6	n/a
Waiheke High School	11 Donald Bruce Rd	372 8938	secondary	state	co-ed	4	459
KINGSLAND							
Kowhai Intermediate	26 Onslow Rd	846 7534	Intermediate	state	co-ed	6	466
MEADOWBANK							
Michael Park School	55 Amy St	579 3083	all levels	state integrated	co-ed	9	382
Mt Carmel School	6 Mt Carmel Place	521 5161	primary	state integrated	co-ed	10	197
Ellerslie School	12 Kalmia St	579 5477	prim+interm	state	co-ed	7	477
St Mary's School	58 Main Highway	579 8937	prim+interm	state integrated	co-ed	5	219

CENTRAL

Name	Address	Phone	Level	Funding	Gender	Decile	Roll
MT ALBERT							
Hebron Christian College	1 McLean St	846 2159	all levels	private	co-ed	9	312
Edendale School	419 Sandringham Rd	846 6340	primary	state	co-ed	5	597
Gladstone School	8 Seaview Terrace	846 9744	primary	state	co-ed	7	843
Marist School	14 Kitenui Ave	846 7408	primary	state integrated	co-ed	6	289
Mt Albert School	Sainsbury Rd	846 9288	primary	state	co-ed	4	173
Owairaka District School	113-115 Richardson Rd	846 5091	primary	state	co-ed	2	347
Te Kura Kaupapa Maori O Nga Maungarongo	140 Haverstock Rd	815 6349	prim+interm	state	co-ed	3	94
Marist College	31 Alberton Ave	846 8311	secondary	state integrated	girls	6	732
Mt Albert Grammar School	Alberton Ave	846 2044	secondary	state	co-ed	5	2474
MT EDEN							
Good Shepherd School	30 Telford Ave	620 4962	primary	state integrated	co-ed	7	199
Maungawhau School	Ellerton Rd	638 8829	primary	state	co-ed	10	633
Mt Eden Normal School	Valley Rd	630 0009	primary	state	co-ed	9	578
Balmoral S D A School	10 a Wiremu St	638 7903	prim+interm	state integrated	co-ed	4	133
Balmoral School	19 Brixton Rd	638 7960	prim+interm	state	co-ed	8	639
Ficino School	27 Esplanade Rd	623 3385	prim+interm	private	co-ed	10	101
St Therese School	463 Mt Albert Rd	620 9441	prim+interm	state integrated	co-ed	2	133
Auckland Normal Intermediate	Poronui St	630 1109	Intermediate	state	co-ed	10	665
MT ROSKILL							
Sunnydene Special School	48 Smallfield Ave	620 7680	special	state	co-ed	3	62
Dominion Rd School	Quest Terrace	620 9483	primary	state	co-ed	3	392
Hay Park School	670 Richardson Rd	625 9531	primary	state	co-ed	1	222
Hillsborough School	Belfast St	625 7307	primary	state	co-ed	9	415
Marshall Laing School	Marshall Laing Ave	626 5103	primary	state	co-ed	7	431
May Rd School	504 Richardson Rd	626 8021	primary	state	co-ed	2	297
Mt Roskill Primary School	Frost Rd	620 5050	primary	state	co-ed	5	779
Three Kings School	944 Mt Eden Rd	625 7208	primary	state	co-ed	7	432
Waikowhai School	381 Hillsborough Rd	627 9665	primary	state	co-ed	3	198
Wesley School	Potter Ave	620 9261	primary	state	co-ed	1	227
Christ The King School	288 Richardson Rd	626 7123	prim+interm	state integrated	co-ed	3	159
Monte Cecilia School	72 Hillsborough Rd	625 5018	prim+interm	state integrated	co-ed	7	183
Mt Roskill Intermediate	Denbigh Ave	620 8508	intermediate	state	co-ed	4	896
Waikowhai Intermediate	Richardson Rd	620 1600	intermediate	state	co-ed	5	423
Wesley Intermediate	Sandringham Rd Extension	620 9367	intermediate	state	co-ed	1	166
Lynfield College	White Swan Rd	627 0600	secondary	state	co-ed	7	2151
Mt Roskill Grammar	Frost Rd	621 0050	secondary	state	co-ed	4	2432
ONEHUNGA							
Onehunga Primary School	122 Arthur St	636 6256	primary	state	co-ed	3	320
Te Papapa School	219 Mt Smart Rd	634 5252	primary	state	co-ed	1	231

Name	Address	Phone	Level	Funding	Gender	Decile	Roll
St Joseph's School	125 Church St	636 8102	prim+interm	state integrated	co-ed	2	294
Onehunga High School	Pleasant St	636 6006	secondary	state	co-ed	3	1509
Penrose High School	421 - 451 Great South Rd	579 5049	secondary	state	co-ed	3	892
ONE TREE HILL							
Cornwall Park School	193 Greenlane West	524 6574	primary	state	co-ed	9	639
Oranga School	21 Rangipawa Rd	579 4189	primary	state	co-ed	2	338
Royal Oak School	Chandler Ave	624 2800	primary	state	co-ed	7	573
Royal Oak Intermediate School	74 Symonds St	636 5667	Intermediate	state	co-ed	3	611
PANMURE							
Sommerville School	7a Bengazi Rd	570 9787	special	state	co-ed	5	129
Carey College	21 Domain Rd	570 5873	all levels	private	co-ed	9	63
Panmure Bridge School	76 Kings Rd	527 6462	primary	state	co-ed	1	185
Pt England School	130 Pt England Rd	527 6247	primary	state	co-ed	1	432
Ruapotaka School	10 a Taratoa S	527 6244	primary	state	co-ed	1	263
Tamaki School	Alamein Rd	527 6345	primary	state	co-ed	1	188
Bailey Rd School	19 Bailey Rd	579 4619	prim+interm	state	co-ed	3	447
Destiny School	18 Allright Place	570 7150	prim+interm	private	co-ed	n/a	22
Panmure District School	87 Mount Wellington Highway	527 7659	prim+interm	state	co-ed	2	182
St Patrick's School	5 Church Crescent	527 7016	prim+interm	state integrated	co-ed	1	163
Stanhope Rd School	2 b Harris Rd	579 6434	prim+interm	state	co-ed	4	512
Sylvia Park School	Longford St	527 6526	prim+interm	state	co-ed	2	255
Tamaki Intermediate	80 a Tripoli Rd	527 6525	Intermediate	state	co-ed	1	330
PARNELL/NEWMARKET							
ACG Parnell College	39 George St	308 1666	all levels	private	co-ed	n/a	362
Newmarket School	7 Gillies Ave	520 2959	primary	state	co-ed	9	232
Parnell School	St Stephens Ave	379 3008	prim+interm	state	co-ed	10	418
PONSONBY							
Bayfield School	2 - 12 Clifton Rd	376 5703	primary	state	co-ed	10	329
Freemans Bay School	Wellington St	378 6904	primary	state	co-ed	7	342
Ponsonby Primary School	Curran St	376 3568	primary	state	co-ed	10	339
Richmond Rd School	Richmond Rd	376 1091	primary	state	co-ed	7	288
Marist School	82 Kelmarna Ave	376 7173	prim+interm	state integrated	co-ed	6	181
Ponsonby Intermediate	50 Clarence St	376 0096	intermediate	state	co-ed	9	478
St Mary's College	11 New St	376 6558	secondary	state integrated	girls	5	705
St Paul's College	183 Richmond Rd	376 1287	secondary	state integrated	boys	3	318
REMUERA							
Corran School	514 Remuera Rd	520 1400	all levels	private	girls	n/a	488
Dilworth School	2 Erin St	523 1060	all levels	private	boys	5	498
Mt Hobson Middle School	131 Remuera Rd	523 1241	all levels	private	co-ed	n/a	44
Meadowbank School	Waiatarua Rd	520 3739	primary	state	co-ed	10	628

CENTRAL

	Name	Addresss	Phone	Level	Funding	Gender	Decile	Roll
CENTRAL	Remuera School	25-33 Dromorne Rd	520 2458	primary	state	co-ed	10	613
	St Michael's School	6 Beatrice Rd	520 0933	primary	state	co-ed	10	217
	Victoria Ave School	282 Victoria Ave	520 0602	primary	state	co-ed	10	467
	Kings School	258 Remuera Rd	520 7770	prim+interm	private	boys	10	653
	St Kentigern Primary School	82 Shore Rd	520 7682	prim+interm	private	boys	10	501
	Remuera Intermediate	Ascot Ave	522 9890	intermediate	state	co-ed	9	790
	Baradene College	237 Victoria Ave	524 6019	secondary	state integrated	girls	9	945
HELENSVILLE	Westbridge Residential School	488e Don Buck Rd	832 4918	special	state	co-ed	2	54
	Tau Te Arohanoa Akoranga	162 Awaroa Rd	420 9300	all levels	private	co-ed	n/a	34
	Helensville School	Rata St	420 8005	prim+interm	state	co-ed	4	408
	Kaukapakapa School	Kaipara Coast Highway	420 5477	prim+interm	state	co-ed	7	258
	Parakai School	Fordyce Rd	420 8494	prim+interm	state	co-ed	3	181
	Wainui School	492 Waitoki Rd	420 5127	prim+interm	state	co-ed	9	202
	Waioneke School	South Head Rd	420 2884	prim+interm	state	co-ed	7	49
	Waitoki School	1119 Kahikatea Flat Rd	420 5244	prim+interm	state	co-ed	10	115
	Woodhill School	State Highway 16	420 8108	prim+interm	state	co-ed	6	102
	Kaipara College	Rautawhiri Rd	420 8640	secondary	state	co-ed	7	670
HENDERSON / WEST	Arohanui Special School	Tirimoana Rd	838 6696	special	state	co-ed	4	143
	Nga Kakano Christian Reo Rua Kura	333 Great North Rd	835 3626	all levels	state	co-ed	2	50
	Edmonton School	Edmonton Rd	838 9318	primary	state	co-ed	5	236
	Flanshaw Rd School	Flanshaw Rd	834 7224	primary	state	co-ed	5	358
	Freyberg Community School	Roberts Rd	838 9664	primary	state	co-ed	5	374
	Henderson North School	Norval Rd	838 8229	primary	state	co-ed	3	481
	Henderson School	Montel Ave	838 9667	primary	state	co-ed	3	240
	Henderson South School	Garelja Rd	838 8766	primary	state	co-ed	1	241
	Henderson Valley School	389 Henderson Valley Rd	837 0545	primary	state	co-ed	6	406
	Matipo Rd School	Matipo Rd	834 6909	primary	state	co-ed	5	390
	Peninsula Primary School	Waipani Rd	834 6711	primary	state	co-ed	4	383
	Pomaria Rd School	Pomaria Rd	836 4919	primary	state	co-ed	3	489
	Rutherford School	7 Toru St	834 5467	primary	state	co-ed	4	270
	Summerland Primary	62 Summerland Dr	836 7460	primary	state	co-ed	8	428
	Sunnyvale School	Ribblesdale Rd	838 9248	primary	state	co-ed	4	427
	Tirimoana School	Kokiri St	838 9737	primary	state	co-ed	6	574
	Western Heights School	Sturges Rd	836 1213	primary	state	co-ed	8	569
	Holy Cross School	8 Lavelle Rd	838 8802	prim+interm	state integrated	co-ed	4	487
	Taupaki School	Cottle Rd	810 9855	prim+interm	state	co-ed	10	259
	Waitakere S D A School	26 Corban Ave	836 6330	prim+interm	state integrated	co-ed	3	42
	Bruce McLaren Intermediate	Bruce Mclaren Rd	836 3175	intermediate	state	co-ed	3	596

Name	Address	Phone	Level	Funding	Gender	Decile	Roll
Henderson Intermediate	70 Lincoln Rd	838 8529	intermediate	state	co-ed	3	528
Rangeview Intermediate	Keru Pl	838 9468	intermediate	state	co-ed	6	898
Te Atatu Intermediate	Harbour View Rd	834 5371	intermediate	state	co-ed	4	246
Henderson High School	Henderson Valley Rd	838 9085	secondary	state	co-ed	3	781
Liston College	16 Edwards Ave	838 9350	secondary	state integrated	boys	5	726
Rutherford College	Kotuku St	834 9790	secondary	state	co-ed	5	1451
St Dominic's College	29 Rathgar Rd	839 0380	secondary	state integrated	girls	6	884
Waitakere College	Rathgar Rd	836 7890	secondary	state	co-ed	4	1435
KUMEU/HUAPAI							
Hare Krishna School	Highway 28	412 6325	prim+interm	state integrated	co-ed	4	50
Huapai District School	40 Station Rd	412 5042	prim+interm	state	co-ed	9	362
Jireh School	Access Rd	412 6386	prim+interm	private	co-ed	n/a	18
Riverhead School	21 School Rdl	412 9105	prim+interm	state	co-ed	7	257
Waimauku School	Muriwai Rd	411 8222	prim+interm	state	co-ed	9	650
NEW LYNN							
Kelston Deaf Education Centre	Archibald Rd	827 4859	special	state	co-ed	3	140
Oaklynn Special School	20 Mayville Ave	827 4748	special	state	co-ed	4	105
Te Kura Kaupapa Maori O Hoani Waititi	441 West Coast Rd	818 2317	all levels	state	co-ed	3	236
West City Christian College	4341 Great North Rd	838 7710	all levels	private	co-ed	5	104
Arahoe School	Arahoe Rd	827 2710	primary	state	co-ed	5	601
Fruitvale Rd	Croydon Rd School	827 2752	primary	state	co-ed	3	278
Glen Eden School	3 Glenview Rd	818 6686	primary	state	co-ed	4	283
Glendene School	Barrys Rd	838 8603	primary	state	co-ed	3	152
Kelston School	5 Archibald Rd	827 2187	primary	state	co-ed	3	401
New Lynn School	Hutchinson Ave	827 4382	primary	state	co-ed	3	238
Prospect School	Rosier Rd	818 5219	primary	state	co-ed	3	513
St Leonards Rd School	15 St Leonards Rd	818 7717	primary	state	co-ed	3	404
TKKM Pumau Ki Te Reo O Ngapuhi	3 Archibald Rd	827 0937	prim+interm	state	co-ed	2	33
Kelston Intermediate	Vanguard Rd	818 5544	intermediate	state	co-ed	3	340
Kelston Boys' High School	Archibald Rd	818 6185	secondary	state	boys	3	1174
Kelston Girls' High School	Great North Rd	827 6063	secondary	state	girls	3	1021
SWANSON							
Ranui School	Ranui Station Rd	833 6286	primary	state	co-ed	2	480
St Paul's School	498 Don Buck Rd	832 7200	primary	state integrated	co-ed	5	296
Birdwood School	Karepo Cres	833 8479	prim+interm	state	co-ed	1	285
Colwill School	Kintara Dr	833 6081	prim+interm	state	co-ed	4	462
Don Buck School	124 Don Buck Rd	833 6005	prim+interm	state	co-ed	3	274
Lincoln Heights School	Keegan Dr	833 7480	prim+interm	state	co-ed	4	602
Massey Primary School	326 Don Buck Rd	833 7232	prim+interm	state	co-ed	4	421
Royal Rd School	Royal Rd	833 7675	prim+interm	state	co-ed	3	390

Name	Address	Phone	Level	Funding	Gender	Decile	Roll
Swanson School	703 Swanson Rd	833 3500	prim+interm	state	co-ed	5	645
Waitakere School	10 Bethells Rd	810 9607	prim+interm	state	co-ed	8	376
Massey High School	274 Don Buck Rd	831 0500	secondary	state	co-ed	5	2423
TITIRANGI							
Kaurilands School	Atkinson Rd	817 5645	primary	state	co-ed	7	756
Konini School	Withers Rd	818 5005	primary	state	co-ed	6	355
Laingholm School	Victory Rd	817 8874	primary	state	co-ed	8	368
Oratia School	Cnr Shaw & West Coast Rds	818 6216	primary	state	co-ed	9	540
Titirangi School	Atkinson Rd	817 8346	primary	state	co-ed	10	484
Woodlands Park School	Woodlands Park Rd	817 5140	primary	state	co-ed	9	177
Green Bay Primary School	Godley Rd	817 6666	prim+interm	state	co-ed	7	522
Titirangi Rudolf Steiner School	5 Helios Pl	817 4386	prim+interm	private	co-ed	9	160
Glen Eden Intermediate	Kaurilands Rd	817 0032	intermediate	state	co-ed	8	1065
Green Bay High School	Godley Rd	817 8173	secondary	state	co-ed	7	1093
WEST HARBOUR							
Hobsonville School	Hobsonville Rd	416 8619	prim+interm	state	co-ed	9	631
Marina View School	97-99 Marina View Dr	416 7524	prim+interm	state	co-ed	10	705
Timatanga Community School	9 Mamari Rd	416 6000	prim+interm	state integrated	co-ed	7	17
West Harbour School	Oriel Ave	416 7105	prim+interm	state	co-ed	3	504
Whenuapai School	14 Airport Rd	416 8779	prim+interm	state	co-ed	10	375
ALBANY							
Kristin School	360 Albany Highway	415 9566	all levels	private	co-ed	10	1607
Pinehurst School	75 Bush Rd	414 ph60	all levels	private	co-ed	n/a	804
Albany School	6 Bass Rd	415 9668	primary	state	co-ed	10	579
Coatesville School	Mahoenui Valley Rd	415 9218	primary	state	co-ed	10	304
Greenhithe School	Isobel Rd	413 9838	primary	state	co-ed	10	444
Kyle Rd Primary School	Kyle Rd	n/a	primary	state	co-ed	n/a	44
Oteha Valley School	Medallion D	477 0033	primary	state	co-ed	10	44
Ridgeview School	Cutts Cres	413 9808	primary	state	co-ed	9	95
Dairy Flat School	State Highway 17	415 9071	prim+interm	state	co-ed	10	323
BEACH HAVEN/BIRKDALE							
Beach Haven School	Tramway Rd	483 7615	primary	state	co-ed	3	406
Birkdale North School	213 Birkdale Rd	483 8674	primary	state	co-ed	4	205
Birkdale Primary School	Salisbury Rd	483 7767	primary	state	co-ed	5	368
Kauri Park School	McGlashen Pl	483 6539	primary	state	co-ed	6	350
BELMONT/BAYSWATER							
Bayswater School	Bayswater Ave	445 6226	primary	state	co-ed	8	144
Belmont School	3a Harrison Ave	445 6605	primary	state	co-ed	9	341
Belmont Intermediate	188 Lake Rd	489 4878	intermediate	state	co-ed	10	554

WEST

NORTH

Name	Addresss	Phone	Level	Funding	Gender	Decile	Roll
DEVONPORT							
Devonport School	Kerr St	445 0183	primary	state	co-ed	10	278
St Leos School	4 Owens Rd	445 9339	primary	state integrated	co-ed	10	120
Stanley Bay School	15 Russell St	445 2510	primary	state	co-ed	10	275
Vauxhall School	Morrison Ave	445 0052	primary	state	co-ed	10	274
AppleTree Education Centre	87 Victoria St	445 6172	prim+interm	private	co-ed	n/a	8
GLENFIELD							
Wairau Valley School	102 Hillside Rd	444 5552	special	state	co-ed	8	90
Bayview School	Bayview Rd	444 2222	primary	state	co-ed	7	353
Glenfield Primary School	101 Chivalry Rd	441 8730	primary	state	co-ed	7	460
Manuka Primary School	Manuka Rd	444 8775	primary	state	co-ed	8	352
Marlborough School	Wykeham Pl	481 0365	primary	state	co-ed	7	341
Target Rd School	Target Rd	444 8493	primary	state	co-ed	6	399
Windy Ridge School	Seaview Rd	444 3105	primary	state	co-ed	7	230
Westminster Christian School	31 Westminster Gardens	444 1983	prim+interm	state integrated	co-ed	10	161
Glenfield Intermediate	Chivalry Rd	444 6582	intermediate	state	co-ed	8	800
Glenfield College	Kaipatiki Rd	444 9066	secondary	state	co-ed	8	1415
HIBISCUS COAST							
Kingsway School	100 Jelas Rd	427 0900	all levels	state integrated	co-ed	10	737
Orewa North School	Centreway Rd	426 4849	primary	state	co-ed	7	398
Orewa School	Riverside Rd	426 5548	primary	state	co-ed	8	471
Red Beach School	20 Albert Hall Dr	426 8915	primary	state	co-ed	9	606
Stanmore Bay School	Waiora Rd	424 5540	primary	state	co-ed	7	639
Whangaparaoa School	39 Ladies Mile	424 9029	primary	state	co-ed	9	663
Gulf Harbour School	65 Alec Craig Way	428 0202	prim+interm	state	co-ed	9	550
Silverdale School	Foundry Rd	426 5510	primary	state	co-ed	9	144
The Happy Rainbow Primary School	293 Wainui Rd	426 4411	primary	state	co-ed	9	53
Orewa College	Riverside Rd	426 4075	secondary	state	co-ed	9	1673
Wentworth College	65 Gulf Harbour Dr	424 3273	secondary	state	co-ed	n/a	105
Whangaparaoa College	15 Delshaw Ave	428 4724	secondary	state	co-ed	9	n/a
LOWER EAST COAST BAYS							
Campbells Bay School	Aberdeen Rd	410 7444	primary	state	co-ed	10	668
Mairangi Bay School	Agathis Ave	478 8424	primary	state	co-ed	10	394
Murrays Bay School	Clematis Ave	478 6239	primary	state	co-ed	10	641
St John's School	87 a Penzance Rd	478 7734	primary	state integrated	co-ed	10	293
Murrays Bay Intermediate	Sunrise Ave	477 2121	intermediate	state	co-ed	10	964
NORTHCOTE							
Birkenhead School	Mokoia Rd	480 7365	primary	state	co-ed	10	364
Chelsea School	Onetaunga Rd	418 0082	primary	state	co-ed	10	330
Northcote School	2 Lake Rd	480 7376	primary	state	co-ed	9	399

NORTH

Name	Address	Phone	Level	Funding	Gender	Decile	Roll
Onepoto School	Fraser Ave	480 7469	primary	state	co-ed	1	119
Verran Primary School	Verran Rd	483 7052	primary	state	co-ed	6	192
Willowpark School	Compton St	480 9236	primary	state	co-ed	9	611
St Mary's School	115 Onewa Rd	418 4333	primary	state integrated	co-ed	7	413
Te Kura Kaupapa Maori OTe Raki Paewhenua	58 Akoranga Dr	489 9390	prim+interm	state	co-ed	4	59
Birkdale Intermediate	200 Birkdale Rd	483 9168	intermediate	state	co-ed	6	624
Northcote Intermediate	Lake Rd	419 4700	intermediate	state	co-ed	6	344
Birkenhead College	140 Birkdale Rd	483 9039	secondary	state	co-ed	6	1046
Hato Petera College	103 College Rd	480 7784	secondary	state integrated	co-ed	2	134
Northcote College	Kauri Glen Rd	481 0141	secondary	state	co-ed	9	1533
TAKAPUNA							
Wilson School	1 St Leonards Rd	489 5648	special	state	co-ed	8	59
Hauraki School	Jutland Rd	489 4568	primary	state	co-ed	10	333
Milford School	34 Shakespeare Rd	489 7216	primary	state	co-ed	10	491
St Joseph's School	2 Taharoto Rd	489 4994	primary	state integrated	co-ed	10	358
Sunnybrae Normal School	36 Sunnybrae Rd	443 5058	primary	state	co-ed	7	407
Sunnynook School	Lyford Cres	410 6534	primary	state	co-ed	8	526
Takapuna School	23 Auburn St	489 6339	primary	state	co-ed	9	326
Takapuna Normal Intermediate	54b Taharoto Rd	489 3940	intermediate	state	co-ed	10	653
Carmel College	114 Shakespeare Rd	486 1132	secondary	state integrated	girls	10	984
Rosmini College	36 Dominion St	489 5417	secondary	state integrated	boys	10	991
Takapuna Grammar School	210 Lake Rd	489 4167	secondary	state	co-ed	10	1590
UPPER EAST COAST BAYS							
The Corelli School	50 Anzac Rd	476 5043	all levels	private	co-ed	10	58
Browns Bay School	Masterton Rd	479 4301	primary	state	co-ed	10	630
Glamorgan School	Glamorgan Dr	473 6453	primary	state	co-ed	10	612
Long Bay School	Ralph Eagles Pl	473 6077	primary	state	co-ed	10	302
Pinehill School	Hugh Green Dr	478 0301	primary	state	co-ed	10	571
Sherwood School	Sartors Ave	478 3024	primary	state	co-ed	10	470
Torbay School	Deep Creek Rd	473 8603	primary	state	co-ed	10	420
Northcross Intermediate	10 Sartors Ave	477 0167	intermediate	state	co-ed	10	1225
Long Bay College	Ashley Ave	473 2500	secondary	state	co-ed	10	1549
Rangitoto College	564 East Coast Rd	477 0150	secondary	state	co-ed	10	3284
WESTLAKE							
Forrest Hill School	50 Forrest Hill Rd	410 8939	primary	state	co-ed	9	411
Wairau Intermediate	Becroft Dr	410 7805	intermediate	state	co-ed	8	505
Westlake Boys' High School	Forrest Hill Rd	410 8667	secondary	state	boys	10	2170
Westlake Girls' High School	2 Wairau Rd	489 4169	secondary	state	girls	10	2244
WARKWORTH							
Kaipara Flats School	School Rd	422 5819	primary	state	co-ed	8	86

NORTH

Name	Addresss	Phone	Level	Funding	Gender	Decile	Roll
NORTH							
Leigh School	Hauraki Rd	422 6031	primary	state	co-ed	5	72
Matakana School	Main Rd	422 7309	primary	state	co-ed	8	391
Warkworth School	35 Hill St	425 8300	primary	state	co-ed	8	554
Ahuroa School	Ahuroa Rd	422 5898	prim+interm	state	co-ed	2	17
Mahurangi Christian School	406-410 Mahurangi East Rd	425 6878	prim+interm	state integrated	co-ed	7	87
Tauhoa School	Naumai Rd	422 5722	prim+interm	state	co-ed	7	36
Mahurangi College	Woodcocks Rd	425 8039	secondary	state	co-ed	8	1254
BEACHLANDS/MARAETAI							
Beachlands School	18 Bell Rd	536 6757	prim+interm	state	co-ed	9	388
Maraetai Beach School	154 Maraetai Dr	536 6570	prim+interm	state	co-ed	9	234
BOTANY DOWNS							
Botany Downs School	Mirrabooka Ave	534 9848	primary	state	co-ed	9	470
Botany Downs College	575 Chapel Rd	273 2310	secondary	state	co-ed	10	311
BUCKLANDS BEACH							
Pakuranga Health Camp School	1-9 Pigeon Mountain Rd	534 9412	special	state	co-ed	1	n/a
Waimokoia Residential School	Thurston Place	538 0036	special	state	co-ed	2	35
Bucklands Beach Primary School	107 Clovelly Rd	534 6543	primary	state	co-ed	10	327
Macleans Primary School	Wycherley Drive	534 5191	primary	state	co-ed	9	359
Pigeon Mountain School	22 Wells Rd	534 9765	primary	state	co-ed	10	531
Bucklands Beach Intermediate	247 Bucklands Beach Rd	534 2896	intermediate	state	co-ed	10	758
Macleans College	Macleans Rd	535 2620	secondary	state	co-ed	10	2400
HALF MOON BAY							
Wakaaranga School	18 Butley Dr	576 8205	primary	state	co-ed	9	613
HOWICK							
Elim Christian College	159 Botany Rd	538 0368	all levels	state integrated	co-ed	9	553
Cockle Bay School	Sandspit Rd	534 8333	primary	state	co-ed	10	707
Howick Primary School	Willoughby Ave	534 6082	primary	state	co-ed	9	375
Mellons Bay School	140 Mellons Bay Rd	534 4363	primary	state	co-ed	10	511
Owairoa School	Nelson St	534 6107	primary	state	co-ed	10	880
Point View School	Kilkenny Dr	274 0637	primary	state	co-ed	10	777
Shelly Park School	Sunnyviews Ave	535 8784	primary	state	co-ed	10	403
Star of the Sea School	14 Oakridge Way	534 6766	primary	state integrated	co-ed	10	460
Willowbank School	Gracechurch Dr	271 1077	primary	state	co-ed	9	599
Howick Intermediate	Botany Rd	534 3922	intermediate	state	co-ed	6	817
Somerville Intermediate School	39 Somerville Rd	535 1070	intermediate	state	co-ed	10	951
Howick College	Sandspit Rd	534 4492	secondary	state	co-ed	10	2371
Sancta Maria College	319 Te Irirangi Dr	274 4081	secondary	state integrated	co-ed	7	319
PAKURANGA							
Anchorage Park School	Swan Cres	576 9175	primary	state	co-ed	4	205
Elm Park School	46 Gossamer Dr	577 0070	primary	state	co-ed	7	564

EAST

Name	Address	Phone	Level	Funding	Gender	Decile	Roll
Pakuranga College	Pigeon Mountain Rd	534 7159	secondary	state	co-ed	9	2247
Pakuranga Heights School	77 Udys Rd	576 9209	primary	state	co-ed	7	485
Riverhills School	13 Waikaremoana Place	576 8105	primary	state	co-ed	6	132
Riverina School	30 Millen Ave	527 7377	primary	state	co-ed	3	279
St Mark's School	334 Pakuranga Rd	576 5296	primary	state integrated	co-ed	8	301
Sunny Hills School	17 The Crest	576 8031	prim+interm	state	co-ed	10	587
Farm Cove Intermediate	Butley Dr	576 6624	intermediate	state	co-ed	9	628
Pakuranga Intermediate	43-49 Reeves Rd	576 1860	intermediate	state	co-ed	4	478
Edgewater College	Edgewater Dr	576 9039	secondary	state	co-ed	3	1262
St Kentigern College	130 Pakuranga Rd	576 9019	secondary	private	co-ed	n/a	1504

WHITFORD

Name	Address	Phone	Level	Funding	Gender	Decile	Roll
Brookby School	West Rd	530 8569	prim+interm	state	co-ed	7	81
Clevedon School	13 North Rd	292 8654	prim+interm	state	co-ed	9	353

SOUTH

MANGERE

Name	Address	Phone	Level	Funding	Gender	Decile	Roll
Sir Keith Park School	33 Robertson Rd	275 4455	special	state	co-ed	1	106
Al-Madinah School	8 Westney Rd	275 5195	all levels	state integrated	co-ed	2	359
Southern Cross Campus	Buckland Rd West	255 0404	all levels	state	co-ed	1	1680
Te Kura Kaupapa Maori O Mangere	7 Comet Crescent	275 1821	all levels	state	co-ed	2	234
Westmount School	47 Rennie Rd	256 2266	all levels	private	co-ed	8	476
Zayed College for Girls	44 Westney Rd	255 0904	all levels	private	girls	5	66
Favona School	Wakefield Rd	275 8449	primary	state	co-ed	1	388
Jean Batten School	6 Imrie Ave	275 5733	primary	state	co-ed	1	494
Kingsford School	54 Raglan St	275 9447	primary	state	co-ed	1	390
Mangere Bridge School	Coronation Rd	636 7304	primary	state	co-ed	3	410
Mangere East School	Yates Rd	276 4689	primary	state	co-ed	1	618
Mountain View School	81 Mountain Rd	636 5410	primary	state	co-ed	1	244
Nga Iwi School	60 Mascot Ave	275 4921	primary	state	co-ed	1	476
Papatoetoe North School	Graeme Ave	278 6153	primary	state	co-ed	2	697
Waterlea Public School	House Ave	636 4233	primary	state	co-ed	4	400
Calvin Christian School	22 Rosella Rd	276 7272	prim+interm	private	co-ed	3	32
Koru School	71 Robertson Rd	275 9194	prim+interm	state	co-ed	1	589
Mangere Central School	254 Kirkbride Rd	275 9979	prim+interm	state	co-ed	1	323
Mary MacKillop School	12 McNaughton Ave	257 1435	prim+interm	state integrated	co-ed	1	334
Robertson Rd School	205 Robertson Rd	275 6224	prim+interm	state	co-ed	1	492
Sutton Park School	89 Vine St	276 4560	prim+interm	state	co-ed	1	535
Viscount School	Viscount St	275 4699	prim+interm	state	co-ed	1	803
Sir Douglas Bader Intermediate School	Court Town Close	275 4332	intermediate	state	co-ed	1	320
Ambury Park Centre for Riding Therapy	66 Wellesley Rd	634 0763	secondary	private	co-ed	n/a	29
Auckland Seventh-Day Adventist HS	119 Mountain Rd	275 9640	secondary	state integrated	co-ed	2	318
De la Salle College	81 Gray Ave	276 4319	secondary	state integrated	boys	1	892

Name	Address	Phone	Level	Funding	Gender	Decile	Roll
Mangere College	Bader Drive	275 4029	secondary	state	co-ed	1	750
MANUKAU/CLOVER PARK							
The Bridge Academy	Cnr Murphys & Flat Bush School Rd	535 0574	all levels	private	co-ed	n/a	15
Everglade School	64 Everglade Dr	262 0244	primary	state	co-ed	7	547
Redoubt North School	Diorella Dr	263 9060	primary	state	co-ed	2	516
Weymouth School	23 Evans Rd	267 3569	primary	state	co-ed	3	492
Tangaroa College	Haumia Way	274 5764	secondary	state	co-ed	1	1053
Wiri Central School	Inverell Ave	262 0594	prim+interm	state	co-ed	1	464
Baverstock Oaks School	Baverstock Rd	278 6741	prim+interm	state	co-ed	10	n/a
MANUREWA							
Homai National School for the Blind	Browns Rd	266 7109	special	state	co-ed	3	48
Manukau Christian School	150 Great South Rd	266 4444	all levels	private	co-ed	n/a	130
Clayton Park School	Coxhead Rd	267 0077	primary	state	co-ed	3	475
Clendon Park School	145 Rowandale Ave	267 6671	primary	state	co-ed	1	396
Finlayson Park School	85 John Walker Dr	266 5558	primary	state	co-ed	1	855
Hillpark School	57 Grand Vue Rd	267 6252	primary	state	co-ed	7	504
Homai School	89 Browns Rd	266 8918	primary	state	co-ed	2	341
Leabank School	Dr Pickering Ave	267 6939	primary	state	co-ed	2	474
Manurewa Central School	Hill Rd	266 8782	primary	state	co-ed	4	571
Manurewa East School	Scotts Rd	266 9487	primary	state	co-ed	2	302
Manurewa South School	Tawa Crescent	266 8341	primary	state	co-ed	2	398
Manurewa West School	McKean Ave	266 8631	primary	state	co-ed	2	397
Roscommon School	Burundi Ave	266 5731	primary	state	co-ed	1	568
Rowandale School	73 Rowandale Ave	267 6663	primary	state	co-ed	1	445
Te Matauranga	206 Finlayson Ave	266 9493	primary	state	co-ed	1	355
Randwick Park School	Riverton Dr	267 0112	prim+interm	state	co-ed	2	683
St Anne's School	124 Russell Rd	269 0023	prim+interm	state integrated	co-ed	2	519
Te Kura A aori O Manurewa	17 Trounson Ave	268 2031	prim+interm	state integrated	co-ed	1	72
The Gardens School	101 Charles Prevost Dr	269 0041	prim+interm	state	co-ed	10	377
Greenmeadows Intermediate	Greenmeadows Ave	267 6255	intermediate	state	co-ed	3	639
Manurewa Intermediate	Russell Rd	266 8268	intermediate	state	co-ed	2	829
Weymouth Intermediate	Palmers Rd	266 7455	intermediate	state	co-ed	1	554
Alfriston College	550 Porchester Rd	269 0080	secondary	state	co-ed	4	277
James Cook High School	Dr Pickering Ave	268 3950	secondary	state	co-ed	2	1424
Manurewa High School	67 Browns Rd	268 3888	secondary	state	co-ed	3	2078
Te Wharekura o Manurewa	81 Finlayson Ave	266 0158	secondary	state	co-ed	1	34
OTAHUHU							
Mt Richmond School	30 Albion Rd	259 1425	special	state	co-ed	2	141
Dingwall Trust School	8 Dingwall Place	278 3675	all levels	private	co-ed	n/a	13
Tyndale Park Christian School	206 Murphys Rd	274 9771	all levels	private	co-ed	n/a	105

SOUTH

Name	Address	Phone	Level	Funding	Gender	Decile	Roll
Fairburn School	Pukeora St	270 1130	primary	state	co-ed	1	682
Otahuhu School	41 Station Rd	259 0109	primary	state	co-ed	1	517
Panama Rd School	Panama Rd	276 8508	primary	state	co-ed	1	305
Papatoetoe Central School	Great South Rd	278 7557	primary	state	co-ed	4	672
Papatoetoe East School	Tui Rd	278 5446	primary	state	co-ed	3	532
Papatoetoe South School	Milan Rd	278 5231	primary	state	co-ed	3	541
Papatoetoe West School	Hillcrest Rd	278 6274	primary	state	co-ed	2	749
Puhinui School	116 Puhinui Rd	278 8703	primary	state	co-ed	3	540
Holy Cross School	Carruth Rd	278 8224	prim+interm	state integrated	co-ed	2	579
South Auckland S D A School	42a Puhinui Rd	278 6055	prim+interm	state integrated	co-ed	2	303
St Joseph's School	29 High St	276 4563	prim+interm	state integrated	co-ed	1	310
Kedgley Intermediate	Portage Rd	278 4202	intermediate	state	co-ed	2	681
Otahuhu Intermediate	22-24 Luke St	276 6421	intermediate	state	co-ed	1	480
Papatoetoe Intermediate	Motatau Rd	278 9763	intermediate	state	co-ed	3	970
Aorere College	Portage Rd	278 5608	secondary	state	co-ed	2	1262
Kings College	Golf Ave	276 0600	secondary	private	boys	10	962
McAuley High School	26 High St	276 8715	secondary	state integrated	girls	1	627
Otahuhu College	Mangere Rd	270 1170	secondary	state	co-ed	1	1399
Papatoetoe High School	Nicholson Ave	278 4086	secondary	state	co-ed	4	1831
OTARA							
Bairds Mainfreight Primary School	Edward Ave	274 8271	primary	state	co-ed	1	367
Chapel Downs School	Cnr Chapel & Dawson Rds	274 8002	primary	state	co-ed	2	657
Dawson School	Haumia Way	274 5390	primary	state	co-ed	1	490
East Tamaki School	Preston Rd	274 9246	primary	state	co-ed	1	327
Flat Bush School	Flat Bush Rd	274 8279	primary	state	co-ed	1	407
Mayfield School	Pearl Baker Dr	274 9374	primary	state	co-ed	1	488
Rongomai School	20 Rongomai Rd	274 6055	primary	state	co-ed	1	141
Sir Edmund Hillary Collegiate Junior School	2 Franklyne Rd	274 8269	primary	state	co-ed	1	383
Wymondley Rd School	Wymondley Rd	276 7241	primary	state	co-ed	1	197
Yendarra School	Bairds Rd	274 7431	primary	state	co-ed	1	375
St John The Evangelist School	14 b Otara Rd	274 7558	prim+interm	state integrated	co-ed	1	351
Te Kura Kaupapa Maori O Otara	52 Alexander Crescent	274 6687	prim+interm	state	co-ed	1	78
Ferguson Intermediate	Ferguson Rd	274 8471	intermediate	state	co-ed	1	464
Sir Edmund Hillary Collegiate Middle Sch	2 Franklyne Rd	274 5782	intermediate	state	co-ed	1	234
Sir Edmund Hillary Collegiate Senior Sch	2 Franklyne Rd	274 5782	secondary	state	co-ed	1	500
Clover Park Middle School	51 Othello Dr	274 5807	secondary	state	co-ed	1	1316
PAPAKURA							
Rosehill School	50 Rosehill Dr	298 4569	special	state	co-ed	2	80
Cosgrove School	10 Cosgrove Rd	298 8365	primary	state	co-ed	2	561
Kelvin Rd School	Kelvin Rd	298 8417	primary	state	co-ed	1	486

SOUTH

Name	Address	Phone	Level	Funding	Gender	Decile	Roll
Papakura Central School	23 Ray Small Dr	299 6009	primary	state	co-ed	6	391
Park Estate School	Park Estate Rd	298 4139	primary	state	co-ed	1	139
Ararimu School	7 Steel Rd	294 8372	prim+interm	state	co-ed	9	123
Ardmore School	Clevedon Rd	299 6228	prim+interm	state	co-ed	6	293
Conifer Grove School	Evanda Crescent	299 7490	prim+interm	state	co-ed	8	482
Edmund Hillary School	Hunua Rd	298 9132	prim+interm	state	co-ed	1	148
Hunua School	Lockwood Rd	292 4889	prim+interm	state	co-ed	9	127
Karaka School	Blackbridge Rd	294 8166	prim+interm	state	co-ed	8	167
Opaheke School	Tasman Dr	298 5410	prim+interm	state	co-ed	7	615
Orere School	Orere Point Rd	292 2736	prim+interm	state	co-ed	3	32
Papakura Normal School	143 Porchester Rd	298 7524	prim+interm	state	co-ed	3	577
Papakura South School	58 Beach Rd	296 9040	prim+interm	state	co-ed	1	146
Paparimu School	7 Matheson Rd	292 5861	prim+interm	state	co-ed	10	46
Ramarama School	126 Ararimu Rd	294 8795	prim+interm	state	co-ed	10	154
Redhill School	Redcrest Ave	298 4377	prim+interm	state	co-ed	1	238
St Mary's School	Clark Rd	298 4450	prim+interm	state integrated	co-ed	6	455
Takanini School	School Rd	299 9349	prim+interm	state	co-ed	2	341
Te Hihi School	Linwood Rd	292 7706	prim+interm	state	co-ed	10	239
Mansell Senior School	Settlement Rd	298 8737	intermediate	state	co-ed	1	318
Rosehill Intermediate	Jupiter St	298 5827	intermediate	state	co-ed	5	368
Papakura High School	Willis Rd	296 4400	secondary	state	co-ed	2	1371
Rosehill College	5 Edinburgh Ave	295 0661	secondary	state	co-ed	7	1893
PUKEKOHE							
Parkside School	184 Wellington St	238 9689	special	state	co-ed	4	95
ACG Strathallan	Hayfield Way Karaka	295 0830	all levels	private	co-ed	n/a	897
Pukekohe Christian School	82 Yates Rd	238 6449	all levels	private	co-ed	7	57
Mauku School	Union Rd	236 3654	primary	state	co-ed	8	63
Pukekohe East School	137 Runciman Rd	238 8708	primary	state	co-ed	10	149
Pukekohe Hill School	Green Lane	238 6374	primary	state	co-ed	5	541
Puni School	Waiuku Rd	238 7403	primary	state	co-ed	4	194
Valley School	East St	238 8774	primary	state	co-ed	5	349
Buckland School	72 George Crescent	238 9419	prim+interm	state	co-ed	7	194
Kings Gate Primary School	53 Victoria St	239 0297	prim+interm	private	co-ed	n/a	27
Paerata School	Tuhimata Rd	238 7050	prim+interm	state	co-ed	4	115
Pukekohe North School	Princes St	238 8552	prim+interm	state	co-ed	1	275
St Joseph's School	94 Seddon St	238 7745	prim+interm	state	co-ed	6	343
Waiau Pa School	Waiau Pa Rd	232 1753	prim+interm	state	co-ed	8	349
Pukekohe Intermediate	Queen St	238 6568	Intermediate	state	co-ed	5	628
Pukekohe High School	Harris St	238 6089	secondary	state	co-ed	6	1493
Wesley College	State Highway 22	238 7014	secondary	state	girls	2	352

SOUTH

For serious house hunters

If you're thinking about property you'll need **Heraldhomes**, the new and improved real estate guide for serious house hunters. With thousands of homes listed every week in a new easy format and helpful features on hot properties and market trends, it has everything you need to find the home that's right for you.

The New Zealand Herald

nzherald.co.nz

Misson Bay	47	Royal Oak	84
Morningside	65	Sandringham	74
Mt Albert	71	Shelly Park	193
Mt Eden	74	Silverdale	153
Mt Roskill	78	Snells Beach	171
Mt Wellington	87	Somerville	184
Muriwai	127	St Heliers	47
Murrays Bay	157	St Johns	68
Narrow Neck	143	St Lukes	71
New Lynn	116	St Marys Bay	94
Newmarket	90	Stanley Bay	146
New Windsor	44	Stanley Point	146
Newton	37	South Head	104
North Harbour	136	Sunnnynook	175
Northcote	160	Sunnyhills	190
Northcross	168	Sunnyvale	108
Northpark	184	Swanson	120
Okura	168	Takanini	220
Omaha	171	Takapuna	164
One Tree Hill	84	Tamaki	87
Onehunga	81	Te Atatu Peninsula	108
Orakei	47	Te Atatu South	108
Oranga	81	Te Papapa	81
Oratia	123	The Palms	150
Orewa	153	Three Kings	74
Otahuhu	215	Titirangi	123
Otara	218	Torbay	168
Owairaka	71	Totara Heights	209
Pahurehure	220	Unsworth Heights	150
Pakuranga	197	Upper East Coast Bays	168
Panmure	87	Vauxhall	146
Papakura	220	Waiake	168
Papatoetoe	215	Waiheke Island	61
Parakai	104	Waikowhai	78
Parau	123	Waimauku	112
Paremoremo	136	Wairau Park	150
Parnell	90	Waitakere	120
Penrose	81	Waiatarua	123
Piha	127	Warkworth	171
Pinehill	168	Waterview	41
Point Chevalier	57	Wattle Downs	212
Ponsonby	94	Wesley	44
Pt England	54	West Coast Beaches	127
Pt View Park	184	West Harbour	131
Puhinui	209	Western Heights	108
Pukekohe	222	Western Springs	65
Rakino Island	61	Westlake	175
Randwick Park	212	Westmere	57
Ranui	120	Weymouth	212
Red Beach	153	Whangaparoa	153
Red Hill	220	Whenuapai	131
Remuera	98	Whitford	200
Riverhead	112	Wiri	209
Rosebank	41	Wood Bay	123
Rosedale	136		
Rosehill	220		
Rothesay Bay	157		